TERENCE R. ANDERSON

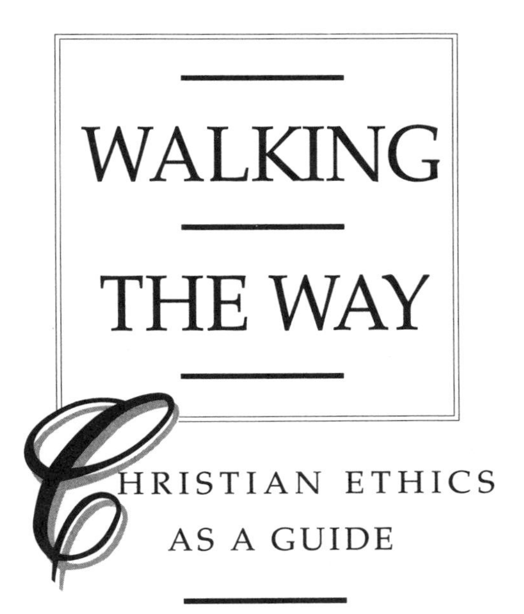

THE UNITED CHURCH PUBLISHING HOUSE

Grateful acknowledgement is made for permission to reprint from copyrighted material, including the following:

From *Community and Alienation: Essays on Process Thought and Public Life* by Douglas Sturm. Copyright © 1988 by University of Notre Dame Press. Reprinted by permission.

From *Faith and History* by Reinhold Niebuhr. Copyright 1949 Charles Scribner's Sons; copyright renewed © 1977 Ursula M. Niebuhr. Reprinted with the permission of Charles Scribner's Sons, an imprint of Macmillan Publishing Company.

From *Christian Ethics and the Community* by James F. Gustafson. Used by permission of The Pilgrim Press.

From *A Community of Character: Toward a Constructive Christian Social Ethic* by Stanley Hauerwas. Copyright © 1981 by University of Notre Dame Press. Reprinted by permission.

From *Bible Ethics in the Christian Life* by Bruce C. Birch and Larry L. Rasmussen. Copyright © 1976 Augsburg Publishing House. Used by permission of Augsburg Fortress.

Canadian Cataloguing in Publication Data

Anderson, Terence R. (Terence Roy), 1931-
Walking the way

Includes bibliographical references.
ISBN 1-55134-003-8
1. Christian ethics. 2. Conduct of life.
I. Title.
BJ1278.A3A54 1993 241.5 C93-093633-7

The United Church Publishing House
85 St. Clair Avenue East
Toronto, Ontario
M4T 1M8

Publisher: R.L. Naylor
Editor-in-Chief: Peter Gordon White
Book Design: Dept. of Graphics and Print
Cover Design: Jo-Anne Slauenwhite
Printed in Canada by: Hignell Printing Ltd.

5 4 3 2 1 93 94 95 96 97

CONTENTS

PREFACE

What is the Way that God calls us to live in these challenging and perplexing times? This book explores Christian ethics as a guide to that Way. It is intended for any interested, serious enquirer rather than primarily for scholars of ethics.

With those of other faiths, Christians share a presupposition that distinguishes their approach to ethics from that of secular thought. They believe that there is a divine purpose for the cosmos. They believe there is a divine intention for human beings in particular. They believe there is a true Way to follow.

How are we to discern this Way amid the bewildering array of new problems and choices that confront us and the many conflicting values and voices vying for our allegiance? Christian ethics is the enterprise of systematically reflecting on the Way. It seeks a method for moving from the Christian faith to moral decisions. It asks, What is God requiring us to do? What is God enabling us to be? A wealth of Christian thought on these questions has accumulated and an ongoing lively engagement persists.

Christian ethics is not a guide, however, in the sense of providing precise directives or of solving every moral dilemma. Rather, it can guide us by informing our thinking about the Way, deepening our understanding of God's will and purpose, helping us to shape our minds and hearts. In this fashion, Christian ethics can prepare us to perceive the Way in our context and to respond faithfully when moral dilemmas confront us.

We begin by looking at what is entailed in the moral life and at why many have found themselves having to be more conscious of the Way they seek to live. The core of this book identifies five aspects of the complex, dynamic reality we call the moral life. These are used as base points for ethical reflection. They provide a framework that will be useful, whatever your experience and persuasion may be. My main aim, however, is to provide some substantial samples of the rich Christian thinking concerning each of these base points, including some of the differences and debates about them. The selection of samples represents a range of views but is neither comprehensive nor perfectly balanced. Similarities and contrasts between Christian views and prevailing ideas in modern societies will be examined. The idea is to provide a feel for Christian ethics at work, rather than a survey of the discipline.

In the last section of the book, I discuss how the different aspects of the moral life (base points) relate to each other. How can all of this be brought to bear upon difficult moral decisions?

I employ "the Way" as the main metaphor for the moral life. It is a metaphor familiar not only in the Bible but in a variety of different cultures. Each of the five aspects of the moral life can serve as a distinctive navigational assistant for indicating the Way. I also liken the moral life to a large orchestra. We can explore the "distinctive sound" of each section (base point) and its place in the orchestra. We can discern the relationship needed between them to produce harmonious music and not discord.

I have been engaged in the study of Christian ethics for nearly thirty-five years. Throughout this venture, my wife Daphne has been my constant companion, inspiration, and mentor. In major respects, this book is a joint effort. My dedicating it to her is therefore no sentimental gesture, but an inadequate acknowledgement. Looking back, we both recognize that this book began in our first pastoral charge at Sundre, Alberta. A lively Bible study group there kept raising questions as to how their faith should guide them in matters confronting them in their daily life. That started me on the study of Christian ethics. A Bible study group in a very different context, in Glen Ridge, New Jersey, asked similar vexing and probing questions, keeping me at the enterprise.

Since then, I have been privileged to struggle, as consultant and teacher, alongside a great variety of people in different occupations and from diverse cultures as they sought to discern a morally responsible course of action. The matters they faced ranged from actions of civil disobedience to allowing a newborn to die. I thank all of them for their moral passion and commitment to thinking carefully about the Way and for all I have learned from them about ethical reflection. Many of their questions and some of their dilemmas and insights are in this book. Especially important have been my relationships with Native peoples and the influence of the late Robert K. Thomas, a Cherokee anthropologist, with whom I have been privileged to live, work, and travel. And, of course, students who have endured my courses in Christian ethics have also taught me much. Over the years, some of them have encouraged me to write a book on Christian ethics that would be useful to both individual laity and congregational study groups. With this in mind, I have prepared a glossary in which I comment on the meaning of certain words and phrases that occur when we talk about Christian ethics.

This work started out as a pamphlet designed to accompany a video series, produced by the Vancouver School of Theology, entitled "Ethical Questions: Faithful Responses." The series aired several times on British Columbia's Knowledge Network and on Canadian Vision TV. Those planning to employ this book in study groups may find it helpful to use it, as originally envisioned, with the video series with which it is integrated. The series is available on video cassette through the Vancouver School of Theology and The United Church Publishing House.

Peter Gordon White, editor-in-chief of the United Church Publishing House, first suggested that the pamphlet be enlarged into a book. Through his support and encouragement, he then made that suggestion a possibility. I thank him for that and for his insightful advice and patient editorial assistance, always graciously rendered.

I also thank those who provided the opportunity for me to write: the Vancouver School of Theology for sabbatical leave; and the McGeachy Foundation for financial support. A number of colleagues and friends read earlier drafts and provided helpful suggestions: Arthur Van Seters, Melva Ratcliff, Bill Crockett, Sally Clinton, Gordon Pokorny, Melu Scott, and Mac Watts. My thanks also to Elizabeth Phinney and, again, to Peter White. Their diligently applied editorial skills helped to refashion my work so it would be as readable as possible.

Terence R. Anderson
Vancouver, B.C.
March 1993

Introduction: Ask for the Paths

"Stand at the crossroads, and look,
and ask for the ancient paths,
where the good way lies; and walk in it,
and find rest for your souls."
(Jeremiah 6:16, NRSV)

Moral life has to do with the way human beings relate to one another. It spells out what a community assumes it means to be human. In times of change, people become aware of their operating morality. We are in such an era of real-life perplexities. This is an opportunity to articulate a Christian foundation for moral living. Knowing that reality is complex and dynamic, we look to Christian ethics as a guide to systematic reflection. To this end, five base points are identified.

The Charts

The first of seven charts gives an overview of the five base points. Each of the next five charts shows key considerations of the base point being examined. These charts arrange the base points in a fashion that displays their interrelationship (as noted throughout the book, especially in part 6), rather than according to the order in which they are discussed in the text. The final chart is a repeat of the first, with detail added to offer an integrated view of the enterprise as a whole.

A MODEL FOR ETHICAL REFLECTION

Moral Agent in Community

Basic Commitment

Analysis of Self as Agent

Moral Character

Worldview and Basic Convictions

Moral Norms and Standards

Analysis of the Social Setting

The Context

Economic, political, cultural, religious

The Situation

Alternate courses of actions and probable consequences

Authoritative Sources

Authoritative Sources

Resolution

Decide/choose
Formulate
Assess
Advise

- Course of Action
- General Position
- Policy Goal
- Programme of Action
  - Objectives and Strategy
  - Strategy

Personal
or
Corporate

Action – Reflection on – Preparation for – Action

AN INVITATION TO THINK ABOUT THE MORAL LIFE AND ETHICS

The two of us sat in silence while the VCR rewound the tape. The violent ending of the film had been a shock. My Cherokee friend watched closely for my reaction.

The movie was based on *The White Dawn,* a novel by James Houston. The story is a true incident in the late nineteenth century. Three men from a whaling expedition lost in the Arctic are rescued from certain death by a small Inuit community. They are shyly but warmly welcomed into the full life of the community.

Like all human societies, this Inuit community has a particular set of customs and morals, a Way of life so taken for granted that people have no need to say what it is. They just know how things are done, the way things should go. Following that Way is simply what it means to be human. So too, the three strangers have their own taken-for-granted understanding of what is an appropriate Way to be and to behave.

The sharp contrast between these two different Ways throws each into vivid relief. The tension builds towards a tragic conflict between them. The strangers function in a fashion that would be expected, even admired, in their own era and culture. Unlike the Inuit, the newcomers display a restless aggressiveness that hovers on the edge of violence. They have a ruthless, competitive style, whether playing games or hunting. Lust and greed taint the eroticism in their relations with the Inuit women. True, they display great courage in their daring but fruitless effort to find a way back to "civilization." But their self-interest shows a complete disregard for the needs of the Inuit people. Without permission, they help themselves to scarce, precious food from the community for their journey.

Finally, and fatally, the strangers show disrespect towards what is held sacred by their rescuers. They scorn the shaman. In the Inuit world, the shaman is essential for maintaining harmony with creation and therefore for locating game. The very survival of the community is threatened. Inevitably this leads to a solemn decision. The strangers who at first had been rescued and welcomed must now be killed.

My companion broke the silence. "Those newcomers violated everything important in that community's Way of life. Like poking a crowbar into a fine Swiss watch!"

The Way in Times of Stability. Every human community has a particular Way, as it is often called in the Bible and also in a variety of cultures. The *moral life* is what ethicists call it. This moral life has to do with the way human beings relate to one another. It also has to do with the way they relate to the sacred and the way they relate to other creatures and things. It spells out what a community assumes it means to be human and to be a member of the community. It involves both the kind of person one should or should not be and the actions in which one should or should not engage.

Good *being* has to do with what are deemed desirable qualities or traits for a person or a people, traits such as generosity, kindness, and courage, as well as those deemed undesirable, like greed or envy. Right *doing* pertains to actions that are deemed appropriate, such as telling the truth and seeking the best for another, and those actions deemed wrong, like murder or stealing. Children are socialized into the moral life of their people or society. In adulthood the moral life is reinforced in various ways.

The Way in Times of Change. In everyday living, most of us do not think very much or often about "the moral life." We do not worry about "the Way" when our community or society is relatively like-minded, when there is little social change. Moral life is largely taken for granted. There is little or no dispute regarding what is the good or the right. The main concerns are how to motivate and empower people to do what everyone "knows" should be done. When accepted patterns of behaviour are violated, we make an effort to restore broken relationships and to bring about harmony. Under such social conditions there is usually a clear and taken-for-granted *morality,* which means behaviour according to custom or code.

In times of change, however, people are pressed into awareness of their operating morality. They must reflect on it under conditions of interaction with other cultures, religions, belief systems, and values, as we saw dramatized in the story *The White Dawn*. Familiar ways are challenged. Questions regarding *right conduct* and *good being* now demand attention and conscious deliberation.

In North America, most of us live in social conditions that require ethical reflection. Indeed, change and social turmoil have marked European and related societies for the last three to four hundred years. The changes in Eastern Europe in this decade alone remind us of the many shifts in political boundaries and systems that have transpired there since the French Revolution. A current cartoon pictures two men in an antique shop looking at a world atlas. One says to the other, "This one goes all the way back to last Tuesday."

More than geography has changed. We have experienced shifts in family life, in childhood, in the relations of men and women, in the place of religion and the church in society and public life, in the patterns of daily work. We know the impact of the electronics and information industries, with all the ramifications for family and community life. The microchip is everyone's everyday reality. New and perplexing moral issues arise from this commonplace fact.

With increasing rapidity, new knowledge and technologies create undreamed-of possibilities. In his youth my grandfather rode horseback to deliver the mail. In his old age we watched men walking on the moon! How these new possibilities are to be pursued are questions that older moralities and traditions could not possibly anticipate. I am not saying that they are necessarily inadequate for guiding us in new matters. My point is that if they are to do so, we must consciously seek to relate them. In plain words, we need to engage in ethical thinking.

Let us take an example from medical technology: By the use of equipment it is now possible to sustain vital functions in human beings for an indefinite period of time, often long after such persons have ceased to be conscious. Does proper care for others require us to do this? Because we can do it, should we do it? If so, under what conditions?

Medical and legal ethics committees grapple with these and other end-of-life questions. A woman with the incurable "Lou Gehrig" disease faces a slow, painful, inevitable death. She pleads for assistance to end her life at a time she will choose. Can a moral decision combine compassion with safeguards against wider abuse? Issues of suicide, assisted suicide, and murder need to be re-thought with great care.

Beginning-of-life perplexities face us also. It is now possible to obtain an amazing amount of knowledge about the foetus before its birth, including its gender and certain abnormalities. Recently a new, not-yet-perfected technique has been developed for selectively terminating the life of one of the foetuses where twins are involved. Should we use this capability to preserve only desirable foetuses? Why? How are we to use — or should we use — our growing ability to manipulate the genetic makeup of the very human species itself?

Closer contact with peoples of other cultures and religions (and certainly with differing views of the moral life) is yet another aspect of the social upheaval experienced by European and North American societies. I have a personal story that illustrates my point. When you rent a car, you are asked to state your occupation. Well, I teach Christian ethics at a theological school. Twenty years ago, in any large Canadian airport, stating this presented no difficulty for the clerk. About ten years ago I was asked to spell "theology." And to explain what it is: "No, it is not geology." More recently (yes, back at the same car rental agency), I was asked to please spell — and explain — the word "Christian"!

Such pluralism, of course, is the hallmark of North American dominant societies. No group can simply take for granted its assumed Way, its traditional morality. So which of the many views of the good life and righteous living should we adhere to as we respond to new moral questions? On what grounds do we decide this?

Consider a specific group of people facing the following situation: The Dene people are five tribes who live in the northern part of Canada. They have recently experienced the arrival of European culture in an intense form. Most Dene communities have operated with this assumption: during the appropriate season everyone contributes fish and game to the community storehouse; then everyone draws upon that common resource according to their need. However, some of these people now work for money. They do not hunt or fish, yet are able to purchase all kinds of other goods. Others who do not participate in this wage economy have little cash for those goods. How now should the "fruits of labour" be held? What would be a right distribution of them? New conditions are demanding a more conscious awareness of their traditional moral life. They struggle to apply the old familiar "morality of sharing" to a new situation.

At all levels, thought must be given to the patterns of human interaction. Intentionality is required regarding "habits of the heart."

A CHRISTIAN FOUNDATION OF THE WAY

"Tis grace that brought me safe thus far..."

The Christian motivation and basis for this endeavour is vitally important. It colours, shapes, and informs both the approach to and the substance of the enterprise itself. *Why* we seek the Way affects *what* we discern it to be. Of course, I shall need to use the language of faith and the Bible to describe a Christian perspective regarding the foundation of the moral life and ethical reflection on it. Let me now briefly outline that foundation as I see it.

God's Grace

The foundation for the Way and for ethical reflection upon it is God's grace. Grace means God's freely offered, steadfast, and enduring love. "For great is his steadfast love toward us; and the faithfulness of the Lord endures for ever" (Ps. 117). God's grace comes to us as a gift first of all in creation and life itself. It also comes as the gift of one's people and the gift of the land. The psalmist expresses it with the repeated refrain, "for his steadfast love endures for ever" (Ps. 136).

This free gift of creation, of land, of one's people, of life itself has been called in some Protestant traditions "common grace." It is thought of as God's creating and sustaining power. God's "steadfast love" that "endures forever" is shown also in God's mercy towards a disobedient and fallen humankind.

Grace comes to us as a liberating, renewing power. Israel experienced it as being freed from the slavery of Egypt, and as the gift of the Law to guide and direct them in their new life and new land. Again, Psalm 136 extols this: "who led his people through the wilderness."

As Christians we believe that the mercy of God to the whole of humanity is revealed and effected supremely in Jesus Christ. There, God's mercy comes to humanity as forgiveness of sin, and as the inauguration of a new creation, a fresh beginning for all. It also comes to us personally in Jesus Christ as the power of God to lead a new life of faith, hope, and love. And it comes as the promise to complete the new creation that was inaugurated in Jesus Christ. Completion is envisioned as the second coming of Christ, bringing a new heaven and a new earth. The profoundest peace (shalom) will be fully realised: the right relationship of all of creation with God, the right relationship of human beings with each other, and the right relationship of human beings with other-than-human creation. In short, well-being, harmony, and justice for all.

This grace in Jesus Christ is what Christians have come to call God's "saving grace." Christians have glimpsed and identified the power of this saving grace in their own lives and have found the possibility of starting anew. In responding to it they find themselves bound together in a new community, seeking to live and witness to the new creation which God has begun in Christ, all of which evokes praise and thanksgiving. John Milton expresses this simply and joyfully in his hymn based on the 136th Psalm:

> *Let us with a gladsome mind,*
> *praise the Lord, for he is kind:*
> *for his mercies aye endure,*
> *ever faithful, ever sure.*

What Shall I Return to the Lord?

Amidst this praise and thanksgiving one is moved to ask, "What shall I return to the Lord for all his bounty to me?" (Ps. 116). The response of the community of people so moved is to joyously walk in the Way that God has called them to walk. Indeed, one could, without great distortion, sum up the message of the entire Bible, both Old and New Testaments, in the phrase "trust and obey." For Christians, then, the moral life is something we wish to live as a response to what God has already freely done for us. Martin Luther says it with typical gusto:

> *Though I am an unworthy and condemned man, my God has given me in Christ all the riches of*

> *righteousness and salvation without any merit on my part, out of a pure, free mercy, so that henceforth I need nothing whatever except faith which believes that this is true. Why should I not therefore freely, joyfully, with all my heart and with an eager will, do all things which I know are pleasing and acceptable to such a Father, Who has overwhelmed me with His inestimable riches? I will therefore give myself as a Christ to my neighbour just as Christ offered Himself to me.*[1]

The community of faith, the church, and not only individuals, is called to live the moral life in Christ amid a still alien and fallen world. Can the church so order its life as a "colony" of the Way that the world might look at it and know that God is busy redeeming humanity, reconciling the world to himself in Christ?[2]

The apostle Paul wrote a letter to the followers in Rome. In the first part, he points to the mercy of God in Jesus Christ and then goes on to say, *therefore,* now live in the light of those mercies (12:1). What that means is to present your bodies, your very selves, as a living, holy sacrifice. To be a holy sacrifice to God means to be consecrated to God, which in turn means to be possessed by Christ, to let the power of Christ renew one's self. This is the appropriate response to God's grace.

Then Paul continues, "Do not be conformed to this world" — that is, according to the present passing era and culture in which one lives — "but be transformed by the renewing of your minds" — by a whole new way of thinking so that you can discern what conforms to God's will.

This is the essence of Christian ethics. It is to work out our own salvation, as it were. It is to let the power of Christ come in and work with us so that our minds and our entire way of thinking are transformed. Then we can hope to discover what it means to live out the new creation that Christ has begun in us.

Christian ethics is an ongoing enterprise of examining the morality of the culture in which we were socialised. We look to see what of it is in accord with obedience to Jesus Christ and may be preserved, enhanced, strengthened. And we look to see what of it needs to be set aside, because it belongs to this passing age and not to the new creation in Christ. Christian ethics, then, is the disciplined reflection on the question, What is God requiring and enabling me to be and do?[3]

A "Because of" Ethic

Note that we are freed to undertake this enterprise with a gladsome mind, as a joyous, not an anxious task. Christian ethics is a "because of" ethic, not an "in order to" ethic. By this I mean that Christian ethics is an enterprise undertaken because of what God has freely done for us in Jesus Christ. It is not one undertaken in order to win our salvation or in order to preserve our souls from damnation or to achieve glory and success in this life.

I can hardly overstate the importance of this foundation of Christian ethics. Our basic certitude, our very identity, is grounded ultimately in God and Jesus Christ alone. It is not in the righteousness or wisdom of our culture or of our church, and certainly not of ourselves. We are liberated into moral honesty. We need no longer pretend that we know the right and the good more fully than we really do. Released from these idolatrous pretensions, we are more likely to have the courage to recognise our own shaky record. Further, we are more likely to be able to respond with understanding and compassion to others when they fall short of a good moral life, when they deviate from or stumble along the Way.

At the same time, we are better able to avoid the opposite tendency. This is the sentimental and dangerous illusion that violations of moral standards do not matter. Sound and discerning moral judgements about actions and qualities of character must be stated. They do not imply moral condemnation of persons. They do affirm a place to stand.

Trust in God's grace is an exhilarating liberation. It frees us to discern correctly and admit openly the moral wisdom to be found in other peoples, other cultures, and other faiths. Truth is greeted gladly in all forms, from all sources.

To put it plainly, to the extent that we are rooted in this certitude of God's grace, we will be free from the twin hazards that haunt all discussions about morality and the moral life. The first is a humourless self-righteousness, the kind that arrogantly assumes we fully know the right and good and do it better than anyone else. The second is a cynicism and despair, the kind that says there is no objective moral order. Or says that if there is a moral order, nobody is able to perceive it, let alone follow it. Or says that, therefore, one Way is as good as another.

Now that we have looked at a Christian foundation of the Way, we can ask, What aspects of our beings are actually engaged in living a moral life? We will use these aspects as *base points* for ethical reflection.[4]

ASPECTS OF THE MORAL LIFE: BASE POINTS FOR ETHICAL REFLECTION

Reflecting on a true case that presents a moral dilemma will help us to identify, in a preliminary way, the various aspects of the moral life. A crisis in our life, a back injury, for example, can help make us aware of activities that we usually do automatically: how we walk, stand, sit, or lie. Similarly, situations that present us with difficult and relatively uncommon moral decisions can make us aware of the moral life that we usually take for granted. Such cases can serve as windows, enabling us to see how we make decisions and to glimpse the makeup of the moral life. Imagine that this woman is your mother.

> Verna, a seventy-five-year-old woman, was always fastidious in her dress and personal appearance. She was extremely active mentally and physically, even after the death of her husband (your father), until one year ago when she entered hospital because of bleeding from the bowel. Investigation revealed that she had a cancer of the lower bowel. In the doctor's opinion, "cure" was possible by an operation involving removal of the lower bowel and creation of a new outlet for the bowel on the abdominal wall. At that time, Verna said that she would rather die than have such an abnormal opening. However, she finally consented.
>
> Her in-hospital physical convalescence was remarkably uneventful, although she obviously found it repulsive to care for her bowel outlet (colostomy). She was very depressed in spite of the assurance of the doctor that he was hopeful the entire growth had been removed. [To you, however, he confided that extension had already occurred to lymph nodes and that he was not at all sure that removal had been complete.]
>
> Following discharge, she withdrew completely from her previous full life. No doubt this was partly due to occasional "accidents" with the colostomy, which were apparent only to Verna (although she could never be convinced of this). She confided on many occasions that she wished she were dead.
>
> Approximately a month ago she began to have lower

> abdominal pain, which radiated down the back of the left leg and progressively increased in severity. On re-admission to hospital, it was found she had lost twenty pounds and was virtually not eating. By this time, her will to live had completely left her, and she pleaded for permanent relief from her pain and her colostomy through death. Drugs, however, gave her sufficient relief so that she appeared to rest, although this required medication every three hours or pain became intolerable.
>
> She was discharged home at her own request, with the medical opinion that she did not have long to live. One pill relieved her pain reasonably well, but two would probably be fatal. Supposing you were responsible for giving her the "pain pills," should you give her two, the fatal dose? Why?

I have listened to various groups engaged in moral discussions about this actual case. The following sorts of comments usually emerge, but not necessarily in this order. Most people, of course, feel torn about what they should do in this situation. They feel that they should seek the highest well-being of their mother and at the same time respect her free choices. But do these obligations not conflict in this situation? A related tension is the conflict between the moral precept to "honour your mother" and respect her decisions on the one hand, and the imperative not to kill or take the life of an innocent person on the other. Suicide is usually wrong. Is it always wrong? Is giving assistance to somebody who wants to take their own life the same as actually killing that person? If we are to honour our mother and respect her decisions does she not need to be informed about her true condition? Is there an obligation to tell her the truth? To bring some order into this, let us group and name the kinds of considerations that have arisen.

Moral Norms and Standards

All of these statements and questions are about moral obligations. They appeal to moral norms and standards that require or prohibit certain kinds of actions or behaviour. There are many different kinds. Some, for example, are quite specific (rules), others are very broad in the guidance they give (principles). There are various views over where these norms should come from, what kind of authority is claimed for them, which should take precedence when they conflict, and how they should be applied in specific situations. Indeed, in recent years a good deal of philosophical ethics in Western thought has focused on these questions. In any case, moral norms and standards focus on the "doing" aspect of moral life. They are one important kind of ethical consideration. There are others. Let us continue with Verna's case.

Character

There is another major segment of the moral life, namely, moral "being," which is usually designated as moral character. This refers to a distinctive constellation, an enduring structure of the self which relates it in a consistent way to values and to the community. But moral being and doing interact on each other. In this particular case, we need to ask what virtues or qualities of character are required. What response would both reflect and foster trustworthiness, truthfulness, kindness, patience, and the like? In the case of Verna, how do we act in a way that manifests and helps to create a community that cares for people who are dying, one that generates a sense of self-worth in persons even though they are no longer productive, the sort of community that enables us to see death as an ending we need not hasten?

Basic Convictions

The two aspects of the moral life identified so far are shaped or informed by certain foundational beliefs. These have been called "control beliefs." They are basic convictions about who we are, what is the good life, what is wrong about the human condition, and what can be done to set it right. So we might ask, are suffering and death completely contradictory to the good life or well-being of this woman? What constitutes human well-being? How do we understand the nature of family relationships? Do we believe that life is sacred and inviolable or merely a central value among competing values in human existence? Here then, is yet another aspect of the moral life and therefore a base point for ethical reflection. I call it basic convictions.

Analysis of the Situation and Wider Context

There are other matters involved in trying to decide whether or not to give Verna the lethal dose of medication. More information about her condition and prognosis would help us. Is her condition definitely terminal? How long is she likely to live? Are there other ways and forms of medication that could control her pain? How much pain and suffering is she likely to have to endure? What would be the effect on the rest of the family of her taking her own life or of some family member assisting her to do this? What is the probable impact on the general ethos of the community? These questions about alternative courses of action and their likely consequences draw us into thinking about the wider social context. For example, in Verna's case what is the law regarding suicide? How does the culture and ethos of the society regard elderly people and those either temporarily or permanently impaired or disabled? Who bears the financial cost and burden of different forms of health care? These sorts of matters bear upon and shape our response and decision in ways of which we may or may not be aware. Our understanding of what is going on in the world around us obviously affects what we think we should and can do. It forms yet another aspect of the moral life, an additional base point for ethical reflection.

Authoritative Sources

Moral norms or standards. Moral Character. Basic convictions. Analysis of the situation and the wider social context. These then are the main kinds of considerations that enter into moral decisions and more general reflection on the moral life or the Way. But what should be the content of each? Granted that moral norms and standards, for example, are an important aspect of the moral life and a factor in making moral decisions, which moral norms and standards should these be? This leads to a fifth base point; namely, authoritative sources. These are the sources we go to when we say which qualities of character we deem virtuous, which convictions we think are sound, which moral norms and standards should guide us, and what an accurate perception is of the situation and context. Human reason, experience, scripture, a natural law found in the basic constitution of the universe are some of the sources that have been given such authority.

So we have identified five kinds of considerations that emerge in thinking about moral decisions and about the moral life in general, the Way. These five considerations point to enduring features of the moral life. It is not known, of course, whether these features are universal to humanity. They are conceptualized differently, if at all, in various cultures and eras. But each refers, I believe, to some real and important aspect of the moral life as it is widely experienced. Every one of these elements can serve, therefore, as a base point for reflection on the moral life. We turn now to explore more carefully each of these five base points.

One

Moral Norms and Standards: A Lamp unto Our Feet

A look at what moral norms and standards are, their various types and functions. Examples of three different types of norms are examined by exploring various Christian interpretations of their meaning and application. The three types are: obligations, which include love of neighbour and trusteeship of creation; values and goods, which include the common good and middle axioms; and moral rights, which include individual rights, collective rights, and animal rights. Following this, we discuss briefly the limits, importance, and place of norms in the moral life.

A MODEL FOR ETHICAL REFLECTION

Moral Agent in Community

Basic Commitment

Analysis of Self as Agent

Moral Character

Worldview and Basic Convictions

Moral Norms and Standards
- Obligations – right relations
  - Love of Neighbour
    - Ten Commandments
    - Justice
    - Liberty
    - Additional Principles
  - Trusteeship of Creation
    - Respect for Intrinsic Worth
    - Sustainable Use
    - Well-Being of Creatures

- Values and Goods – consequences and ends
  - Beneficence or well-being
  - Common Good
  - Middle Axioms – social goals

- Moral Rights – moral claims
  - Individual Rights
  - Collective Rights
  - Animal Rights

Analysis of the Social Setting

The Context

The Situation

Authoritative Sources

Authoritative Sources

Resolution

INTRODUCTION

All cultures have moral norms or standards; a collection of these is referred to as moral law. They are navigational markers that point to a Way. They require or prohibit certain behaviour and thereby provide direction for the moral life.

Let us look at the example of the Cherokee people, who say that they received the "Four Mothers Law" from the Creator, probably between 1000 and 500 B.C. "It was a law of peace and harmony, peace among one another and between all the different tribes," explains a Cherokee narrator. "Before that time, that law was just taken for granted." The Cherokees had migrated from the Atlantic coast through the mountains to the Ohio river basin around 2000 B.C. They began to develop more sophisticated arts and crafts. "Since they were starting to develop and get smarter," continues the Cherokee, "the Creator got a little worried. He figured the Cherokees needed a stronger law."

Stronger here means a more detailed and elaborate set of moral norms. The elder Cornsilk, the agent who brought this new law, told this prophecy: "As long as the Indians held to God's law they would live the good life. However, if they strayed off the white path of peace then a new nationality would come here to North America. They would overcrowd the country and life would become hard."[1]

The Cherokees kept this moral law for about a thousand years. They decisively broke it by going to war against the Delaware who had tried to cross Cherokee territory. Years of war and forced migration resulted for the tribes caught up in the ensuing struggles. The Cherokees eventually wound up in what they came to consider their homeland, an area in the Great Smoky mountains where the states of North and South Carolina and Tennessee now meet. Several hundred years after this move (around 700 A.D.), on the mountain now called Klingmans Dome, the elders received a vision: "God told them that ... they had followed a path that would lead them to destruction if they kept on. Then God said that He was going to give them a second chance and give them a second and stronger law of peace which He called the Seven Clan Law."

The Creator made the world and human beings in a certain way, explains the elder. "He gave us a Law to go by which fitted our nature as a People and, which given our nature, sets up the right kind of good feelings between one and another, and between us as a People and all the rest of the Universe — the Earth, the animals and plants, the spirits.... That Law gives us a way to go that is natural and normal.... God wants us free, and prospering, and happy. Harmony is the base that His creation rests on and the Law keeps that harmony and love firmly in place."[2]

This understanding of moral law accords well with the

Christian view. Indeed, the narrative is reminiscent of God's gift of the moral law to Israel at Mount Sinai, following the exodus from Egypt. It is a part of the covenant that is so central to Israel's identity and well-being. The elaboration and enrichment of the Sinai law now found in the Bible's book of Deuteronomy is also like a "stronger" law to guide the people in a changing and more complex situation. These precepts, together with the liberation from Egypt, are a gift of God's grace for the people's well-being. Writes the psalmist, "Great peace have those who love your law.... My soul keeps your decrees; I love them exceedingly. I keep your precepts and decrees, for all my ways are before you" (Ps. 119:165-168).

In Western societies today, people appeal to a variety of moral standards in choosing and justifying their actions. The proliferation of professional and business "codes of ethics" indicates that secular societies also feel the need for guideposts to an appropriate way to live, in response to rapid social change. We now see attempts being made in North America to spell out norms for behaviour in order to guard against sexual harassment. This is a contemporary example of the need for a "stronger" or more detailed moral law. The discovery of this need is notable in a society that rebelled against standards, such as those regarding fornication, adultery, and lust, that limited free sexual expression. The Cherokee elder is right; the smarter people get, the more they need a "stronger" moral law!

Norms and standards, then, are a major ingredient of the moral life. They are a central base point for ethical reflection. If we picture the moral life as an orchestra, norms and standards are the brass section; like the big brass, everyone is aware of them. A large part of ethics, Christian or secular, is concerned with the grounding, selecting, ordering, and applying of various kinds of moral norms or standards. This means fashioning and interpreting moral law. Much wisdom about the moral law has accumulated over the years, as various peoples have wrestled with the complexities of human relationships under diverse circumstances. How do we sort and sift this rich material? There are some categories developed by ethicists that can be helpful. For instance, norms that designate qualities of moral being as good (virtues) or unworthy (vices) can be readily distinguished from those that deal with moral conduct, what we are to do and not do.

We will discuss virtues and vices later in the section on moral character. Our first undertaking is to examine standards that are guides for action. It is useful to distinguish between three types of action guides, called, respectively: *obligations, values* or *goods,* and *moral rights*. We now turn to explore each of these types to see how they may guide us in the Way.

OBLIGATIONS

Everyday human interactions entail certain mutual responsibilities if people are to live harmoniously. Particular kinds of behaviour are required to maintain the necessities of shared existence. *Obligations* are a type of moral norm that attempts to name the kinds of actions that are essential for any flourishing human community. One should tell the truth, one should keep promises, one should not harm others, and the like. Such obligations establish the basic ground rules of action.[3] The moral law of the Cherokee, of most tribal societies, and of the Bible are alike in this. They focus on right relationships between humans, between human beings and God, and between human beings and creation. They differ significantly on the content of norms.

Their moral precepts, however, contain more of this obligation-type of moral norm than any other type.

In peasant societies, and even more in modern, bureaucratic societies, obligations tend to take on a different association. Instead of expressing and maintaining the web of basic human relationships, they connect more to roles and functions. They are then formulated as rigid, abstract duties. This is vividly displayed in the work of eighteenth-century philosopher Immanuel Kant, who greatly influenced subsequent Protestant ethics. He viewed the norms that define duty as entirely separate from instinct, inclination, or even concerns about consequences. An action is to be regarded as moral and right, he claimed, only if it is done not because of desire but out of a sense of duty. And duty is determined by reason.[4] However, the type of standards for behaviour called obligations are properly understood as designating acts that are deemed to be responsibilities entailed in right relations rather than merely duties associated with roles.

It is useful to distinguish kinds of obligations according to how specific they are in their guidance. "Do not harm" and "respect the autonomous choices of others" are examples of obligation-type norms that give only general direction. Such broad standards are usually called *principles*. More specific obligations, such as, "Never withdraw life-sustaining nutrition from a patient," are usually called *rules* or *guidelines*. They give more precise guidance by spelling out the implications of principles. One of the ongoing and important discussions in Christian ethics is what rules and guidelines best express the enduring principles in new or different cultural contexts. In our examination of obligations, we will concentrate on principles.

What are the particular obligation-type norms that, from a Christian perspective, mark the Way God intends us to live? There are two basic principles that serve as a summary of various additional ones. The first, the Great Commandment to love God and neighbour, is acknowledged in all strands of the Christian tradition. The second, the principle of trusteeship of creation, is not as generally recognized or as fully developed.

Love of Neighbour: The Ten Commandments

The command from God to love our neighbour is central for Christians. Agape (ah-gah-pay)is the distinctive Greek word used in the New Testament to describe this kind of love. This basic norm is pervasive throughout the New Testament. In the tradition about Jesus found in the Gospels of Matthew, Mark, and Luke, it is expressed as "the Great Commandment," sometimes called "the double commandment" (Mark 12:28-34; Matt. 23:34-40; Luke 10:25-37). In Mark's account, one of the scribes comes up to Jesus and asks him,

> *"Which commandment is the first of all?" Jesus answered, "The first is, 'Hear O Israel: the Lord our God, the Lord is one; you shall love the Lord your God with all your heart, and with all your soul, and with all your mind, and with all your strength.' The second is this, 'You shall love your neighbour as yourself.' There is no other commandment greater than these."*

In Mark, obedience to this double commandment is more important than performance of correct ritual. In Matthew, this summary commandment provides the key to the meaning of the interpretation of the entire law, while in Luke, it is linked with the parable of the good Samaritan. We are exhorted to go and do likewise. What counts, Jesus makes clear, is not merely knowledge of the law but obedience to it.

The first commandment, to love God, is foundational to the entire enterprise of Christian ethics, as we saw earlier. In this section on norms, we shall focus on the second commandment, love of neighbour, as the key expression of a right response to God.

God's command to love our neighbour is pervasive throughout Paul's letters and the entire New Testament. God's new commonwealth has been initiated in Jesus Christ, his life, death, and resurrection. In Christ is seen the promise of new life, a new creation. Likewise, in Christ is found the command of that new life; namely, to love our neighbour. The fruit of the Spirit is this love. It gives life to the new age and, by it, we are to walk (Gal. 5:16). Indeed, "the whole law is filled in a single commandment, 'You shall love your neighbour as yourself'" (Gal. 5:14. See also Rom. 13:8-10).

According to the Gospel of John, Jesus' mission is to lead the world out of darkness and death into light and life eternal. The new commandment that goes with life and light is, "Just as I have loved you, you also should love one another" (John 13:34b). Jesus has set the example of the Way by his washing of the disciples' feet, and we are also called upon to do "as I have done to you" (John 13:15). Such love provides the identity of the new community of disciples. The book of Revelation is filled with antipathy towards the persecuting Roman state and is concerned with the integrity and survival of the struggling community of faith under times of tribulation. Yet even there, love is seen as the very heart of faithful endurance and the key characteristic of the Christian life (Rev. 2:4-5; 12:17; 14:12).

But what kind of love is this? Is it different from or related in any way to the familiar kind of human love that seeks to draw the other to oneself? Is it similar to the companionable mutual liking that marks friendship? If either is so, how can I be commanded to have such love, especially towards my enemies? In light of these questions and the centrality of the command to love our neighbour, it is not surprising that there has been much deliberation by Christians as to what this love means. Many volumes have been written on the subject.[5] Nevertheless, considerable agreement has emerged, both about certain essential features of agape and certain obligation-type principles that embody this fundamental norm. We shall examine each of these in turn.

The Essential Qualities of Agape. The model for agape is God's love for us in Jesus Christ (John 13:34).[6] God's love in Jesus Christ is:

1. unconditional: all human beings are loved for their own sake. God both creates and affirms the worth of all human beings. God's love is motivated by human worth. If it were otherwise, it would be arbitrary and unintelligible. But the worth is bestowed on all human beings by God in the very fact of creating us. God's love is not dependent on any form of attractiveness that a person may inherit or acquire. Nor is it dependent on moral or any other kind of achievement, though of course God finds satisfaction in human moral goodness and well-being.

   Therefore the command to love our neighbour in such a manner entails looking on all other persons as children of God, with ultimate worth in God's eyes. It means that nothing a person does or is qualifies or disqualifies them from respect and active help. It means "identification with [the neighbours'] interests in utter independence of the question of attractiveness."[7]
2. unlimited: unrestricted to all persons, the unconditional love of God is extended to all of humankind and, in a different sense, as we shall see later, to all of creation. There

are no limits or boundaries on God's love, no in-group and out-group. The church as the community of faith intentionally responding to this gift of love has a special calling, but God's love is not confined to its boundaries. We are called to love neighbours — and neighbours are understood in the New Testament as the next person we meet — even if he or she is an enemy.

3. equal: in God's sight one person is as valuable as another. God loves not simply the whole of humankind but each one of us individually. Thus each person is valued irreplaceably in the sense that no other person can be substituted for any one of us. Of course, God's satisfaction is greater with the faithful and upright person than the faithless and the evil doer. Further, God gives a strategic priority to victims and the oppressed. But God's commitment is equally strong to all of us.

   This aspect of agape generates difficulties as we seek to emulate it in our relationship to our neighbours. On the one hand, the many differences among human beings should not affect our respect and care for them. On the other hand, because each is irreplaceable, we need to attend to the peculiarities of each individual, including their needs, any special relationships we may have with them, and the like. Equal means the same in our regard for them but not necessarily identical actions towards them.

4. steadfast, reliable, stable: God's love for us endures. It is, as stated in the psalm quoted earlier, "ever faithful, ever sure." God is faithful to the covenant relationships to which he calls humankind. To love our neighbour like this means to be persons whose being and word others can depend on. It means accepting long-term responsibility for our actions and their consequences.

5. seeking the well-being of others in order to meet their true needs: throughout both the Old and the New Testament, God is continually portrayed as one who cares for human well-being and who seeks to meet people's deepest and truest needs. This includes liberation from bondage, sustenance in the wilderness, a law that sustains and guides them in their life together, judgement to bring them back from erring ways, and forgiveness and restoration to a right relationship of community with God and each other. Following the command to love like this, therefore, means actively seeking the well-being of all other persons. Well-being includes: the requirements for physical survival; the things necessary for true human agency, such as development of talents and gifts; and a right relationship and covenant with God and fellow human beings.
6. community forming: God's love for us is a covenant love; that is, a love that binds us together as members of a covenant community with God. We have been created as social beings, capable of community and in need of it. "The labor of [God's] love is to overcome the pride and covetousness that estrange people alike from God and from one another and to bring them to that state of mutual attachment and mutual dependence which is proper to a family."[8] Thus, when we are commanded to love like this, we are "summoned to one another." As Paul puts it, we are to be reconciled to one another within the community of love. We have a ministry of reconciliation to bring others into such community. Harmony and peace will be important aspects of the well-being we seek for others, reconciliation wherever alienation exists, restoration of community when it is threatened and breaks down. To love as God loves us, then, is to exercise a reconciling love.

7. forgiving, restoring: God's love, which we are called to imitate, is a forgiving and restoring love. This is closely connected with the community-forming and reconciling quality just described. "But God proves his love for us in that while we still were sinners Christ died for us" (Rom. 5:8). Forgiveness is quite different from mere indulgence, which simply overlooks wrongdoing as if it did not matter. Forgiveness recognizes the significance of wrongdoing but nevertheless extends the possibility of reconciliation and seeks the offender's transformation and return to full acceptance and their place in the covenant community. This is how we are to care for one another, with a willingness to forgive and receive forgiveness that entails repentance, change, and reconciliation.

There is, then, general, though not universal, agreement among Christian thinkers that these are the essential characteristics of agape. These characteristics already begin to give form and substance to the broad norm of love of neighbour. They entail certain qualities of being and appropriately so, for we are not only to engage in acts of love but to be loving persons (I Cor. 13). I shall later examine some of the debated features of what it means to be such a person in the section on moral character.

The Ten Commandments. What about love of neighbour as an action guide? Is it all-embracing or does it lead to recognition of other norms that spell out in more detail what actions are appropriate to such love? Answers vary. Some Christians believe further norms are unnecessary. A few say they are positively detrimental to true agape: we are to discover what the right thing to do is in a particular situation solely by bringing a loving will to the circumstances. Each situation is so unique that no guiding generalizations can be properly made. In this approach, love of neighbour becomes virtually the only norm or else disappears as an action guide altogether and is seen as only a quality of character.[9] I shall return to this matter in a discussion about the general place of norms in the moral life.

For now, let us follow the most pervasive view in Christian thought: we are given certain binding norms that embody love of neighbour, though they do not exhaust the meaning of it. The Great Commandment is, after all, a summary of the teachings of the law and the prophets and not a substitute for them. It is also, according to Matthew, a summary in the sense that it provides the intent and direction of these teachings. Therefore, it is a basis for interpreting them. We can expect to find in these biblical teachings about the moral law, then, additional norms that tell us some of the action-implications of the command to love neighbour.

The Ten Commandments (Ex. 20:1-17; Deut. 5:6-21) form the core of the covenant. This is "the binding together of God and human community on the basis of the prior redeeming grace of God." The commandments give the ordering of life that belongs to this definitive relationship for human existence. They are "instruction for life, the teaching of God about what is necessary to do in order for the community to live according to God's way and in harmony with one another."[10] They indicate clearly and succinctly both what is *not* to happen and what are the most basic requisites of communal life if the human community is to survive and flourish.

The teachings of the Ten Commandments or the Decalogue are not confined to the covenant and law tradition in the Old Testament. The prophets applied these teachings in their own setting and discovered deeper moral meanings in them. Violation of these instructions was viewed as a sign that knowledge of God was absent in the land (Hos. 4:2; see also Jer. 7:9-10; Micah 6:11-12; Amos 3:5-12; Isa. 5:23 and 10:1-2; and Ezek. 22:1-12). The Ten Commandments are also key to the moral teachings of the New Testament, as we shall see later.

The exclusive worship of God is central to a right relation with God. The first three commandments elaborate on what it means to have this ultimate commitment to God alone. As already indicated, this is the very foundation of a true moral life from a Christian perspective. The next seven commandments have to do with love of neighbour.

The sabbath commandment is the centre of the Decalogue. It is the bridge from God to neighbour. The sabbath is for remembering and for rest. In Exodus, God's rest on the seventh day of creation is recalled; in Deuteronomy, God's deliverance of Israel from slavery in Egypt, where there was no rest from toil. In this day of remembrance, then, people celebrate their liberation and their creaturehood as they remember God who is both creator and redeemer.

Like the other commandments, this one gets elaborated into more specific rules, in this case, ones governing the use of the sabbath (e.g., Ex. 23:12; 31:12-17). But, also typically, the meaning of the commandment is broadened over time as new implications and understandings are discovered. Thus, this commandment has come to include not only provision for human beings to have rest but also rest, relief, and humane treatment for draft animals. Eventually, even the land is given a rest under this provision (Lev. 25:2-7; Ex. 23:10-11). In Deuteronomy, the concept of sabbath rest is extended to include relief from the burden of debt and the release of bond slaves (Deut. 15:1-6, 12-18). "The sabbatical principle prohibits a permanent slavery or an enduring poverty. It resists the acquisitive instinct that would keep others from having the opportunity to live good and satisfying lives in God's creation."[12] Jesus' recognition that the sabbath was made for human beings, not human beings for the sabbath, was one that followed in the line of this same interpretive "trajectory," rather than a repudiation of this commandment.

The commandments to honour father and mother, to not murder, to not commit adultery, to not steal, to not bear false witness against your neighbour, and to not covet, all directly pertain to right relationships between human beings. It is essential to remember, of course, that right relationships with human beings are intrinsic to right relationship with God.

In the New Testament, this second set of commandments, the so-called "second table," are viewed as a partial explanation of what obedience to Christ means (Mark 10:17-22; Matt. 19:16-22; Luke 18:18-23). In Mark, Jesus demands both observance of these commandments and a complete surrender to the life of discipleship. In Matthew, the second table is extended into a more radicalized version as found in the six antitheses of the Sermon on the Mount (Matt. 5:27-48). One of the things that Jesus has done, in the language of contemporary ethics, is to take the obligations expressed in the second table of the Ten Commandments and further push their demands for certain kinds of action into qualities of moral being. For example, not only is the act of murder wrong, as Jesus reminds us, but he calls us away from the dispositions of anger and scorn that underlie it. We will discuss these virtues later when we come to the "base point" of character. Paul also makes clear that the "law of Christ" entails not only the love commandment but its articulation in the second table of the Decalogue (Rom. 13:8b-9).

Each of these commandments has become a summary of a rich moral tradition, a tradition that includes case law regulations coming from centuries of Israel's working out the implications of each norm for daily life under diverse conditions. While our social context is sufficiently different so that some of the more specific rules would no longer properly express the particular commandment (for example, specific guidance regarding rest from labour for both humans and animals on the sabbath), we can learn more about the commandment from these applications.[13] We will then be better able to interpret what it requires of us today. Each commandment also brings with it a history of interpretation along a clear trajectory, as we saw with the sabbath commandment. The meaning of the commandment is thereby broadened and deepened. Each commandment becomes an even more helpful action guide, delineating what is entailed in love of neighbour.

A brief look at the sixth commandment, "you shall not kill" —which leads off the second table of the Decalogue—will serve as an illustration of this.[14] Killing a fellow human being violates the first commandment by assuming the prerogative of God, who alone creates life and who made human beings in God's own image. It is also contrary, of course, to love of one's neighbour. Murder is the ultimate violation of one human being by another. All relationship with the victim is irrevocably broken. There is no going back. But only certain kinds of killing, namely arbitrary and illegal killing destructive of the community of Israel, were referred to by the Hebrew verb "to kill." That is why it is sometimes translated as "murder" rather than "killing." Nevertheless, from its earliest formulations, the sixth commandment sets a clear direction for the protection of human life. Any taking of human life is very difficult to justify morally.

Ancient Israelites, like modern Christians, had to wrestle with whether there were any circumstances when the taking of human life might conceivably fall outside this prohibition. The early tradition said this was so only when the community could legitimately claim it was acting on God's behalf: in the case of war, only those wars permitted or ordered by Yahweh; in the case of taking the life of another individual, only one who has shed the blood of another human being — a murderer, blasphemer, or exorcist. However, the general direction of the development of this commandment throughout scripture and much of the Christian tradition is one of extending its coverage. It gradually comes to protect an increasingly wide range of human life. Fewer and fewer exceptions are permitted.

The matter of vengeance provides an illustration of this development. The common practice in ancient times was to seek vengeance against the entire family of those who had committed a murder. In the Bible, this retaliation is limited to an "eye for an eye, a tooth for a tooth." Those who kill accidentally or unintentionally are protected by the provision of places or cities of refuge for them (Ex. 21:13). Even murderers are not to be treated as "an unprotected species." Thus Cain receives from God a mark, "so that no one who came upon him should kill him" (Gen. 4:15). In the New Testament, the law of revenge is handed over to God: "Beloved, never avenge yourselves, but leave room for the wrath of God; for it is written, 'Vengeance is mine, I will repay, says the Lord'" (Rom. 12:19). However, this passage in Romans goes on to call us to feed the hungry enemy and thereby prevent the threatened destruction of life. Jesus himself urges us to seek reconciliation even with accusers (Matt. 5:25). We are admonished to overcome anger and scorn towards others that so easily generates violence in ourselves or others (Matt. 5:21f).

The great sixteenth-century Reformers John Calvin and Martin Luther further developed this interpretation of the sixth commandment. They state the need "to struggle against every 'murderous spirit' by taking both preventative and supportive measures." If there is anything that makes for the peace of our neighbour's lives, we are to see to it, says Calvin, in commenting on the sixth commandment. And Luther claims that we are challenging this commandment whenever we fail to do the good we could in clothing the naked and feeding the hungry, or when we acquiesce in the wrongful sentencing and killing of others.[15] It is not only actual deeds of killing that violate the sixth commandment, but also our neglect of others in need. The sixth commandment calls us to address the "killing conditions" that prevail in both our immediate and more remote neighbourhoods.

This commandment provides, then, one "signpost" for what it means to love our neighbour as God loves us. It comes strongly into play in decisions regarding euthanasia, suicide, capital punishment, abortion, and war. In many specific situations involving these matters, it may seem to be in conflict with other important norms, such as honouring the wishes of parents or combating injustice, that also embody the basic commandment to love our neighbour. We will return to the question of how we are to weigh and compare and apply various norms, especially in situations where they conflict.

The sixth commandment is expressed in differently formulated norms that receive support from circles much wider than Christian or Jewish. One of the basic principles, for example, that is used for assessing appropriate actions in the field of health care is the principle of nonmaleficence — you shall not harm or injure. Obviously this includes the prohibition against killing, but some philosophers would also extend this principle to embrace the prohibitions against stealing, committing adultery, and bearing false witness.

We may summarize by saying that, from a Christian perspective, the foundation of a sound moral life and the whole enterprise of Christian ethics is the first Great Commandment, to love

God. The first three of the Ten Commandments elaborate on what this means. The fundamental obligation-type norm is the second Great Commandment, love of neighbour. The last seven commandments are principles that provide additional direction regarding what actions express love of neighbour. These standards for behaviour are obligations in the sense that their observance is integral to right relationships among humans. They are essential to the good functioning of human communities. They do not exhaust the meaning of the moral life or of obedience to Christ or even of what constitutes love of neighbour. They do, however, provide "signposts to freedom." They are God's gift, liberating us from chaos and confusion.

Love of Neighbour: Justice

"Frustrating and unnecessary" — that is how a group of young people described the regulations governing their common life at a church training centre in the 1960s. As Christians who had come to know and care for one another, they felt that they did not require such rules. The leaders of the centre, under pressure, finally agreed to experiment with living together for a time according to the vision of the young people. There would be no formal requirements. Everyone would rely on spontaneous love and concern for one another. Several weeks later, I arrived to teach a course and found that anger, resentment, hostile camps pervaded the place. Only a few were doing all the daily work of meal preparation, clean up and the like, and had begun to resent it. Programmes had virtually ground to a halt because participation was so irregular and unpredictable.

What had gone wrong? It was obvious that they had forgotten to take human sin into account. Disaster! In the terms of moral norms, the group had emphasized the importance of love of neighbour, which certainly includes the principle of liberty. But they had forgotten (or ignored) the fact that it also includes the principle of justice. Justice has to do with rendering to each person his or her due and with balancing the interests and claims of individuals and groups. Love without justice is sentimentality. Clearly we need to examine the obligation-type norms of justice and liberty more closely.

Justice is a widely recognized major moral norm. It is a powerful warrant for action, but it is a complex norm with many sides. Not surprisingly, there is important and vigorous discussion regarding its meanings. For some, justice refers to a total social ideal, almost the equivalent of the good society or even the good life. Thus liberation theologians tend to include political freedom, socio-economic equality, and even renewed religious faith in their concept of justice. For our purposes, I am following the more usual practice of identifying justice as a norm. As a norm, justice is only one important criterion for determining a good society and is the prime standard for assessing political and economic life.

Aspects of Justice. One of the great scandals of our society is the fact that many women receive lower pay than men for doing the same work. This is a clear violation of one aspect of the norm of justice. This particular facet of justice is referred to as *compensatory* or *commutative* justice. It has to do with assessing the treatment individuals accord to each other in various kinds of transactions. Does each person in the transaction receive their due portion or a fair share? Fair prices for goods and services exchanged, fair wages for labour and services rendered, fair compensation for goods stolen or injuries inflicted, all are matters having to do with compensatory justice.

Another facet of justice is concerned with the relation of

individuals to the community. A British Columbia physician withheld that portion of her taxes used by the government for military purposes, because, on the basis of her religious conscience as a Quaker, she is opposed to military action. She claims that, in the name of justice, she should not have to pay for such activities. What do individuals owe the community or its agent, the state? What is its due? This is the citizenship aspect of justice and bears on questions like obedience to laws, jury duty, willingness to serve in wartime, and the like. This is sometimes referred to as *general* justice.

A third aspect of justice comes increasingly to the fore in a highly bureaucratized society. It is referred to as *administrative* justice and is concerned with whether the administrative bodies of a state administer their responsibilities fairly so that each person receives his or her due. Black Canadians in Halifax and Toronto, Aboriginal peoples in Manitoba and Nova Scotia, have recently claimed, with an impressive amount of evidence, that they have not been treated justly in the administration of the law. Is the welfare system we have in place, whatever its strengths or weaknesses, being administered in such a way that all those eligible receive their proper due?

I want to focus here, however, on a facet of justice referred to as *distributive* justice. This is a set of standards brought to bear on how the community as a whole relates to its individual members. Those young people who tried to live without regulations violated this aspect of justice in their failure to distribute justly the burdens of the community's life. Small children have a vivid sense of distributive justice in matters such as whose turn it is to do dishes or other household chores. There are, in any society or community, both material goods and moral goods and values that have to do with the group as a whole — fellowship in the sense of solidarity, peace and harmony with nature, clean air, the basis of self-respect. These cannot be divided or allotted but belong to the group as a whole. I will discuss these further in the next section in connection with a norm called the "common good."

However, there are also material and moral goods and values that can be distributed among the members of a community or society. These include things like various liberties or forms of freedom and different kinds of wealth. There are also burdens and responsibilities of community life that can be allocated. By what criteria should these benefits and burdens of social cooperation be distributed to the members of a community or society? This is the question of distributive justice.

What are the grounds for distributive justice and what are the principles that provide more specific criteria for distribution? There are a number of theories that provide "windows on justice," a frame for viewing it, but thereby permit only a partial angle of vision.[16] These theories of justice are actually "fragments" from the broader moral theories and philosophies that underlie them. I shall not examine any of them in detail here but, as noted, will refer to some of them later, since they impinge upon the general operating views of justice in our culture and have also influenced many Christian thinkers.

Christian Grounds for Justice. From a Christian perspective, the ground for justice is the justice of God, Creator, Sustainer, and Redeemer. God is righteous, and this is seen in God's covenanting relationship with the people and is manifest in both justice and compassion towards them. As humans, we too should seek to be righteous. This comes about when a person seeks "to fulfill the possibilities of given or assumed relationships in a way that is fair and favourable to others."[17] In the prophets of Judah of the eighth century B.C., the prophetic stance on justice receives its classic expression. For these prophets (Amos, Isaiah, and Micah), justice is a norm with an assumed meaning, and they use it to cry out against the social conditions of their times. Both the economic order and the legal system are deemed corrupt, because they permit the gap between rich and poor to increase and ignore the needs of the latter.

The transfer of land ownership from many small kinship groups to a few wealthy individuals is the centrepiece of economic injustice. "Ah, you who join house to house, who add field to field, until there is room for no one but you, and you are left to live alone in the midst of the land!" (Isa. 5:8-10). Ownership of land was important not only for economic reasons but because it was part of the inheritance God had given to Israel. By it, "the will of God to have free people on free land bound only to loyalty and obedience to his sole majesty was made possible."[18]

Ownership of land, therefore, was central to people's sense of identity and assurance of a place in the salvation history of Israel. Community rights and obligations went with this inheritance. Hence, when a family lost its land, much more than economic loss was the result. It was the loss of the foundation of freedom, the possibility of full participation in society. This understanding of land is startlingly similar in many respects to that held by most Aboriginal peoples in North America, for whom the loss of land has equally far-reaching implications. For them also, it is the central issue of justice.

The problem with the judicial system, said the prophets, is that the laws enacted made the change in land ownership legal, thereby violating the values and normative tradition that belonged to Israel's history of salvation. In addition, the judiciary was becoming corrupt under the temptation of money and bribes offered by the wealthy. The ordinary person could not be assured of justice in the courts.

In all of this, however, the key litmus test for assessing justice in Israel was the actual treatment of the poor and the vulnerable, such as widows and orphans. In an earlier stage of its history, Israel was more of a tribal society, characterized by strong kinship relations in which there were habitual, reliable ways of caring for the weaker or less fortunate members of the family (e.g., the book of Ruth). But in the more commercially developed, peasant-type society of the eighth century B.C., these patterns were eroded. The disadvantaged and poor were left vulnerable. Their plight was the criteria used by the prophets to assess Judah as an unjust society. "The Lord enters into judgment with the elders and princes of his people: It is you who have devoured the vineyard; the spoil of the poor is in your houses. What do you mean by crushing my people, by grinding the face of the poor? says the Lord God of hosts" (Isa. 3:14-15).

In the voices of these eighth-century prophets, we have a passion for social justice in the name of God's justice. This is representative of a central concern throughout scripture. The enduring core of this message is that

> *all citizens should have a share in the control of the society's basic economic good as the instrument of their status, access to rights, and freedom. The administration of order should protect and support this distribution against economic and political processes that erode it. Institutional law should be subject to interpretation and correction by the worth of persons and moral values. Wealth which prejudices the welfare and rights of others is unjust. Treatment of the least favoured in the society is the fundamental criterion of the achievement of justice.*[19]

In the Bible, then, there is a strong concern for all four of the aspects of justice we have identified: commutative, administrative, legal, and distributive. But in addition, there is a broader, more dynamic understanding of justice that is not fully captured even by the sum total of these four facets, nor adequately reflected in modern secular theories of justice.

Justice and the Poor. The central focus of justice according to this broader understanding has to do with the treatment of the least favoured. It is about actions to correct the societal conditions that generate and exacerbate oppression and helplessness. This entails an extended responsibility with an open-ended quality. There is widespread agreement among Christian theologians and ethicists that God has a special regard for the poor and the oppressed, seeks justice for them, and calls the church to the same kind of regard and action.

Liberation theology, especially from Latin America, has lifted a "preferential option for the poor" to high visibility. But it is important to recall, as does Julio de Santa Ana, a Methodist theologian from Uruguay, how strong this motif is in Christian tradition — Orthodoxy, medieval Catholicism, and the Protestant reformers. The attention to systemic injustice and the need for more just political and economic systems was prominent in strands of the Social Gospel of the late nineteenth century. Ecumenically oriented Protestants who gathered at Edinburgh in 1910 for the World Missionary Conference had already wrestled with free market capitalism and Marxist socialism. They were struggling with the relation of the faith to economic questions, such as the "rationalization" of production, urbanization, colonization of the Third World, the rise of robber barons, and a new underclass.

Among Christian thinkers today there is also considerable agreement that God's special concern for the poor is not because they are more virtuous but simply because they are in need. A summation of Latin American liberation theology views on this states that "the poor are not assured of a place in God's kingdom because of the historical accident of their belonging to a given social class under particular socio-historical circumstances that made them disadvantaged and oppressed. Nor are the poor more virtuous in any morally and religiously significant way.... God does justice to the poor solely because they are in need and calls upon God's people to do the same."[20]

I find a slightly different formulation of this central belief more helpful and less subject to misunderstandings than that implied by the phrase "preferential option." The key phrase of the formulation is "strategic concentration." "God's love for all persons implies a *strategic concentration* on the victims of society, on the weak, the exploited, the neglected persons who are a large majority of the human race."[21]

But who are the poor whose neglect and continued oppression is the hallmark of an unjust society? They are not, Julio de Santa Ana reminds us, the poor whose laziness, idleness, and hedonistic pursuits have resulted in their own poverty and to whom the exhortations found in a number of biblical texts, especially Proverbs, are directed. Rather, they are the poor described in Psalm 146, the *anawim*, a Hebrew word meaning the oppressed, the prisoner, the blind, the "bowed down." Other words for poverty in the Hebrew language connote persons in material need, or refer to the low, weak, and powerless. The widow, orphan, and sojourner are frequently listed. There appears to be a common characteristic possessed by each of these types. Like the widow and orphan, they "have no one to speak on their behalf, no one to plead their cause.... Each of these types is someone who is without a voice before the legal, economic, political and cultural structures."[22] It is those, then, who are in some way powerless and excluded from a significant place in the community or society, the destitute and the marginalized.

Most of us have experienced, or likely will experience, this kind of helplessness at some time in our lives. At those times, God has a special concern for us. Hopefully, so do fellow Christians. But there are those who are systematically oppressed, excluded, and subject to such conditions. The measure of justice is appropriate action to effect the necessary changes in an economic, political, and judicial system to correct this situation.

There is widespread agreement among Christian thinkers that the poor thus described are the most knowledgeable about injustice because they are the ones who suffer most directly from it. More controversial and debated claims made about the poor are the following: because of their condition, they have a special understanding not only of injustice but also of the meaning of justice; they have a distinctive knowledge of God; their struggles constitute a special incarnation of the Holy Spirit that is a vehicle of God's saving power. There is some scriptural warrant for these kinds of claims, but they entail theological convictions about the nature of sin, the way God works in history, and the meaning of salvation that have far-reaching implications and about which Christians differ significantly.

All such matters point us to another whole section of the "orchestra of the moral life," the string section; namely, basic convictions. It is worth observing at this point that there is danger of romanticizing the poor. We who are more fortunate can easily lay upon them a messianic task that no human being is able to fulfil. This leads eventually to disillusionment, anger, and despair. Some of the claims made for the poor would lead one to think that it was a disservice to work in any way for people's removal from that marvellous condition! Reinhold Niebuhr, a prominent American theologian and ethicist of this century, provides a needed corrective. He reminds us that the power of sin is operative in all human beings, even if it shows itself in different ways among the poor than it does among the powerful and wealthy.[23]

Yet a special receptivity to the gospel and distinctive insights into the character and ways of God are often forthcoming from the dispossessed. Perhaps the mistaken claim is that conditions of poverty inevitably and automatically generate these qualities and that all those who are poor will therefore exhibit them. Rather, these conditions afford possibilities for a different knowledge of God that wealth and power do not, for which wealth and power are, indeed, impediments. Santa Ana suggests that the Lukan version, "Blessed are you who are poor" (Luke 6:20), is supplemented, not contradicted, by the Matthew version, "Blessed are the poor in spirit" (Matt. 5:3). Poverty comprises both a material and a spiritual aspect. Being poor does not by itself ensure entrance into the kingdom, but the person who has been deprived may be more open to receive the mercy of God and its blessedness. "Wealth makes it difficult for a person to enter into the proper spirit of helplessness, which is required of those who are to yearn for the reign of Jesus.... Those who possess economic power, then, must be brought to a point where they see that power as being of no *avail* ... which is felt so much more easily by the poor. And it is precisely those experiences of helplessness which give the powerful some basis for experiencing solidarity with the poor."[24]

There is another important aspect of justice as it is understood in the Bible. It is implicit in the land distribution issue addressed by the prophets, examined earlier in this section. Justice entails that the poor, indeed all persons, have not only their basic needs met but also find a place of dignity, belonging, and respect in the community. (Remember that land was necessary for this in ancient Israel.) This includes an opportunity to contribute significantly to the life of the community. Reinhold Niebuhr's approach to justice includes at least part of this aspect. He claims that greater equilibrium of power among individuals and between groups is integral to justice. Not only goods and services but also power must be distributed more equitably.[25]

Niebuhr gives another reason for this more equitable distribution of power. The pervasiveness of sin and finitude makes it impossible for humans to arrive at any objective and unbiased set of criteria or principles of justice. They always reflect, to some degree, the interests and biases of the particular group that formulated them. Yet such principles are needed. How else can we assess in any situation what a just outcome, i.e., a fair distribution of goods, services, and burdens, would be? This problem of determining what a just outcome would consist of is most evident in disputes between large groups. In such cases, it is almost impossible to find any truly disinterested party that could determine an objective standard for assessing what a just solution would be. The Middle East, conflicts between states of the former U.S.S.R., the Quebec-Canada debate come to mind. The poor and dispossessed must be empowered with a more equal voice in shaping these standards of justice, Niebuhr claims. Only then will the criteria themselves and the resulting calculations of a just outcome be more adequate.

Justice and Power: Procedural Justice. In ethics a distinction is made between "end-state justice" and "procedural justice." End-state justice is concerned with fair or just outcomes with regard to the distribution of goods and services. Procedural justice is concerned with establishing fair procedures for making decisions and adjudicating between the conflicting interests and claims of different persons and groups. Take the thorny issue of First Nations' comprehensive land claims, for example. These are claims involving First Nations that have not previously entered into any treaty or agreement with a Canadian government regarding land. End-state justice entails pursuing a right distribution of land, resources, and governmental power. Procedural justice entails establishing a fair procedure for ascertaining what this might be. Will the procedures assure that all the parties get an equal hearing and have their legitimate interests weighed fairly, or will the procedures be dominated by the more powerful parties? In the case of First Nations' land agreements, it is not easy to establish unbiased criteria for assessing end-state justice or to draw a very precise picture of what it would be. The importance of procedural justice, therefore, is increased.

In other cases, like that of the distribution of emergency medical supplies, we may have a clear and relatively objective standard for measuring a just end-state. They should be distributed according to those who have the greatest need. However, procedural justice is still important for determining who meets that criterion and therefore for assuring the right outcome.

Distinguishing between these two aspects of justice helps us to understand better some of the disputes currently surrounding issues of distributive justice. The business community, for example, is characteristically concerned with procedural justice. The much-discussed "level playing field," that is, conditions under which all parties can enter into equal and fair competition, is a type of procedural justice. In the sphere of international trade, for instance, appeals are made on these grounds against special subsidies, monopolies, government taxes, and environmental regulations that burden corporations in some counties more heavily than in others. Unfair procedures lead to unfair distribution.

Typically, those who emphasize this aspect of justice to the virtual exclusion of other aspects focus on equal opportunity. A society is just if it provides equal opportunity for all to acquire goods and pursue their own goals. One of the chief barriers to this form of justice is a state that interferes excessively with such pursuit by having numerous regulations. Since this approach to justice is so pervasive in Western societies, we may well pause for a brief description of one of the better known theories espousing it and some of the criticisms it generates. In the process, we will also gain a glimpse into the kind of argument that goes on around the norm of justice, which in turn underlies important political and economic debates and ideological disputes.

Robert Nozick, an American philosopher, provides one of the most sophisticated theories of justice along these lines.[26] His analysis is rich and complex, but his core argument is clear. How do modern societies in actual fact disperse goods and services to their members? It is not done through a central agency. Rather, goods and services are distributed by many different individual and group exchanges, buying, selling, giving, and the like. The key question, therefore, is whether the *procedures* by which people's original holdings were acquired and then transferred to others are just. If so, then the results will be just. This is true even if it turns out that some become much wealthier than others. Unequal results are only unjust if the rules of fair procedure were violated somewhere along the route of acquiring and exchanging.

One central rule for just procedures is that goods are acquired and exchanged in a way that does not harm others in the process. Further, there are important matters of what we identified earlier as commutative or compensatory justice. If I have mixed my labour with something (iron, soil, information, etc.) that I acquired fairly, then, in the name of justice, I am entitled to that product or a fair compensation for it. Nozick's next step is to claim that the free market operates in a way that ensures fair procedure. Therefore, he says, the outcome of market exchanges is a just one. Virtually the only function of the state is to make certain that the rules governing these fair procedures are obeyed as much as possible.

One of the prime concerns of this theory of justice is with protecting the liberty of individuals. Nozick believes that all theories that emphasize end-state justice override liberty. Granted, this is a legitimate concern, but does this approach go to the opposite extreme? Is justice collapsed into liberty? I think it is. The critics of this theory — and there are many — acknowledge that it is correct in lifting up the importance of commutative justice, fair acquisition, and exchange of goods and services. Justice entails recognition of the entitlements that flow from such exchanges.

However, the criticisms collect around three main concerns: Criteria and conditions for fair exchanges (just procedures) are more complex than the theory admits. The free market place does not actually function even according to the simple rules of fair exchange proposed by Nozick and therefore is not the just procedure it is claimed to be. Commutative and procedural justice, though important, do not exhaust the meaning of justice. There are other aspects to consider, particularly in light of biblical injunctions. The norm of justice requires attention to just end-states as well as just procedures. What is happening to the poor? Why? Are they receiving their proper due? Do they have a rightfully significant place in the community? These are also vital concerns.

Principles of Distributive Justice. The importance of end-state justice brings us back to the problem of establishing more precise criteria for determining it. By what principles should benefits and burdens be distributed? Equals ought to be treated equally, and those who are not equal may be treated unequally. This is called the "formal principle of justice." What kind of attribute or quality justifies different treatment or unequal allocation of a resource? Should it be special need or contribution to society or hard work? Some would claim that nothing justifies unequal distribution, that all should receive the same. The principles that attempt to establish the criteria for treating persons either the same or differently are called "material principles of justice" because they provide substance to the broad formal norm of justice.

There are various proposed principles for delineating distributive justice more fully. The following is a list of material principles that includes some of the major options advocated by different theories of justice: *(a)* to each person an equal share; *(b)* to each person accordingly to individual needs; *(c)* to each person according to individual effort; *(d)* to each person according to societal contribution; *(e)* to each person according to merit.[27]

Let us use the problem of allocating scarce kidneys as an illustration. Now that this organ can be transplanted so successfully, and there are more candidates for receiving one than there are kidneys available, by what principle should they be distributed? Should they be distributed according to the societal contribution of individuals? This would mean that a sixty-year-old single man with no dependants who is given to periodic episodes of dependency on drugs or alcohol would not be as entitled as a fifty-year-old concert pianist who brings beauty and pleasure to many. But the musician started life with a special gift and was also privileged to develop it. What about the less naturally gifted person who works hard taking care of others?

Perhaps the kidneys should be distributed not according to an individual's accomplishments but according, instead, to his or her effort, to the amount of energy and work a person puts into their own life and community. We can quickly see that each of these principles leads in a significantly different direction for the distribution of this scarce resource. Also apparent, of course, is a host of other questions that they do not answer, such as what should count as societal contribution or how individual effort is to be measured.

To each according to individual need is a material principle of distributive justice that is more congruent with the norm of love of neighbour. This is the principle by which life-sustaining medical resources should be distributed. Fundamental need may be defined as anything which if not obtained will harm a person or detrimentally affect him or her in a fundamental way. But quite likely there will be more people who need a kidney transplant in this sense than there are organs available. What then? This may be the point at which we cannot discover any additional standard for assessing a just outcome. We are pressed to procedural justice. We attempt to find the fairest procedure for deciding among the remaining qualified candidates. This could be some form of lottery, perhaps first-come, first-served. If we have first allocated the kidneys according to a sound material principle of justice and then, if necessary, according to a just procedure, then we can say that the outcome is as just as possible.

The principle of need is surely most fitting for guiding distributions, not only of lifesaving medical resources, but of all the basics of life (though it is surely not appropriate for a just distribution of, say, Porsche cars). Our society's efforts, however inadequate, to provide a welfare net represent an effort to meet this principle. Further, given the equal worth bestowed by God on every person, there have to be very strong reasons from a Christian perspective for any unequal distribution of benefits and burdens. Yet people's needs, even basic ones, differ to some extent. A chronically ill person or an accident victim has different basic needs than a young, healthy person. Therefore distribution according to this principle may require unequal or different treatment. Nevertheless, justice requires *impartial* treatment in the sense that self-interests and preferences should not be allowed to affect the way the needs of others are determined or met.

Other principles, such as to each according to ability, or each according to results achieved, and so on, may be appropriate subordinate criteria for justice in certain cases under certain circumstances. To pay the same amount to those who do no work and to those who do a great deal would hardly seem just, regardless of the respective needs of each. Hence, in certain circumstances, effort or accomplishment are appropriate subordinate criteria. However, they must be kept under the need principle for great injustice would result if work done was the only criterion for the distribution of goods.[28]

One popular rationale in Western liberal societies for unequal distribution is that it provides vital incentives for vigorous production. Human nature being what it is, most people will not work harder or more effectively unless they receive greater rewards for doing so. Unequal distribution, then, is just if it produces the greatest good for the greatest number. This claim is grounded in the utilitarian theory of ethics. From a Christian perspective, it seems contrary to the vital core of justice, namely, to strive to improve the conditions of the poor, the very minority whose well-being is deemed expendable in the name of the good for the greatest number.

In the 1970s, the province of British Columbia appointed a Royal Commission to establish what regulations should govern proposed mining and milling of uranium in the province. Wide public opposition to any mining of uranium had arisen. In the ensuing debates before the Commission, one company in favour of mining appealed to the principle of the greatest good for the greatest number. Yes, there are hazards to the health of workers and communities entailed in such mining, it was admitted, but these could be reduced with proper care. The great benefits to society as a whole justified, it was claimed, some having to bear the dangerous burdens. The communities affected should be regarded as "*zones of national sacrifice*"!

Rather than being another principle of justice, this really sets justice aside in the name of another norm, the common good. (We will look at that shortly.) Nevertheless, the issue of incentive for production is very important. If the economic pie is getting smaller so all receive less, there is small comfort in its fair division. A contemporary philosopher, John Rawls, has formulated a principle of justice that is helpful at this point: "All social values — liberty and opportunity, income and wealth, and the basis of self respect — are to be distributed equally unless an unequal distribution of any, or all, of these values is to *everyone*'s advantage,"[29] adding elsewhere, "and in particular for the least advantaged members of society." This is very different from the formula of the greatest good for the greatest number.

Material principles of distributive justice, then, do have a useful role. We need at the same time to bear in mind Niebuhr's caution about the limitations of all such criteria, and the reminder from liberation theology that justice, biblically understood, cannot be adequately encompassed by such criteria or even their enactment.

Budgets: A Test Case for Distributive Justice. One of the most challenging moral tasks to test any interpretation of the norm of justice is setting a budget. A budget is a form of allocating scarce resources. It is toughest under conditions of shrinking finances. How are institutions like hospitals and churches to justly distribute the burdens of financial cutbacks? I prepared the following guide at the request of a United Church of Canada presbytery committee facing difficult allocation decisions as a result of cutbacks in mission funds. It illustrates a use of the multifaceted norm of justice, including some principles for guiding distribution of burdens.

A. Process of Decision-Making — procedural justice
   1. Are the decision-makers chosen by the church through due process and accountable to them?
   2. Do those most affected by the decisions have a good opportunity to participate in the process?
   3. Is that opportunity equal for all applicants? The different language, culture, and formal education of each applicant group needs to be taken into account to ensure this.
   4. Are the criteria used for allocation of resources available to all?
   5. Do the decision-makers have adequate and relevant information of an equal kind and quality from all applicants? Equal does not need to mean in the same form. Again, language, culture, and formal education, let alone skills and practise in filling in application forms, will affect this. Applicants should be invited to provide needed information in the form in which they are best able to communicate. Note: The considerations and criteria listed below should shape the kind of information sought.
   6. Do we encourage among the decision-makers the cultivation of those virtues that are appropriate to good trusteeship?

B. Allocation — distributive justice

The most difficult kind of decision is choosing among worthy goods that are often so dissimilar they cannot be compared. The formal principle of justice is "similar treatment for similar cases." Are the projects under consideration dissimilar in ways that justify different treatment? The following criteria (stated as questions) may assist in providing an answer.

1. Criteria of promise keeping: What agreements and commitments has the church already made to the project and/or the constituency group?
2. Criteria of appropriateness: does the project
   a) Serve one or more of the Mission goals?
   b) Is it related to a particular historic responsibility of our church, for example, some aspect of mission or some constituency that the wider church looks to the United Church to tend?
   c) Is it related to some special contextual responsibility of the United Church, i.e., are we the branch of the church that happens to be on a particular spot at a crucial time and is the rest of the church depending on our witness and action in this situation?
   d) Is it meeting an emergency or crisis situation that must be addressed either now or be too late?
   e) Is the project designed to pursue mission goals in a way that addresses underlying issues rather than only symptoms?
3. Criteria of need of the constituency served:
   a) What access do the people of this community in general have to funds, resources, and the Gospel of Christ and ministry of the church?
   b) How central to the church's calling and vital to the community's well-being are the goals of the project?

   c) Are the goals of the project being pursued in this context by any other agency? Are they likely to be?
   d) What would be the likely effect on the constituency of reducing this project, or of dropping it?
4. Criteria of need of the project:
   a) Can it significantly benefit from financial assistance? (I once had a youth group that was floundering. It would not have benefited much from more funds. It needed more imaginative leadership.)
   b) What access does the project have to other sources of needed funds?
   c) How critical to the survival of the project is this particular assistance?
   d) How critical to the effectiveness of the project?
5. Criteria of efficiency: Is the project getting the most for its money? Could it find less costly ways of accomplishing the same goals?
6. Criteria of effectiveness: This is one of the most difficult to assess and comparisons can often be misleading. Effectiveness may, for example, be impaired because of inadequate funding, and it would hardly be fair in such a case to deny a project further funding on grounds of ineffectiveness! Further, some projects may have goals more difficult to achieve or be operating in a more difficult context and therefore merit special consideration rather than being penalized for ineffectiveness.
   a) Does the project have a likely chance of achieving its goals?
   b) Has the project made reasonable progress towards its goals, given the nature of its goals, the limits of its resources, and the context it which it operates?

Answering these questions by a fair process should produce an appropriate prioritizing of projects. This means a morally valid justification for dissimilar treatment of projects in terms of allocating resources. If more than one project meets these criteria in the same way, then they should be treated the same, i.e., receive identical portions of the budget (or cutback).

Not only principles of justice are involved in this list, of course. Other obligation-type norms, such as promise keeping, come into play. Two other base points are operative as well. The first is convictions regarding God's creative and redemptive purpose, the mission of the church, and the presbytery's role in this, including its mission goals (hopefully prioritized). The second base point is good social analysis of the context that is served by the presbytery, plus accurate information concerning the projects.

Summary. What is justice? I have been speaking of it as a powerful, multifaceted, obligation-type norm that gives a clear direction for our actions. Justice is integral to love of neighbour, but not identical with it. Other principles are needed to give expression to other considerations entailed in love of neighbour. However, justice may be interpreted as a social ideal or vision, the equivalent of the good society, and as such can be defined in terms so broad that it comes close to embracing all the concerns involved in love of neighbour.

The central focus of justice as a norm, the actions it constrains us to take, has to do with proper treatment of the poor or least advantaged and the establishment of social conditions in which they will have the worthy and dignified place to which they are entitled. Actions that increase the misery and powerlessness of the poor and harden the conditions that perpetuate this are unjust. This central focus of justice should be the basis for formulating and selecting more specific principles of distributive justice. Given the human conditions of finitude and sin, no social conditions ever fully measure up to the norm of justice, and we are called to an ongoing enterprise of seeking better approximations of it.

Deciding which programmes of social change and what kind of political and economic systems will lead to greater justice requires, of course, additional aspects of ethical reflection. These include basic convictions regarding the nature of societies and human beings, social analysis, and other norms such as liberty, peace and harmony, the common good, and trusteeship of creation. We will get to these in later sections.

Love of Neighbour: Liberty

Liberty is another obligation-type norm integral to love of neighbour. My ninety-year-old mother refused to go to tea in the dining room of the geriatric care facility where she was resident for a few weeks. The staff pointed out to me that going to tea was required of all patients because they received both exercise and the stimulus of company. (The staff harboured the strange illusion that I could persuade my mother to change her mind!) "They told me I had to," my mother explained to me. "If they had invited me, I might have gone, but when they demanded that I go, that made me mad!" I wryly and silently reminded myself that one common formulation of the norm of liberty is that autonomous (self-directed), deliberate actions and choices should not be constrained by others. Hence in contemporary philosophical ethics, it is usually called the principle of autonomy. My mother was indirectly appealing to it. In doing so, she was using what for modern Western societies is the lead trumpet of the orchestra of the moral life, the standard that is given overriding importance.

She was also unknowingly tapping into a strong trend in health care of the last twenty-five years. Respect for the autonomous choices of others has become a key principle in determining responsible health care. It has been effectively appealed to as a warrant, especially by women, for correcting paternalistic views of care in which the well-being of patients is pursued unilaterally without regard for their wishes. The standard of informed consent by the patient is now the accepted prerequisite for any medical procedure, from taking a blood sample to administering life-saving devices to enrolling a person in medical experiments. Was this principle violated within this facility only in relatively minor matters like going to tea? Was it set to one side because of the age of the patients?

Autonomy in the form of informed consent calls into play in turn several other principles, including veracity — one should tell the truth and not lie or deceive others (the ninth commandment). Without the truth or at least adequate, accurate information, a person is unable to exercise genuine free choice. No one had told my mother why they thought she should go to tea. Confidentiality, respect for the patient's decision concerning the giving out of information about her thoughts, sentiments, emotions, and physical being, is another aspect of liberty.

The norm of liberty/autonomy is a key action guide for the political sphere. Along with norms like justice and harmony, it is a standard for assessing the way we organize and govern our collective lives. Does the political order respect people's freedom to believe and worship, to express themselves, to form groups, to participate in the formation of government, to own property? These are some of the key political liberties that have been hard won for us in the past in North America. We take them for granted until they are challenged, or until we are reminded of them by those who live in or come from societies where they are absent.

This standard of liberty, however, is properly appealed to by women and various minorities who are systematically and arbitrarily restricted in ways that apply only to their group. Only relatively recently did women win the right to vote, for example. But however imperfect the institutionalization and practice of these liberties is, the moral norm of liberty or autonomy is almost universally recognized within Western societies. An appeal to it carries great moral weight.

There have to be very strong reasons for overriding people's free choice. In the debate within Canada regarding Aboriginal self-government, therefore, the moral burden of proof rests not on the First Nations who seek it but on those who would deny Native peoples, if they so choose, the freedom to continue as distinctive peoples, released from the colonial system now in place and from the pressure to assimilate.

Christian Grounds for Liberty. The norm of liberty or autonomy has a Christian theological basis quite different from that of Western Enlightenment with its assumption about the rational autonomy of the individual. From a Christian perspective, true human freedom comes only from right relationship with God made possible through Jesus Christ. It is the freedom from the power of sin and death, freedom to spontaneously serve God in Christ.

William Temple, the late Archbishop of Canterbury, develops a different but related theological basis for grounding the principle of respect for the free choices of others. Each person is a child of God and one for whom Christ died. As such, each has a worth independent of his or her usefulness or merit. Acknowledging such worth entails giving other persons the widest possible scope for developing and making actual in their lives the quality of freedom that distinguishes human beings as creatures made in the image of God. "It is the responsible exercise of deliberate choice," claims Temple, "which most fully expresses personality and best deserves the great name of freedom."[30] He goes on to observe "how absolute was Christ's respect for the freedom of personal choice. He would neither bribe nor coerce men to become followers" — not even Judas. Alas, Christians have been a long time recognizing this. In more recent history, however, a broad consensus has emerged among Christian churches that to "force consciousness," i.e., to coerce people into religious conformity, violates love of neighbour because it does not respect the autonomous choices of others.

Liberty as a moral standard for the way we organize and govern our collective life finds additional, albeit negative, grounds in the Christian understanding of human sin. All persons and groups, even the "enlightened" and "redeemed" (however defined), observes Reinhold Niebuhr, tend to pursue their own self-interest at the expense of others. Frequently this is done under the guise of serving the public good. No group or person is good enough to be trusted with a great amount of power over others. Devices for both dispersing power and keeping it accountable are therefore essential.

One of the issues in the interpretation of the norm of liberty is determining what constitutes a genuinely autonomous or self-directed choice of action. A community health care nurse attending an elderly man living alone in the inner city discovers that he has serious infection in his leg. He refuses to go to hospital for treatment. Then one night he accidentally floods his apartment and the one below. He explains that, as an old sailor, he likes the sound of running water. He leaves his kitchen tap on at night. On this occasion, the drain had accidentally plugged. The other tenants of the building want him committed for treatment, especially as his leg gets worse, and he becomes, in their opinion, a confused nuisance. Is his continued refusal to go to hospital a genuine free choice or is he incompetent to make such a decision?

In the ongoing debate about the marketing of baby formula in Third-World countries, the defence is made that the mothers there are free to buy it or not, as they choose. But are they? Can their choices be deemed truly self-directed under the combined conditions of great need, the unfamiliar manipulation of advertising, and their relative ignorance about the health hazards entailed?

As well as the question of competency, there is that of voluntariness. When are actions truly autonomous and not the result of powerful alien forces or subtle manipulation? This emerged as a crucial question in a study I conducted on the use of behaviour control mechanisms, ranging from chemicals and behaviour modification programmes to brain surgery, in the treatment of criminals. Prisoners are asked to volunteer. The inducements are powerful; both positive ones, such as reduced prison time; and negative, which may include everything from loss of small privileges to a longer time in solitary confinement. Are the choices made by the prisoners regarding the programmes truly self-directed? Under conditions of prison life, could they ever be?

The answer to the questions posed by these cases depends in part on how freedom itself is understood. Three common but different understandings of freedom may be distinguished.[31] According to the first, only those choices and actions that are not conditioned by anything external or internal to the person are free, including the emotions and reason. They must, as it were, materialize from nothing, be totally spontaneous. None of the choices in the cases above would qualify, and indeed it is hard to think of any that would. The second view of freedom regards only those human actions and choices that are controlled by reason as truly autonomous or free. If they are dictated by desire or passion rather than reason, they are not truly self-directed. This view is found in Plato and is assumed in most liberal thought, including that of philosophers Hegel, Rousseau, and Kant. The key, of course, is how reason is defined. Cultural bias is apt to surface in definitions, even in broad formulae such as "what any reasonable person would do in similar circumstances." In any case, the old sailor's choice would not likely qualify, the prisoners' might, and those of the mothers not likely but possibly.

The third view of freedom would claim that choices and actions are free when controlled by "a moving principle" that belongs to the agent, whether these be desires, emotions, or reason. Choices and actions are not free but rather coerced only when this "moving principle" is external or outside the agent and not integral to his or her identity. "An act is free if the agent identifies with the elements from which it flows; it is coerced if the agent dissociates himself from the element which generates or prompts the action."[32]

Central, then, to this third view of freedom is the understanding of the "true self" or identity. "Tell me a man's identity," says one philosopher, "and I will tell you his freedom, tell me its limits, and I will tell you when he is coerced," because freedom is "the acting out of that identity."[33] This takes into account cultural and religious factors, since they are crucial to identity. External inducements, internal temptations, various forms of influence do not in themselves render self-direction impossible. They do so only if they tap motivating forces within a person that are not recognized as such by the individual. Or they do so if they are both threatening to the core of the person's identity and overpowering in their potency.

More information is needed to assess the three cases in these terms, but it is likely that the sailor's choice is a free one according to this understanding. The mothers' choice is very problematic on the grounds of unawareness of unfamiliar influences at deeper levels. The prisoners' choices are also unlikely to be autonomous by these standards, since the control over their lives by the inviting officials is so extensive that the potential threat to the core of their identity, whatever that might be, is unavoidably present.

If identity is so basic to understanding liberty or self-directed choices and actions, are there features *essential* to any human identity? What is a Christian identity? These questions, thoroughly discussed in theology throughout the history of Christian thought, point to another kind of ingredient of the moral life, another section of the orchestra, which we have identified as basic convictions. In part 3 I shall return to this question of Christian identity. For now, I simply point out that Christian views of the self are not as individualistic as those in Western liberal thought. This leads to a different interpretation of the norm of liberty, with important implications, especially for societal ethics.

This different interpretation bears on another issue with regard to the norm of liberty. In the dominant societies of North America, this norm is accorded overriding moral priority. When this is combined with a highly individualistic sense of identity and a correspondingly restricted view of what constitutes self-directed choice, some negative effects emerge. In health care, for example, the dominance of autonomy is leading to what has been called a "minimalist ethic."[34] The relationship between caregiver and patient may be reduced to one of consumer and supplier: the caregiver does only what is specifically demanded by the patient and takes little further interest or responsibility in the name of respect for free choice.

Is the erosion of public life and any sense of the common good fostered by a preoccupation with individual freedom? Certainly many of the most agonizing moral dilemmas in both personal and political life involve a real or perceived conflict between the greatly valued and high-profile norm of liberty and other norms. Examples spring to mind. Liberty at least seems to conflict with not harming, as in the case of abortion; or trusteeship of creation, as in the case of environmental controls over private enterprise and property; or justice, as in the case of affirmative action in hiring women and minorities. We have already flagged for further discussion the important matter of weighing moral norms when they conflict. However, we have some interesting ground to cover first.

Trusteeship of Creation

The central norm for guiding the Christian life is the Great Commandment to love God and neighbour. We have been examining some of the key principles that indicate what actions are entailed in love of the neighbour. The question arises: Is love of neighbour the only basic principle of the obligation-type to which Christians are called to adhere? Do all other obligations belong to it? For the most part, I agree with those Christian thinkers who have said yes. All other principles of obligation, whether or not they are directly derived from the love commandment, are subsumed under it, transformed by it, and to be interpreted in light of it.

However, there is one other basic norm of obligation, I believe, that supplements the love commandment. It is to care for non-human creation as its trustees or stewards, accountable to God. This norm is also rooted in God's love, but in this case, a love for other-than-human creation. "God creates his creation in grace. The creation itself is a realm of grace."[35] "Common grace," the grace into which everyone is born, includes "the whole giftedness of life, the wonder of life." The appropriate response is to appreciate that grace and "to love the world and care for it to the glory of God."[36] Further, God's love extends to all creatures and to the entire creation, even if the kind of love God exhibits towards human beings has its own distinctive quality as "covenantal love."

The image found in scripture that best expresses the biblical understanding of the relationship of human beings to other-than-human creation is the image of steward or trustee. Douglas Hall, a contemporary Canadian theologian, argues that in our time of growing alarm over massive ecological destruction, this is "a biblical symbol come of age." In the Old Testament, a steward refers to an actual office or vocation in society — a special kind of servant who has major supervisory responsibilities and must make decisions, give orders, and take charge. "The steward is one who has been given the responsibility for the management and service of something belonging to another, and his office presupposes a particular kind of trust on the part of the owner or master."[37]

The steward accountable to Joseph in Genesis 43 and 44 is one example (see also I Chron. 27, 28; Dan. 1:11,16). The steward is entrusted with particular responsibilities but must never forget that he is a servant and accountable to the master for the things that have been entrusted to him (Isa. 22:15-21). Even the king of Israel may be thought of as a steward. If he forgets that he is accountable to God, his master, he is subject to rebuke and even replacement.

In the New Testament, observes Hall, the office of steward takes on a metaphorical and even theological significance that is just starting to emerge in the Isaiah passage. God is the sole master and "owner." But the disciples of Christ are likened to stewards who are called to manage the Christian household on behalf of their master, the risen Christ, and will be held accountable for the exercising of that trusteeship (Luke 12:42ff). Paul likens himself to a steward and implies that the church as a whole has stewardship responsibilities. As servants of the Suffering Servant, Christians are "stewards of God's mysteries" (I Cor. 4:1). Even Jesus Christ is not seen primarily as an owner but as the true steward: "All belong to you, and you belong to Christ, and Christ belongs to God" (I Cor. 3:22-23).

Jesus as servant is a major motif in the New Testament and sometimes he is likened to a special kind of servant, namely a steward of "the manifold grace of God" (I Peter 4:10). As good stewards of Christ, who is the exemplar steward of God, we are therefore called to special responsibilities of trusteeship. These responsibilities are for the mysteries of the gospel and the managing of the household of God's creation. As Ephesians goes on to say, stewards are not regarded as outsiders in this role but as participants in the household of God (Eph. 2:19-22; 3:1-2). Yet we are stewards and clearly not masters or owners of this household. We are accountable to God for our trusteeship of it. "From everyone to whom much has been given, much will be required; and from the one to whom much has been entrusted, even more will be demanded" (Luke 12:48b). As stewards, we are called to be watchful and trustworthy.

This image of steward is congruent with other images in the Bible used for describing, on the one hand, the relationship of human beings to God and, on the other hand, the relationship to other-than-human creation. "Against the frequent human attempt to 'think more highly of ourselves than we ought' it places the great 'I Am' of its Yahweh — and we know again that we are dust. Against the equally frequent human attempt to hide in our frailty and bemoan our finitude, it presents a God who calls us to stand on our feet and be God's covenant partners in the sustaining and enhancing of life."[38] Thus it is appropriate to see the image of steward as a metaphor applicable to humanity as a whole, says Hall. True, the followers of Christ are called to be stewards, but as followers of Christ, they are participating in "the new humanity," putting on the authentic humanity of Jesus (Col. 3:10). Stewardship, then, is a dimension of the true humanity that God intends for us all.

It is important to note that while the English word "dominion" used in translations of Genesis 1:28 accurately reflects the literal meaning of the Hebrew word that strongly connotes domination, it is nonetheless misleading. The model for dominion in the Bible is the rule of God. However, we see this model most clearly, and hence the true meaning of dominion, in Jesus Christ, who "emptied himself, taking the form of a slave" (Phil. 2:5-11). A better rendering of the Genesis passage, suggests one theologian, would be "and God said you are to exercise care over the earth and hold it in its proper place." Its proper place means that nature is God's, but it is not God, and is not to be worshipped as such but revered as a precious gift over which human beings are to exercise trusteeship or stewardship, again after the model of Jesus Christ.[39]

Are there additional principles that spell out what it means to be a good steward or trustee of other-than-human creation? Alas, there is not nearly as rich a tradition or literature either in the Bible or in the history of Western Christian thought in this regard, compared to that surrounding the norm of love of neighbour. Christians in tribal societies, in particular, notice this lack. They find themselves needing to draw upon the accumulated wisdom of their own peoples for guidance as to what is proper action towards plants and animals.

We can expect much more discussion of and elaboration on this norm. For the purpose of such discussion and further testing, I offer three principles. First, human actions in regard to any particular part or entity of the rest of creation — animals, plants, land, etc. — should manifest *respect for the intrinsic worth of that entity*. This is to act in a way that "honors a thing for what it is, to consent to its being what it is and not another thing."[40] This does not rule out the use of nature to meet human needs, but it does mean using it in a way that is congruent with the intrinsic being of the creature or thing.

This principle of respect may be contrasted with the prevailing one of utility, which assesses our actions with regards to other-than-human creation only in terms of their usefulness to human purpose. The principle of respect would, for example, cut against the practices of "factory farms," which "produce" and raise chickens and cattle in assembly line fashion. Issues regarding the elimination of whole species and issues pertaining to genetic manipulation need to be assessed in terms of this principle.

The second principle I offer is that human use of other-than-human creation *should be sustainable*. To be good stewards of God's household entails concern for the continuation of species, the fruitfulness of the land, purity of water and air, and the like. This is so that animals and plants may continue and other entities may be an ongoing resource for the life of future generations of humans and other creatures.

This principle is reflected in the World Council of Churches' phrase, "sustainable society," coined in response to reflections on the growing environmental crisis and the limits to growth debate of the early 1970s. To be sustainable is "to be capable of a definite existence." The focus of the World Council of Churches was on respecting the finitude of the planet and on the need to sustain the life-support systems of the earth and the resources on which they depend.

This principle may be contrasted with the generally operative standard of maximizing the harvest and production of goods and services for the use of the present human generation. The application of the sustainability norm to questions of economic growth and development has been very controversial.

The third principle is that humans should *tend to the well-being* of other-than-human creation in accord with God's purpose. This is the most problematic of the three sub-principles of trusteeship because it evokes an obligation to actively pursue the well-being of plants and animals, and thus goes much further than respecting their right to be and their place in the interdependent scheme of things. The problem is in ascertaining what well-being in this case means and the limits of such obligations. What I am trying to lift up here is our obligation to preserve and enhance well-being in ecological terms, that is, in terms of relationships. In the case of some animals and living organisms, well-being may include preserving the possibility of their experiencing their own worlds, thus entailing care for a species' natural habitat, for example. However, much work remains to be done in developing this principle.

GOODS AND VALUES

A nurse who works in a hospital extended care unit ponders whether she should cross the picket lines of her own union. The strike is one for which she voted. She might ask, "In this situation, what are my responsibilities to my patients and friends?"

As a nurse, she has made an implicit promise to care for her patients in need, and she is especially worried about one ninety-four-year-old woman whose emergency care has been assured by the union. The patient is nevertheless very anxious and really requires constant care for minimal comfort and safety. As a member of the union, the nurse has obligations pertaining to solidarity with her sister nurses and a commitment to justice for underpaid fellow workers. She is faced with a moral dilemma because important obligation-type norms appear to be in conflict.

However, she might also ask, "Of the different courses of action open to me, which would result in the best consequences?" She could then compare and weigh the goods and the evils that are likely to result from crossing or not crossing the picket line. What values would be achieved or damaged in regard to her patients, to the hospital, to the other nurses, to her family?

We have been examining obligations; that is, moral standards that require or prohibit actions and practices on grounds of their own inbred qualities. They are standards deemed authentic to right relations and a strong social fabric for human community. Actions may also be morally appraised, however, by the more immediate consequences they produce or by the ends to which they ultimately contribute rather than by whether they are right or wrong in themselves.

Standards used to assess the consequences of action are called "values," or in more traditional language, "goods." The focus of obligations is on actions with regard to the web of relations. The focus of values or goods is on actions in regard to what we should seek to bring forth, where we should be going. Value- or good-type norms define objects or end-states thought to be worthy of human pursuit: one should always act in a way that promotes the well-being of others or act in any situation so as to maximize the pleasure of all concerned.

What values and goods are to be pursued? What evils and disvalues are to be avoided? Needless to say, there are different theories about the nature and source, identification and ranking of values or goods. In philosophy, there are two main schools of thought on this question. The first claims that a value is a subjective standard and is simply constituted by the feelings aroused in a person. An object, such as a tree, or a state of affairs, such as harmony, acquires value only when an interest is taken in it. A value, then, is "any object of any interest." This is the so-called subjective theory; it is usually associated with the term "value" rather than "good."

The other main view is the objectivist theory, and it more often employs the word "good" rather than value. This view claims that either term refers to characteristics belonging to the objects themselves. The good or value of something is discovered, not created or assigned by the minds of persons.

In the discussion of values or goods, a distinction is made between intrinsic and extrinsic values. An intrinsic value is one we wish to possess and enjoy for its own sake and not for something it produces. Examples of this value include health, friendship, happiness. Extrinsic values are values or goods that we seek as means to something else, such as the acquisition of money, scientific research, a proven surgical procedure. Most theories of ethics that focus primarily on assessing consequences are concerned with delineating intrinsic values as criteria.

Christian Grounds for Goods and Values. There is little direct reference to this type of norm in the Bible, where, as we have seen, the focus is on obligations. Yet most Christian ethicists today would grant that the consequences of our actions are morally important. There are ample materials in scripture for interpreting what constitutes the goods that we should seek.

However, the bulk of thought in Christian ethics regarding this type of norm is found in the Roman Catholic tradition.

Thomas Aquinas, the great medieval theologian who was and continues to be a pivotal figure in the formation of Roman Catholic tradition, set forth the basic premise. Human beings have a natural desire to achieve their true fulfilment or perfect good. But the true end of human beings, their perfect good, is to be found only in God. Actions flowing out of this innate tendency and contributing to the realization or actualization of this ultimate good are morally sound.

The good to be sought, then, is not happiness, as some Greek philosophers claimed, or pleasure, as for hedonists, but is God. "Anything else is good only in relation to God as a reflection or mediation of God.... All other forms of goodness are always a derived goodness dependent upon the prior goodness of God."[41] To establish anything else as the centre of value is idolatrous. This approach appraises all norms, actions, and character in terms of whether or not they are congruent with and conducive for the true end of human beings created in God's image.

However, behaviour in any particular situation must, to be reckoned as morally right, meet other kinds of criteria in addition to producing good results. Hence, many contemporary Roman Catholic ethicists use a term such as "premoral" good when speaking about values or goods to be sought as the consequences of actions.[42] According to these ethicists, an action is morally good only when it meets a variety of criteria in addition to the criterion that it produce consequences with "premoral" goods.

What are the goods and values that, from a Christian perspective, should be used to evaluate the consequences of actions? The well-being of others is one prime example. The principle of beneficence, familiar in health care and widely acknowledged, calls for actions that seek such a consequence. Of course, our view of well-being will depend primarily on basic convictions regarding the good life, salvation, and the nature and destiny of persons. It will also depend on the distinctive needs and characteristics of the individual for whom it is sought. But the experience of Christians who have wrestled with its meaning in the past has helped to sketch a broad physiognomy of well-being.[43] Physical health, basic knowledge and skills, affection from and community with others, and self-respect are all important aspects. Seeking another's well-being also involves having regard for that person's identity and freedom. From a Christian viewpoint, however, a very important dimension of human well-being is a right relationship with God. Actions may be morally assessed, then, by whether or not they are likely to foster ends or result in consequences of this kind.

Peace and harmony, friendship, beauty, health, justice (in the social ideal sense) are examples of goods or values that are typical of qualities that we deem worthy for society to pursue. Working to transform society in accord with goods such as these was the prime agenda of the Social Gospel movement, present in the large Protestant denominations of North America in the latter part of the nineteenth and first half of the twentieth centuries. These goods were judged to be integral to the kingdom of God — the fulfilment of God's purpose for creation. Social programmes and political ideologies were assessed in terms of their efficacy in "Christianizing" the social order or bringing it "under the law of love." This meant creating an order of justice, equality, fraternity, and democracy or at least guiding and directing the latent forces working for these goals.

One of the great theologians of the movement, Walter Rauschenbusch, measured the capitalist economic system of his time by these standards and found it wanting: "Our economic organization will have to be transformed in these directions. It is unchristian as long as Men are made inferior to Things, and are drained and used up to make profit. It will be Christian when all industry is consciously organized to give to all the maximum opportunity of a strong and normal life."[44]

Norms that assess ends or consequences of actions, i.e., values or goods, are frequently brought to bear on societal matters through one of two basic concepts: the common good and "middle axioms." I now turn to examine each of these in more detail.

The Common Good

The "common good" is a broad, umbrella kind of norm representing the shared values or goods of a political or economic association, such as a nation, a corporation, a union, the United Nations. It is also referred to as the public good or public interest or general welfare. Public policies, legislation, political and economic practices are judged in light of this norm. The papal document *Mater et Magistra* (1961) describes the common good as "the sum total of those conditions of social living, whereby human beings are enabled more fully and more readily to achieve their own perfection."

In the ancient and medieval eras of Western societies, the common good was an important concept in political thought and ethics. Since the rise of liberal modernity in the seventeenth century, it has been much in dispute. In the twentieth century, it has, on the whole, been neglected in both secular and Christian ethics. The exception is in the Roman Catholic tradition, where it has remained an important moral norm for political ethics. However, there has recently been renewed interest in this norm by both Protestant and secular ethicists and by political philosophers as well.

As a norm, the common good helps us to scrutinize important but neglected concerns of our society, from environmental matters to the very social fabric that is necessary to sustain communities. These are precisely the things that the present ethos of liberal individualism, with its emphasis on individual rights and autonomy, provides no framework for addressing.

The ongoing Canadian struggle to hammer out a viable constitution acceptable to all the various peoples or societies, regions, diverse minorities and other groups is related to the question of a common good. Are there any values held in common by these conflicting parties? Perhaps even a shared desire for a peaceful pluralism could be a starting point. However, if there are very few or none, the viability of Canada is doubtful. Discussions about the possibility of pluralistic, liberal societies having any sense of a common good to function as a guiding norm are, therefore, especially pertinent for Canadians.

The disputes centre around not only the particular content of this norm but whether it is a viable concept as a norm at all. Underlying the questions of the validity, understanding, and use of the norm of the common good are differing views of the human self, society, and political life. Once again, we are pointed to a whole other aspect of the moral life, basic convictions, and pressed to anticipate our discussion of it, to be found in a later section. Two distinct understandings (basic convictions) of the relation of the self to community and world ground the rival social visions entailed in an ongoing debate in Western thought. On the one hand, there is what is labelled the classical liberal tradition; on the other hand, there is what is called the communitarian tradition. This discussion has recently re-emerged with renewed vigour. Each view leads to different understandings and claims concerning the common good as norm.

In the classical liberal tradition, society is viewed as nothing other than the complex of individuals and groups that compose it. Thus it is virtually meaningless to speak about society as some kind of totality that might pursue certain ends and values. In any case, there is no such thing as the true interest or good of the public as a whole. Canada, to continue our illustration, cannot hope, therefore, to sort out its constitutional matters by reference to some public vision or values formulated as a common good.

Rather, any society, that of Canada included, really consists of many different sub-groups of similarly interested individuals. These individuals diverge widely in their judgement as to whether the results of any particular political struggle are to be deemed good. Even the procedures for bargaining between groups with conflicting interests cannot be designated as a public good since those used are a matter of conflict and controversy.

Therefore the term "common good" or "public good," claim classical liberals, functions simply to justify and give moral legitimation to the interests of a particular faction within the society. In Canada's case, we can think of particular political entities such as Quebec or the central region or First Nations or Alberta. Contemporary defenders of this kind of liberalism argue that using a norm of common good for guiding society will inevitably result in one part of a pluralistic society attempting to secure their special version of the good society at the expense of the others. The result would be tyranny.

The communitarian vision, on the other hand, is based on the assumption that the human person is essentially a social being. A person's identity, survival, and fulfilment are dependent upon social relations. The kind of social relationship and communal participation found in any particular society, therefore, will profoundly affect both the well-being of its members and also how persons will perceive they ought to live. What kind of relationships do we wish to foster in Canadian society? The common good attempts to describe what kind of social relationship and communal participation are to be valued as good in themselves. "The communitarian stresses the need for cooperation and compromise 'for the sake of some larger public interest or the common good'. It recommends the design of social mechanisms that coordinate the activities of various participants in society as a whole so that they lead towards this common good."[45]

Communitarians are concerned with what they perceive to be the erosion of the very fabric of North American societies and the decline of public life, engendered by the predominance of "liberated and autonomous selves" with no vision of or commitment to a larger public good. This excessive individualism can either lead to anarchy or alternatively to a new form of authoritarian tyranny designed to hold this fragmented culture together.

Is there a way of interpreting the common good that will meet the challenges of liberalism? Two Christian ethicists, David Hollenbach, a Roman Catholic, and Douglas Sturm, a Protestant, say yes. Both of them begin with a view of the human self that is relational rather than individualistic. They also share the basic argument that the genuine welfare of the individual is served by a healthy community and by attending to features of connectedness both between human beings and between human beings and nature. Yet a healthy community requires free and creative individuals. The public good, writes Sturm, "is the good of the relationships through which the members of the community sustain one another, contribute to one another, and constitute a creative center for the ongoing life of the community. To act in the public good is not to deny the individuality of persons or associations, but it is to reject the indifference to others of individualism."[46]

Both property rights and civil liberties, then, are to be viewed from the perspective of their service to the public good so understood, claims Sturm. "Possession, control and use of property of all forms, tangible and intangible, should be evaluated by their contribution to the formation, maintenance, and quality of character of an open society."[47] Civil liberties are essential, not only as a means of protecting individuals from despotic power, but because they are necessary for effective participation by individuals in communal decisions. Freedom of expression and thought, for example, are essential if people are to contribute creatively with fresh ideas and styles of life to the ongoing community. With this interpretation, the common good is a useful norm by which to assess political and economic systems and the place and function of corporations.

Hollenbach is especially sensitive to the values of pluralism. Like Sturm, he believes that the dignity of persons can be realized only in community while, at the same time, genuine community can exist only where the dignity of persons is secured. This includes "respect for the freedom and dignity of persons and for the many forms of relationship in which persons can participate: friendships, families, voluntary association, civil society; and the human community as a whole."[48] The common good, therefore, entails full respect for these many different forms of interrelationship. It is a pluralistic ensemble of goods, and no one of them should be absolutized or allowed to dominate the others. Each has its own place.

Hollenbach is also fully aware of the danger of imposing one particular view of the good life, in the name of the common good, on a pluralistic society. Yet, as a Roman Catholic, he fully subscribes to the view that the true good of both individual human beings and society is to be found, finally, only in God. How can these seemingly conflicting concerns be held together? A true commonweal is a people bound together by faith in Christ, love of God, and the neighbour in God. But such a true commonweal cannot be realized on this earth but only in the coming kingdom. Christians, then, should have "lower expectations about the pursuit of the full human good through political means." Only some aspects of this commonweal can be realized in different groups and associations in society and in the political community. Christians should therefore not feel compelled to impose their particular view of the good life on any earthly society. The common good of civil society is analogous to the full communion of the kingdom of God but is only "that measure of the communion of persons that is achievable in history."

Thus for both of these ethicists, human rights, civil liberties, and a pluralism of associations, all so important to liberals, are incorporated into a communitarian vision of society based on a relational understanding of the self. Such an understanding of the common good calls for social, political, economic, and cultural conditions "that make it possible for persons to participate in the life of the community to a degree that respects at least the most basic demands of their personhood." As such, the common good is a possible ethical resource for discovering new bases for Canada as a nation state and a norm for ethically reflecting on proposed constitutions and future policy.

This is how it was used by the Canadian Catholic Bishops in their "Ethical Reflections on the Economic Crisis," published on New Year's Day of 1983 in response to the high unemployment of that time. Their proposals generated much controversy, but the heart of their message is a call for "public dialogue about alternative visions and strategies." Choices must be made "about values and priorities for the future direction of this country." Here is a call for formulating a common good. The "special value and dignity of human work in God's plan for creation" and the "goal of serving the human needs of all people in our society" are but two of the values that the Bishops set forth as proposals for what that common good should include.[49]

Middle Axioms

Another variation of the "value or good" type of norm that delineates consequences and ends to be pursued has been named (or as most ethicists agree, mis-named) "middle axioms." Middle axioms are "goals which represent the purpose of God for our time."[50] They are agreements that the church, or perhaps some wider grouping, reaches on the general direction that social policy should take. They thereby form a guide to opinion and action.

Elimination of unemployment and critical support of the United Nations are middle axioms that were espoused by the ecumenical movement in the 1940s. Middle axioms embody goods and values but are more specific than general norms, such as the common good or well-being. They are an attempt to work out some of the implications of such broad norms for a particular time and place. While middle axioms are concrete social goals, they remain general in scope. When guided by these, we must still make decisions about the means, including strategy and tactics, to employ to achieve them.

The concept of middle axioms emerged in the course of preparatory work for the ecumenical conference on Church,

Community, and State held at Oxford in 1937 (an important precursor for the World Council of Churches).[51] The concern was with finding some kind of standard for public policy direction and setting out social action that was more specific and concrete than broad principles, yet less detailed than actual policies or strategies. The latter embody so many empirical uncertainties and are so tied to particular contexts that churches, as corporate bodies or as ecumenical coalitions, are unlikely to reach agreement about them.

The problem of racism provides an illustration. Love of neighbour and the norm of justice lead the churches to condemn racism, but this is very broad guidance indeed! A further step is agreement on the middle axiom — a concrete social goal — that "in our time, the system of apartheid should be abolished." This is specific as to what consequences we should seek. However, the middle axiom does not include specific strategies for accomplishing this. Possible means for doing it are numerous. Responsible choices will depend to some degree on time and place; Christians can legitimately differ about such means. Wide agreement on them is unlikely and perhaps even unwise, given the various circumstances in which Christians find themselves called upon to act.

Middle axioms proved very useful for churches and influenced most of the ecumenical studies in social ethics emanating from the Oxford Conference of 1939 up until the 1960s. After falling into relative disuse with the shift to a different approach to social decisions and action in the World Council of Churches, there has recently been renewed interest in this type of standard. It has been more carefully formulated by Ronald Preston, an Anglican ethicist and economist.

Central to understanding middle axioms, as Preston points out, is the process by which they are arrived at. The starting point is the broad principles that flow from the gospel and the commandment to love our neighbour. An effort is then made to discern what these principles mean in a given time and place. This entails, of course, "discerning the signs of the times," an analysis of the social context and situation. It means getting at facts and interpretation of facts—in short, dealing with the base point that we have designated as "situation and context." This is where Christians, who usually have varying experiences, perceptions, and expertise, differ the most.

However, claims Preston, given a good consultative process, with a representative group of persons most connected with the issue under discussion, "it is possible that as a result of this co-operative work broad agreement may be reached in suggesting in what direction it is possible to foster change, whilst those who agree on this may differ on the precise policies by which it should be fostered."[52] This agreement on goals and direction of change is what constitutes middle axioms. In this way, it is sometimes possible for the churches to indicate what the significant issues are among the welter of issues, what trends need encouraging or discouraging, what the broad possibilities of action are and their likely consequences.

In sum, middle axioms are not easy to formulate. Indeed, on some issues it may not be possible for the churches to arrive at enough of a consensus to achieve this. Nevertheless, possibilities include goals such as the abandonment of nuclear weapons; major reduction of water and air pollution; fair, negotiated settlement of Native land claims; dismantling of systems of apartheid; elimination of starvation in Africa.

Middle axioms are, by their very nature, time-bound standards. As Preston observes, much of their authority depends upon the cogency of the process by which they were formulated. Their moral authority, therefore, is clearly more limited than that accruing to the other norms we have been examining. However, if there is thoughtful and genuine consensus among a wide group of Christians regarding such goals, it does at the very least establish a moral "burden of proof." Those who would claim we should act for different ends must present very strong reasons for doing so. In Preston's words, "it is a help to a Christian to have some clarificatory guidance which is more probable than mere opinion, whilst leaving him the essential space for a personal decision on details."[53]

MORAL RIGHTS

The letter called upon a government official of another country thousands of miles away to cease holding three particular persons in prison without trial, and to stop immediately the torture being perpetrated upon them. I signed the letter without qualm. Now that is unusual for an ethicist accustomed to seeing moral ambiguity in most political actions! Hundreds of others also signed. Most of them were like me, I suspect, knowing virtually nothing about this distant country, its laws, or the guilt or innocence of the persons.

Our signing, of course, was an action with virtually no risk to ourselves, but two other factors stilled possible qualms. Amnesty International, the organization sponsoring the letter, has a deserved reputation for accurate and fair information about such situations. In the language of ethical base points, it is a reliable source for "what is happening" in these matters. But most decisive in creating a strong and clear moral imperative was the foreign government's violation of a type of norm different from either obligations or goods, one that functions to protect us; namely, *rights*.

Rights are justified claims that individuals and groups can make upon others or upon society. They are characteristically claims of power, privilege, needed goods and services, those things deemed of basic importance to human life. The right to recognition as a person before the law; freedom from arbitrary interference with privacy, family, home, or correspondence; the right to life, liberty, and security of bodily person were all either in jeopardy or clearly violated by the government to whom the letter was written. The right to own property; the right to work; the right to a standard of living adequate for health and well-being are additional, typical examples of human rights.

Human Rights

What makes such claims justifiable? Moral rights are claims or entitlements justifiable on moral grounds. They may be distinguished from legal rights, which are claims justified by legal principles and rules. Human rights, in earlier times referred to as natural rights, are basically moral claims that are deemed to be universal or applicable to all. They are concerned with matters of permanent importance to human life. This is what gives Amnesty letters their force and legitimacy and why they can appeal across cultural and legal lines. "A human right is an especially important and unalterable kind of moral right belonging to all persons by virtue of what is most basically involved in being human."[54]

Human rights have long had a place in Western thought, becoming especially prominent during the eighteenth and nineteenth centuries with the rise of liberalism. Since the Second World War, they have become prominent in ethical and political thought and discussion. A large and rich literature has emerged, studying and debating the meaning, scope, foundation, conditions of possession, moral weight, and classification of different kinds of rights. Max Stackhouse, a contemporary Christian ethicist, points out that the idea of human rights implies a universal ethic, since it entails moral claims of the sort that everyone, everywhere, ought always to recognize. "The current surge of concern for human rights represents the potential development of a universal 'doctrine' about humanity in community, implying a social ethic." Human rights, he goes on to say, imply "that there is a universal moral order under which all peoples and societies live."[55]

Does this kind of moral norm or standard offer a set of moral criteria and a language that will be recognized and acknowledged by all religions and cultures? Judging from the various understandings and critiques of human rights in Western liberal thought alone, that may be doubtful. However, there is no question that these moral claims have widespread recognition and have helped to advance human well-being throughout the world. The fine work of Amnesty International and the surprising effectiveness of its letters and endeavours is but one modest testimony to this.

Christian Grounding. From a Christian perspective, are human rights a viable type of moral standard, grounded in scripture and the tradition? Surprisingly, there are no direct biblical references to human rights nor is that concept, as such, present in scripture. Some Protestant thinkers, such as Latin American theologian Jose Miguez Bonino, warn that there is no "ready-made, immutable 'Christian doctrine of human rights.'" To claim that this is solely a Christian notion, then, would be historically inaccurate and intellectually dishonest. However, there are sound biblical and theological grounds for Christians to affirm in their faith that "they and others should take human rights seriously."[56]

Max Stackhouse takes this further in claiming that certain themes in scripture and the history of the Christian tradition provide the prerequisites for all the thinking and action of human rights. First and most basic is the concept of a universal moral order rooted in God's righteousness and the conviction that all human beings and creation come under the authority of this universal law. This law is knowable by all human beings. According to the New Testament, it is written on our hearts. Thus family, clan, political associations and powers, and individual persons are all to be assessed, guided, and protected by its precepts.

Second, says Stackhouse, the church as a social institution created a new type of social bonding. This bonding is not based upon the usual foundations of family, ethnicity, or national power, but rather upon commitments to law, hope, and love. It was and is "the place where a new spirit could manifest itself between master and slave, male and female, rich and poor, Jew and non-Jew."[57] The church as this kind of social institution both points to the universal law and by its very existence provides a social space that relativizes all other forms of human association. It also provides checks against the possible totalitarian authority of power concentrated in either family or state.

The dignity and worth bestowed by God on every human person is the central grounding for both Roman Catholic and Protestant Christian support of human rights. No one can legitimately be regarded merely as a means to some larger collective programme or purpose. Both Roman Catholic and Reformed thinkers locate this dignity in the fact that human beings have been created in God's image, though they may differ as to which aspects of human nature constitute that image. Until quite recently, Roman Catholics emphasized that humans are like God in their intelligence and freedom. The Reformed tradition asserts, along with a strand of more recent Catholic thought, that humans are like God in being communal and loving. Other Christian thinkers ground the dignity and worth God has bestowed on human beings in the covenant God has made with "the people God has liberated" or in the universal covenant God has made with all humankind. Lutheran ethicists emphasize that the dignity and worth of human beings may seem, in the light of observable behaviour, to have been forfeited. However, it is rooted not in the way in which we function or in certain qualities of being but rather by the fact that God has freely justified us by grace and bestowed such worth and dignity upon us.

Yet another foundation for Christian support of human rights is located in the Great Commandment to love our neighbour. This, as we have seen, leads to important moral obligations, such as justice. Such obligations can legitimately establish moral claims or rights. "Although the Bible does not have a catalogue of duties called 'human rights,' it does reveal claims of justice which function as rights for each member of the community; some translations perceptively translate the justice terminology at times as *rights* (e.g., Jeremiah 5:28: 'They do not defend the *rights* [*mishpat*] of the needy'. RSV)."[58]

There is, then, a correlation between obligations and rights, albeit an untidy one. All rights entail obligations on the part of another person. In health care, for example, the right not to have anyone invade my body or use it without my permission involves an obligation on the part of health care workers to respect my autonomy and to proceed only if I have given my informed consent. It is not always this clear, of course, as to who has the corresponding obligation. For example, in the case of the broad human right to the basic necessities of food and shelter for sustaining life, it is not readily evident whose responsibility it is to fulfil that obligation. If all rights entail corresponding moral obligations, the reverse is not true. For instance, the obligation to love our neighbour by seeking his or her well-being and even to sacrifice our own interests on that person's behalf does not establish the right of that neighbour to make the moral claim that we owe such sacrifice.

One controversial issue pertains to the classification and prioritizing of human rights. Do certain rights connected with private property take precedence over rights to the basic necessities of life when these conflict or vice versa? Numerous classifications have been offered by both secular and Christian ethicists, and there has been considerable discussion around the relationship between various types of human rights.

A widely used distinction is made between, on the one hand, civil-political rights (such as freedom of religion, assembly, speech, movement, and the right to participate in government) and, on the other hand, social-economic rights (such as rights to food, shelter, basic health care, and education). One main source of the modern human rights tradition is found in a particular strand of liberalism associated with John Locke, a seventeenth-century English philosopher. Locke claimed that human rights are rooted in natural law; that is, built into the very fabric of creation. But Locke was concerned with the protection of individuals from the absolute powers accorded to rulers and the state. This whole liberal tradition has emphasized civil-political rights and ignored or rejected social-economic rights. On the other hand, in the Marxist tradition, especially the Soviet version of it, the civil-political rights of classical liberalism are dismissed as preoccupations of bourgeois capitalists and their acquisitiveness dressed up as universal human rights. True human rights have to do with the socioeconomic needs and rights of human beings.

In contrast to these two traditions, Protestant and Catholic theologians writing on this subject generally "take an inclusive approach to the types of rights."[59] David Hollenbach provides one of the most interesting of the various classifications proposed by Christian ethicists. He distinguishes between person rights, those belonging to the person as such; social rights, which are conditions for the preservation of the well-being of the person; and instrumental rights, having to do with essential conditions in the larger institutions of society. Regarding the vital but troublesome issue of prioritizing rights, he says that the focus should be on the question of whose needs and freedoms should receive preference rather than on what kinds of rights should receive priority. On this basis, he proposes the following three priority principles: 1) the needs of the poor take priority over the wants of the rich; 2) the freedom of the dominated takes priority over the liberty of the powerful; 3) the participation of marginalized groups takes priority over the preservation of an order which excludes them.[60]

To whom do rights apply, and what are the conditions for possessing them? Central to the modern human rights doctrine, as we have seen, is that rights apply universally to all human individuals and cannot be forfeited even if they may be justifiably overridden in certain circumstances. However, there is much debate as to whether or not rights of any kind extend to foetuses and future generations of human beings; animals and plants; groups and collectives. Who or what is to be regarded as an end in itself and not simply as means or of instrumental value? The underlying issue is the extent of the moral community. We need to look briefly at collective rights and animal rights.

Collective Rights

Do the Quebecois and Aboriginal peoples have rights as groups? Does this involve recognition of a distinct Quebecois society and of the First Nations' freedom to continue as peoples with their own form of government? The individual person as rights-holder is the focus of the Western human rights tradition. This is true especially of the typically liberal form (rooted in Lockian liberal theory) in which human rights are justified either in terms of inherent dignity of persons or in terms of their maximizing the overall benefit of society. Further, the individual remains the focus whether the emphasis is on civil-political rights as in classical liberalism, or includes social-economic rights as in welfare liberalism. The rights of groups or collectives have received little attention. In Canada, however, constitutional issues, including the definition of aboriginal rights, have lifted up collective rights for special scrutiny.

Michael McDonald, a Canadian ethicist who has written quite extensively on this issue, draws a distinction between collectivities and aggregates. Both collectivities and aggregates are composed of individual members. Aggregates, however, do not have any group identity or agency. An example is a collection of people with grievances against the same company who join forces to sue for damages. A collective or group, on the other hand, has interests and seeks benefits for the group as such and not simply for its members. The true collectivity, then, has a distinct existence and identity of its own that is more than just the sum total of its members.

McDonald makes a further distinction between two types of collectivities. A shared understanding collects diverse individuals into a group. In one type, persons "identify with a group." They choose to become a citizen of a state or to play with a particular team or to join a particular association. With the second type of group, members recognize a significant commonality with others and acknowledge the existence of a group to which they belong. Families, ethnic communities, peoples, or nations are examples of this second type. This is the type of group that the liberal tradition in all its variants has difficulty understanding or accepting because the very essence of liberalism is choice. For liberals, a valid group or society should have "an array of choices or opportunities open to individuals" and a "critical mass of choosers" able to make free and informed choices.[61] Both "aggregates" and voluntarily chosen groups meet this criteria of choice. In a business enterprise, for example, individuals voluntarily choose to pool their rights, and the group may take on the transferred rights of the individuals. "Classical liberalism" recognizes that such voluntarily formed associations do have the right to at least not be interfered with by the state.

Classical liberalism does not, however, give recognition of collective rights to the second type of group, for example, a First Nation in which discovery rather than the choice of a common identity is involved. In fact, the liberals' insistence that only voluntary assent legitimates a group and that individuals have the right to disassociate from any group, tends to erode communities of this second kind, as Aboriginal peoples will readily testify.

"Welfare liberals" sometimes advocate collective rights for groups of this second type on the grounds that true respect for individual persons entails recognition of the culture, language, and community in which their identity is rooted. As McDonald summarizes, "becoming an autonomous person requires a social context — a context in which one acquires an identity not just as an individual but as a member of a community." Given that language and culture are essential for developing an autonomous identity, welfare liberals recognize "the need for collective rights to provide linguistic and cultural security of the members of a minority cultural, linguistic, religious and other groups."[62] The advantage of the approach of welfare liberalism is that it advocates positive support of communities and groups like the Quebecois and First Nations. The disadvantage is that it does so only for the sake of fostering autonomous individuals. This means that the welfare liberal will extend collective rights only to those cultures that support the formation of autonomous individuals.

A vivid illustration of this surfaced on a television programme produced in the United States. It examined religious communities that believe in and practice plural marriage. The issue in question was not the moral appropriateness of this custom but whether such communities have the right to exist freely and engage in such practice. In every other respect, these communities obey the law; they are self-sufficient and keep to themselves. A social worker stated her conviction that even though these groups did not present a problem to the state or to the surrounding community, they should not be accorded the right to continue. The reason? Because the children within these groups were not raised or taught to be autonomous individuals!

This viewpoint is widespread. Where it prevails, societies like those of Native peoples, which foster the development of a sort of self other than the independent, possessive individual "choosers" so valued by liberalism, will not be regarded as communities worthy of positive rights.

Even more disturbing is McDonald's insight that from the perspective of welfare liberalism's limited support of collective rights, there is good reason for the state to intervene and alter "offending structural and substantive features of the groups' practices including its decision-making structures and its basic tenets." In this way these groups will be forced to "shape up" and provide the social formation crucial to individual autonomy. "Collective autonomy for the minority will be diminished in order to advance the autonomy of individual members of the minority. The result may well be that the existence of minority groups may be more threatened by an activist, welfare liberal state than by the more passive night watchman state of classical liberalism."[63]

Communities, as well as individuals, have basic value. They are also possessors of rights, claims McDonald. However, he offers no way of prioritizing rights when group and individual rights conflict. In challenging the individualistic assumptions of liberalism in all its various forms, the issue of an adequate understanding of human nature is again raised. This is a matter to be taken up in the section on basic convictions. But the conundrum of group rights versus individual rights also points to the inadequacy of using rights as the only type of moral norm. From a Christian perspective, they have a vitally important but limited place in the moral life and in a social ethic.

Animal Rights

The well-being of other-than-human creation is an ancient concern, recently revived in Western thought. However, the issue of whether or not animals are possessors of rights — basic moral claims — has arisen only in the last twenty-five years. Christian perspectives on this subject vary according to different theologies of creation, as we saw in the case of the principle of trusteeship of creation. Yet again that aspect of the moral life I have identified as "basic convictions" comes into play.

From a Christian perspective, animals differ from humans in that they are not created in the image of God. Nevertheless, many of the other grounds for human rights apply equally to animals. First, animals have worth and value in and of themselves as part of God's good creation (Gen. 1:22; Matt. 6:21; Luke 12:24). They share with humanity the ability to praise God (Isa. 43:2-21).

Second, animals are part of God's covenant and exist in a symbiotic relationship with humans (Gen. 9:10). They shared in both the judgement and the hope of renewal in the Noah covenant (Gen. 8:1); they are caught up with humans in God's punishment for unfaithfulness to the covenant and in God's way of bringing covenant partners back into faithfulness (Hos. 4:3; Jer. 7:20; Isa. 50:2). Animals participate in God's redemptive promise and have a place in the vision of restored peace and harmony (Hos. 2:18; Isa. 11:6ff.; Ez. 34:25ff.; Col. 1:20; Eph. 1:10).

Third, as we have already discussed, human beings are placed in a special relationship as trustees or stewards of animals, with particular obligations towards them. It seems reasonable, therefore, to say that animals have legitimate rights or moral claims in terms of their relationship to human beings as their trustees. Indeed, it was only after the flood that God's command included the taking of animals for food, and it appears as a concession to human sinfulness (Gen. 9:3).

What specifically are these rights, and how are they to be weighed when they come into conflict with human rights? Andrew Linzey, an Anglican theologian, is one of the few Christian thinkers who has begun to work carefully through these matters.[64] He suggests that animal rights have primarily to do with human omissions or forbearances (what are called "negative rights") rather than rights entailing human responsibilities and duties to do something (positive rights).

The debated answer to this question, says Linzey, centres around two issues: first, the question of killing animals, whether for purposes of food, sport, or environmental management; and second, the issue of causing pain to animals, whether for purposes of maximizing food production ("factory farms") or experimentation for scientific research or for testing new products. If, as Christians believe, we are called by God to be trustees or stewards of other-than-human creation, including animals, the very minimum of legitimate moral claims to which animals are entitled is protection against arbitrary or frivolous infliction of pain or killing by humans. There have to be morally strong reasons for either killing or inflicting pain. Careful thought needs to be given as to what reasons and what circumstances would legitimately satisfy this moral burden of proof.

Limits of the Rights-Type of Moral Norm

There are a number of critiques of the whole rights approach to ethics in general and to political morality in particular. Many of these date back to the eighteenth and nineteenth centuries and the challenges made to the concept of human rights by Edmund Burke, Karl Marx, and even from within the liberal tradition itself, namely, the critiques of the utilitarian stream of liberalism. The revival and development of human rights since the Second World War benefited from many of these criticisms, and modifications were made accordingly. More recently, however, the communitarian critique of liberal thought, already discussed in connection with the common good, raises anew some of the earlier concerns about rights.

Once again, one of the major charges made by communitarians against contemporary human rights doctrine in all its various forms is its individualistic assumptions regarding human nature and society. The result is an impoverished concept of political morality and social good. An ethos of selfishness and egoism is also generated, "a rather unpleasant and morally unhealthy situation of a lot of self-centered individuals going around querulously making claims against one another all the time, and demanding benefits, protection and remedies from their society in an adversarial and contentious spirit."[65] Communitarians are concerned that putting individual interests at the very heart of the moral life tends to overwhelm all other kinds of moral norms, values and goods. Thereby jeopardized are a variety of precious human relationships, for which individual rights are inappropriate norms.

An example often cited by such critics is marriage. If dependent on the assertion of human rights, it would become a relationship that is something other than a genuine marriage. Something similar might also be said for families, for societies that are kinship centred, and for churches or other covenant communities. This concern is part of what lies behind the recent efforts to develop collective rights, as we have seen. But even if such collective rights were more widely recognized, this would not entirely solve the problem. Collective rights impose duties and obligations on other groups and collectives and not on individual members of the group. There are, in short, a whole variety of values and goods that adhere to communities and groups as a whole, like language, solidarity, and fellowship. These in turn depend on virtuous persons who behave in caring, generous, loyal ways, none of which are addressed by human rights.

The focus on individual interests and claims and their pursuit in an adversarial relationship to others does seem a long way from Jesus' command to love our neighbour. The obligation norms concerned with mutuality and sharing, and the willingness to set aside even one's own interests if such would foster the true well-being of others, are more appropriate to Christian and other kinds of covenant communities. Yet we have seen that basic human rights do point to important goods that should be the concern of anyone who takes seriously the dignity and worth of all human beings.

Developing a modified theory of human rights that accommodates these criticisms, yet is faithful to the best of the rights tradition, is the aim of a number of both secular and Christian thinkers.[66] A more modest claim for the place of human rights in the moral life, especially in political morality, is one corrective step. True, rights do serve to draw attention to certain important individual interests and goods. Thus, "it is awful to be locked up or silent, terrifying to be beaten and tortured, and appalling to be left to starve or vegetate when resources are available for food and education; and one may think these ills so bad that their avoidance should be an overriding aim of any decent society."[67] However, human rights need to be supplemented by other moral norms and standards to show us how we should exercise these claims and under what circumstances.

In addition, all of these writers recognize that human rights should not be seen as final, absolute standards for assessing right action. They may be overridden under certain circumstances by competing goods and norms. Not everything of importance in politics can be connected to the freedom, security, and well-being of individuals, nor can all goods be reduced to individual interests. Some goods adhere to the well-being of the community as a whole. The necessary conditions for genuine human agency expressed through positive participation in the life of society are, not only individual freedom and well-being, but also a context of communal relationships. Perhaps communal relationship and common goods, on the one hand, and individual moral agency requiring certain fundamental rights, on the other, are finally dependent upon each other.

In the language we have been using, basic human rights and collective rights are only one type of norm to guide us, particularly in the political and social spheres of our lives. From a Christian standpoint, they come under the commandment of love for neighbour. Like other norms, they need to be weighed in connection with other kinds of considerations or base points in both the development of the moral life and in decision-making situations.

THE PLACE OF MORAL NORMS IN THE CHRISTIAN MORAL LIFE

We have been examining three types of moral norms: obligations, values or goods, and rights. In the case of each type, I selected a few representative samples and, through them, tried to illustrate the range of rich resources available, plus some of the important debates at issue concerning the selection and interpretation of norms. There are, of course, many more broad standards and a host of specific norms (rules and guidelines) that provide a more precise marking of the Way.

The brass section of the moral orchestra contains more instruments than we are able to explore here. Hopefully, enough have been examined to make its tone and quality recognizable. However, which of these norms is to take priority when we are faced with situations in which all available courses of action entail the conflict of two or more of them? Needless to say, this crucial question has brought forth much discussion and various proposals! In part 6, we will examine this matter in conjunction with the wider question as to how the various sections of the moral orchestra are to be brought together. Here we must face a prior question that has troubled Christians: What is the appropriate place of moral norms in the Christian life?

At one end of the range of views on this question are those who argue that moral norms and standards of any type should not have a place in the life of Christians. The power of the Holy Spirit so transforms those who have "put on Christ" that they are able to know intuitively, in any situation, what is God's will and purpose for them and to spontaneously obey it.

At the opposite end of the spectrum are those who would make moral norms and standards, at least of certain types, the centre, almost the sole content, of the moral life. These standards are seen as God's commands and imperatives. Norms and analysis of the situation are regarded as the only two base points needed — brass and percussion are sufficient.

The major strands of the Christian tradition, however, recognize a solid but limited place for moral norms and standards. I find myself with the mainstream on this issue. There are, however, important variations within that stream regarding which type of standard is appropriate, how central norms are to the moral life, their foundation, and how they should be weighed.

The discussion in Christian thought on the place of moral norms is frequently cast in terms of the relation of law to gospel. The moral law contains collections of moral norms, though strictly speaking it entails more than this, such as qualities of character and other teachings. The gospel, of course, is God's free gift of forgiving and empowering grace in Jesus Christ. What is the relationship of the moral law to the gospel, of moral norms and standards to the spontaneous response to God's grace?

On the whole, in the Old Testament, especially in the tradition of Deuteronomy and certain Psalms, the law itself is seen as a gift of God's free grace. The law clarifies what issues are at stake in our decisions and provides us with guidance in the place of confusion and chaos. It is "a lamp for our feet, and a light for our paths" (Ps. 119:105). But it is also experienced as a burden, the standard by which people are found wanting and therefore justly condemned. This is true especially in some of the sixth-century prophets, such as Jeremiah (ch. 31) and Ezekiel (ch. 36).

In his letter to the Romans, Paul expresses explicitly this seemingly paradoxical nature of the moral law. It is a blessing of God, especially in terms of the covenant, but it is also a curse, especially for those gentiles who stand outside the covenant and yet remain under the law and are found wanting by its terms. To such gentiles, Paul proclaims the Gospel of Jesus Christ, that they may be saved "apart from the law." Ever since the time of Paul, Christians have been debating on whether or not they, as those who have been saved by that Gospel and counted as righteous before God by the work of Jesus Christ, are still bound to the precepts of the law.

The Reformers Luther and Calvin provide us with some helpful reflections on this. Both strongly affirm that salvation is assured by the unmerited forgiveness of Christ and not through the impossible task of adherence to moral law. They further agree that the law has two important, though rather negative, purposes. The first use of the law is as a teacher. When humans attempt to live by its precepts they are soon made aware of their limitations. The law thus serves to reveal the sin of human beings. It leads us to the mercy of Christ. It is, as it were, a mirror in which we can see our own iniquity and shortcomings. The second use of the law is to both prompt and coerce human beings to do the will of God. It functions to curb the violence and excess of a fallen humanity in general and makes possible minimal order and decency among sinful humankind. For Luther, this second use continues to be important for Christians, for though counted as righteous, they continue in practice to be sinners and also must live in a fallen world.

But insofar as Christians are transformed by grace and live within the "realm of redemption," the moral law has no place or function. Rather the Christian is to be guided by the Holy Spirit, through the Bible, the church, and prayer. By this guidance we should learn what the particular needs of neighbours, which are to be met by love, are in a specific situation. Insofar as the Christian must still live as a sinner in the realm of creation, a creation which is fallen, he or she is subject to the moral law of reason and justice, though these can be tempered by faith and love.

For Calvin, there is a third use of the moral law. For those saved by God's grace in Jesus Christ, the moral law can serve as a teacher and a guide so that believers may learn what is the will of God to which they aspire and are now moved to follow. Some Christian thinkers have developed this further and would claim that the moral law now becomes a major part of what "life in the Spirit" looks like.

The position taken in this book follows the tradition of Calvin's third use of the law. Moral norms and standards are a major source of guidance to those who seek to live by the spirit of Jesus Christ. The moral law is, indeed, a "lamp unto our feet" that helps us discern moral issues and guides us in their resolution. It serves as a modest though not foolproof check against rationalizing. Moral norms make it more difficult to justify our own desires and interests in the name of serving God and caring for our neighbour than do easy appeals to the Spirit's guidance.

Further, norms preserve specific concerns integral to love of neighbour or trusteeship of creation that might have to be temporarily set aside when all available options in a situation preclude them. In some circumstances, we are forced to choose between the lesser of evils. For instance, I recall the concern of a nurse working in a long-term care facility, who reluctantly restricted the movements of an elderly woman confined to a wheel chair because she kept knocking other clients down as she travelled about. (She would also periodically raid the dispensary!)

The nurse was clear that in imposing such restraints, she was setting aside the norm of autonomy. She recognized that this action was less than what she deemed right. She therefore tried to respect the free choices of the woman in every other way possible, and even when overriding them, tried to do so in the least offensive way possible. The norm of autonomy in this case preserved an important aspect of love of neighbour (respect of choice) in the nurse's consciousness that she had to temporarily set aside. It also enabled the nurse to call what she was doing by the right name — the lesser of evils — rather than claiming it was simply and completely right in these special circumstances.

Norms also often provide common standards for action among persons and communities of diverse beliefs. In health care, for example, people who may disagree about the grounding and sometimes the application of a norm frequently share a recognition of the standard itself.

The moral law and obedience to it cannot save us or place us in right relationship with God. It does not make bad people good or weak people strong; this can come only through the free gift of God in Jesus Christ. The moral law with its norms and standards does help us to realize how much we need that forgiving grace. Norms and precepts are not sufficient to deal with all of our moral dilemmas. Elaborate schemes of specific rules to cover even more contingencies can become rigid and, in new contexts, may no longer serve the principles and values they were designed to express. Clearly then, norms do not exhaust the meaning of life in the Spirit or of the moral life in Christ, but they do constitute one essential aspect of the moral life and are one key ingredient in reflecting on moral decisions.

The brass section is a strong and rich part of the moral orchestra. The study of norms and standards is highly developed and illuminating. This has involved a rather lengthy examination, more than will be given to other base points or sections of the moral orchestra. However, there are other vital components no less important. Neglect of them impoverishes, even distorts, the moral life. We shall look now, then, at another facet of the moral life, another base point, namely, moral character.

Two

Moral Character: Habits of the Heart

A look at the nature of moral character and how it is understood from a Christian perspective. Two aspects of character are closely examined. The first is posture or stance towards life. The second is dispositions, which are assessed as either virtues or vices. Love and hope are explored as a sample of dispositions that Christians view as key virtues. A glance at a few other virtues and vices is followed by a discussion of how moral character is formed and the church's role in this. Finally, the place of character in the moral life is appraised.

A MODEL FOR ETHICAL REFLECTION

Moral Agent in Community

Basic Commitment

Analysis of Self as Agent

Moral Character
(Habits of the Heart)

Posture or Stance
Doxology

Dispositions
Virtues
Love
Hope
Faith, patience, and others
Vices
Pride, envy, anger,
sloth, gluttony, lust

Worldview and Basic Convictions

Moral Norms and Standards

Analysis of the Social Setting

The Context

The Situation

Authoritative
Sources

Authoritative
Sources

Resolution

INTRODUCTION

So far we have been reflecting on the question of what God is requiring and enabling us to do. We have explored norms and standards, which should serve as markers of the Way and guide us in determining right action. We turn now to a different aspect of the moral life. What kind of *persons* is God requiring and enabling us to become? What should guide us in determining good *being?* The moral agent or person becomes the focus of attention rather than moral actions. Thus we speak of a good person, one who is perhaps gracious, kind, patient, loyal, and courageous. This aspect of the moral life is referred to as moral character.

Character refers to the inner and distinctive core of a person from which moral discernment, decisions, and actions spring. It is an enduring configuration of the intentions, feelings, dispositions, and perceptions of any particular self. This configuration, unique to each individual, relates the self in a fundamental and consistent way to the world. In terms of the Way, a person's moral being is both part of living the Way and a kind of internal antenna for discerning the path to walk. We are moving from considering the brass section of the moral orchestra to exploring the woodwind section. We will attempt to learn its distinctive sound, one that brings its own unique texture to the moral life.

The biblical understanding of "the heart" points to the same distinctive personal core. In biblical understanding, the heart is the central and unifying organ of personal life, the innermost spring. In typical biblical usage, the heart refers to the thoughts, plans, attitudes, fears, and hopes that mark or characterize a particular individual. There is concern in the Bible, then, not only for outward action and right behaviour in accord with God's law or norms, but also for a clean (Ps. 51:10), upright (Ps. 32:11), pure (Matt. 5:8), honest and good (Luke 8:15) heart.

The life of Christian discipleship, the commitment to follow Jesus as it is described in the Gospels, certainly entails, as we saw, obedience to the law and right action. But this is rooted in a commitment of the heart and a transformation of the inner moral being of the person. In Matthew, for example, the moral law is to be internalized in a way that includes feelings and attitudes. One is not only to obey the law but to be a temperate, truthful, loving, and patient person. There is an open-ended thrust towards the total transformation of the person that is typical of all ethics that emphasize good character. We are called to turn enmity and hatred into mercy and mutual forbearance and thereby not only sustain and maintain a righteous community as obedience to law enables us to do, but also to enlarge and extend that community and renew it when it breaks down.

In Paul, the motif of the believer entering into the death of Jesus Christ and rising to a new life in Christ, or the "putting on" of Christ, points to moral being as well as doing. His motif on the new life in the Spirit does likewise. This new relationship of the believer with God in Jesus Christ, and the Spirit out of which the believer now comes to live, entails his or her innermost being, as well as outward actions and doing.

Character has also been a concern of major strands in the Christian tradition. For example, Thomas Aquinas explains this aspect of the moral life at length. The contrary is true for twentieth-century philosophical ethics and, to a considerable extent, theological ethics. They have concentrated on establishing a universally valid set of standards for behaviour. Character has been neglected. Only within the last ten to fifteen years has it resurfaced in these disciplines as a focal point for examining the moral life.

A provocative essay suggests a reason for this neglect; it is that genuine community, the social grounds requisite for character, is badly weakened in modern societies. An over-arching tradition or narrative that makes sense of life as a whole is needed to provide the conceptual framework for nurturing and reflecting on character. Yet a unifying narrative that embraces all the different roles and "life-worlds" in which modern persons typically engage is out of joint with our times. It is not congenial either to the pluralistic social conditions or the relativism and individualism that mark the prevailing dominant ideologies. The tradition of character and moral being "is at variance with central features of the modern economic order and more especially its individualism, its acquisitiveness and its elevation of the values of the market to the central social place."[1] It follows that any critical retrieval of the moral tradition of character and the virtues will be deeply counter-cultural.

The unique configuration of feelings, intentions, dispositions, and the like that mark the character of any person does not readily lend itself to precise analysis. We will explore what have come to be recognized as two main aspects of character, a basic *posture* towards life and relatively stable *dispositions*.

POSTURE OR STANCE

Central to any person's character is their fundamental stance or posture towards life and the world. This can also be thought of as the "determinative perspective" or the point of view from which one looks at one's experiences and evaluates them. At the risk of straining the moral orchestra metaphor, the basic posture towards life may be likened to the oboe; by its sounding note the rest of the orchestra is tuned.

A stance towards life and the world is grounded in basic commitments and loyalties. Some examples: We may have the expectation that all moral acts inevitably ensnare us in the very evil we seek to avoid. This expresses a tragic stance towards life. Or we may view the world, both social and natural, as knowable and controllable through the application of knowledge and reason. This is a view that underlies a triumphant kind of posture. A Native elder explained that this was how his people experienced the British at the height of their imperial power, seemingly totally confident of their culture, their Way, and projects. "How else," he said, "could you describe or explain two unarmed Englishmen riding into an armed Sioux camp and, with great self-assurance, saying to an amazed group of warriors, 'Here, here, we can't have any of this!'"

Or there is a stance like that held by an existentialist philosopher: "Life is like jumping off the Empire State Building," he said to me one evening. "It is simply what you choose to do on the way down. You can compose a poem, admire your reflection in the windows, shout and curse, or whatever." This is a stance of defiant assertion in which the self views the world as essentially meaningless but grasps what significance and meaning it can. Contrast these stances with the posture revealed in the statement of scholar and mystic Rabbi Abraham Heschel: "I did not ask for success; I asked for wonder. And You gave it to me."[2]

These diverse fundamental stances are different orientations to life and the world. Each shapes a distinctive selection of values or goods, of things in which one delights, of longings and desires. Above all, our posture towards life affects our perception, the way in which others and the world are seen and interpreted.

To illustrate this, James Gustafson, a prominent contemporary ethicist, invites us to compare the stance grounded in Augustine's type of Christianity with one rooted in the rival Manichaen sect of that time. The Manichaens claimed that there is an ongoing war in the world between good and evil powers that are clearly distinguishable from each other. Evil has a status and power equal to the good. With such a belief, "one will move from fear to a crusading mentality that forecloses sensitivity to the changing constellations out of which new good can emerge, that seeks to destroy the evil rather than to reform it, that seeks to abolish rather than to reconcile." If, on the other hand, one believes as an Augustinian Christian that "the goodness of God and the goodness of life as created, governed, and redeemed by God are ultimately and really greater than any particular occasion of evil, or all occasions of evil collected, one will live and move with a fundamental confidence in the world, with an openness towards the world, with a sensitivity to change and the opportunities it provides, and without a debilitating despair."[3]

What fundamental stance or orientation to life is generated

by loyalty to Jesus Christ? There is no single answer to that question. In other words, there is no single basic stance towards life that all Christians can be predicted to hold. There are other possibilities besides the Augustinian one described above. The religious context and theological tradition in which a person is formed will affect the way in which they have laid hold of the gospel and the stance that flows from this. Additional variables that are involved in shaping any particular person's stance include: the degree to which other fundamental loyalties and commitments to self, family, and nation impinge upon loyalty to Christ; the way social and cultural conditionings have intermingled with loyalty to Christ; and the degree of faithfulness and loyalty to Christ, which might vary within the same person from one time to another.

Nevertheless, there is a limited range of possible postures that are congruent with loyalty to Christ. In Gustafson's words, "Christians have one point of common life, namely, the centrality of Jesus Christ as the One through whom the ultimate powers and realities of life are known and understood, the One who represents as a historical figure the origin of a continuing historical community of trust and loyalty."[4] In Jesus Christ, we see the character of the mysterious God the creator. We receive God's redemption. We taste the transforming power of the Holy Spirit. This both enables and requires us to become new persons.

Stance of Doxology. Loyalty to this "three-in-one" God evokes a fundamental posture of doxology — praise and thanksgiving. In the words of Charles Wesley's famous hymn, "love divine, all loves excelling, joy of heaven to earth come down" generates a posture of "wonder, love, and praise" and "Thee we would be always blessing, serve thee as thy host above, pray and praising without ceasing, glory in thy perfect love." The stance of doxology generates confidence and openness to this troubled world with the knowledge that the very real powers of evil are not the final word. There is nothing created that God has not redeemed and over which God does not rule. God's love is deeper even than the abyss of death.

At the same time, this stance of doxology generated by loyalty to the one who by the cross of Christ is "all compassion" affords a distinctive angle of vision. It yields a perspective from which all human beings are regarded as beloved children of God. We can see clearly and fearlessly the finitude, brokenness, and sin of the world in which we all participate, its suffering and despair. Yet by the light of the resurrection, this stance brings to view the sustaining love and goodness of ordinary human experience, the awesome beauty of other-than-human creation, the manifestations in people's lives of Christ's saving grace, freely given.

The stance of doxology also enables us to clearly see ourselves as *creatures,* not as the *Creator*. We are a part of God's redemptive story, but neither knowledgeable about nor responsible for the ultimate outcome of that story. Confidence in God's grace helps us to live in the light of the promised kingdom of shalom, witness to it, and, in short, do all for the glory of God in the confidence of the kingdom's final coming in fullness.

DISPOSITIONS: VIRTUES AND VICES

A second dimension of character closely related to, and in fact even expressive of, the fundamental stance is made up of dispositions. A disposition is a persistent tendency or a stable readiness to speak and to act in a certain manner or way. Thus we can identify a hopeful disposition or a greedy, impatient disposition. Such "habits of the heart" or traits of character manifest themselves primarily as a tendency to act in certain *ways*; for example, lovingly or selfishly. The precise content of the action, of course, will vary with the situation and circumstances. Dispositions also affect the *manner* in which we act; for example, patiently or arrogantly. They influence our *perception* of events and their significance for us. Is the cup seen as half empty or half full?

Dispositions or "operative habits" deemed desirable or good are called *virtues*, and those deemed undesirable, *vices*. Which dispositions are judged to be virtues and which are seen as vices depends mainly on one's fundamental commitment of faith, basic posture to life, and the community and its stories that express these. It is also affected to some extent by the social context. Assessments vary with changes in institutional forms and patterns of social life. Certainly, different roles and functions in life lead to a particular prioritizing of those qualities that best enable those roles or functions to be fulfilled: for example, the courage required of a soldier or the patience of a teacher or the loyalty of a citizen and patriot.

As roles and functions change or are rejected, the virtues associated with them may fade from prominence, disappear altogether, or come to be regarded as vices. The honour associated with being a gentleman has practically disappeared with the demise of that social station. Modesty, chastity, and submissiveness, once deemed virtuous for women, are rejected by most in Western societies. Some feminists criticize the assessment of these qualities of character as virtuous on the grounds that they helped to maintain an unjust and inequitable relationship between men and women.

Other feminists warn against too hasty or wholesale an

abandonment of certain virtues associated in the past primarily with women, especially those connected with nurture. These virtues may indeed have been misused for unjust male purposes and be out of joint with our modern culture. Nevertheless, they are vitally important for human flourishing and need to be held up as virtues appropriate for men as well. As feminist philosopher Carol MacMillan states, "it is important to remember that obedience is not the same as subservience; humility is not the same as masochism; and patience is not the same as impotence. The distinction can be expressed by saying that the first category presupposes agency and the second aims to destroy it, so that (for example) obedience differs from subservience by being a case of intentional passivity as opposed to mere passivity."[5]

On what basis, then, are certain qualities of character to be designated as virtues and others as vices with this changing and sometimes bewildering array of candidates? What is required, as stated earlier, is a clear understanding of the purpose of human life and the meaning of the good society, a common narrative or story that makes sense of life as a whole, and a tradition. With these, we are able to select dispositions or habits of the heart, qualities of character, that are congruent with that basic narrative and tradition, that express and facilitate the good life and the good society.

What virtues are congruent with the Christian narrative? Or, put differently, what virtues arise out of a life in Jesus Christ (Phil. 1:27); which exhibit the manner of life and bearing towards one another appropriate to the Spirit (Phil. 2:5)? We are called above all to be trusting, hopeful, and loving (I Cor. 13:13). Christians have reflected much on the meaning of these three virtuous dispositions. Thus, again, there is abundant, valuable material for ethical reflection. We will begin by illustrating some of the prevailing points of discussion in connection with interpreting the virtues of love and hope.

Loving Disposition

Some of the essentials of agape, as this kind of love is referred to in the New Testament, were enumerated earlier. There we were concerned with which standards of behaviour spell out the more general principle of love of neighbour so that we could assess particular actions in light of such standards. Here we are concerned with another whole dimension; namely, what is entailed in a loving disposition or habit of the heart? Both of these are essential to the full moral life. We all know of actions that result in good but are done without affection or thoughtfulness — cold charity. On the other hand, we all have experience of persons of a generous and loving disposition, whose actions, offered in a spirit of genuine spontaneous concern and caring, were not efficacious of true well-being and may even have caused harm.

Self-Love. A useful illustration of the kind of probing that goes on, both concerning the meaning of love as a virtue and its relationship to love as an action guide, is provided by the ongoing debate in Christian thought regarding self-love. Is regard for myself part of a loving disposition that I should seek to cultivate, or is it a barrier to a readiness to give myself in service and in caring for others? This seemingly perennial question has been very prominent in contemporary North American societies. It emerges in one form or another in everything from debates about methods of psychological therapy to concerns about a narcissistic culture and the decline of community and public life.

What a tangled skein the discussion about self-love has become in Christian thought. One difficulty is that the whole matter is variously formulated according to how it is thought to be connected with other matters regarding love. Thus, sometimes it is explicitly discussed in terms of the relation of self-regard to other-regard in love of neighbour. Other times it is interwoven with the closely related issue of whether self-sacrificing love or mutual love is the essential meaning of agape. Or it is embedded in the question of what the relation of agape (modelled on God's love in Christ for human beings) is to various common human loves, especially the kind of love that seeks to draw the beloved to the self (Eros).

The place of self-regard in the quality of true Christian love is, then, entangled in a larger web of issues. These include convictions about the constitution of the human self, the nature and persistence of sin, the means of salvation, the character of God, and the content of salvation! Nevertheless, embracing the risk of over-simplification, one can discern two major strands in this tangle.

The first focuses on self-denial as the centre of Christian agape. Self-love is commonly rejected by this approach, whether in God's love for humans or in our love for God or for neighbour. Alternatively, it may view self-love as natural to humans and as an example of how we are to love others, but not one that needs to be encouraged. Such an approach is usually, though not always, connected to the conviction that there is a sharp distinction between the kind of love we call agape and the ordinary human loves associated with desire and longing for some form of good. Self-love, then, is seen as either *nefarious* and a barrier to true agape or, at best, a *natural* phenomena that provides a useful paradigm as to how we should care for others.

The second strand affirms a place for self-love. This is usually connected with the wider motif in Christian thought that begins with affirming the human desire for the self's own good and happiness. Agape is not the replacement of this desire with disinterested benevolence, as in the first view, but rather the directing of this desire to its true ends, its ultimate goal in God. True happiness is found in caring for the neighbour as an end in him or her self. Even God's love, some though not all exponents of this view would claim, contains its own need for communion, and the view of God as some solitary form of affection without any needs is rejected.

This approach includes many who espouse mutuality (persons finding fulfilment through caring for others and in turn receiving care) as the proper goal of love. "Agape is first and primordially the spirit of *communion* willing the divine relationship between Father and Son as the ground and pattern of the fulfillment of all things."[6] Exponents of "legitimate self-regard" vary as to whether they see such self-love as *necessary* before one is able to love others or in limited forms and degrees merely *permissible* or as a definite *obligation* alongside the obligation to care for others.

Some of the concerns that emerge in various Christian thinkers who espouse the affirmation of self-regard as part of agape are as follows: First, there is a concern that we recognize the goodness of God's creation and that creation is relational at its core. Human beings are intended for communion and relationship that consists not only of joyous giving but also receiving love and care.

Second, the self is never entirely free of some form of self-love or desire for fulfilment, nor can it be. The question is, will this desire for self-fulfilment be properly directed to the one ultimate good truly worthy of desiring, namely, God? God in his redemptive purpose works with rather than against this innate human impulse to seek self-fulfilment and belonging.

A third concern of this approach is that if love is understood in a way that completely excludes self-regard, a preoccupation with self is ironically likely to be fostered. Individuals become preoccupied to the point of morbidity and melancholy in their efforts to be selfless. In fairness, the danger of these self-destructive tendencies is also recognized by those who espouse agape as self-denial.

Fourth, the effort to achieve complete disinterestedness may "make for injustice by encouraging and permitting undue self-assertion in others."[7] Rejection of all self-regard can lead to imbalances in relationships that invite acts of cruelty and manipulation. This is especially the case for women in our society, feminists observe. Women with religious idealism, imbued with the virtue of love understood as readiness to give up self for the sake of the other, are thereby blocked from righteous indignation even when they are abused. A slave morality is engendered that allows men to manipulate them.

In addition, this kind of religious development reinforces, in an unhelpful, even dangerous, way, certain patterns already present in the psychological formation of women. They grow up, according to this feminist theory, being able to identify entirely with those who care for them as children in a way that men do not. This leads to a kind of apathy in women with regard to their own development as persons. Women, therefore, are prone less to the sin of pride and self-assertion than to the tendency to give themselves to others to the point of losing their ability to be centred selves at all.[8]

Finally, there is a concern that the common relations of human life, such as marriage, family, and friendship, "should be at the center rather than at the periphery of Christian reflection and the love theme."[9] Any theory of Christian love should begin with the language and metaphors of familial relations as is true in the Old Testament. When self-denial and disinterested benevolence are made the centre of Christian love, says one exponent, then these "special" relationships present a problem, because to love is to regard everyone equally and nonpreferentially.

This is a formidable list of important matters! What are some of the major concerns connected with the view that *self-denial* is at the centre of true Christian love? It is important to note that not all the diverse Christian thinkers who agree with this view of self-denial would share all of the following concerns. First, there is the claim that the cross of Christ, rather than creation and nature, is the definitive revelation of God's love for humankind. Therefore the love we are commanded to emulate is an undiscriminating and self-sacrificing love. A Mennonite ethicist reflects this tradition faithfully when he calls upon Christians to follow Christ even to the cross. Discipleship places no justifiable limits on self-denial. For others, who agree that the cross of Christ is central in revealing the norm of love, such sacrificial love is not a generally feasible possibility for fallen humankind. Rather it remains as an ideal standard that reveals the partial and tainted nature of all our actions, done even in the name of love.

Yet, some heedless sacrificial love is necessary even for mutual love of reciprocity: "If mutual love is not constantly replenished by impulses of grace in which there are no calculations of mutual advantages, mutual relations degenerate first to the cool calculation of such advantages and finally to resentment over the inevitable lack of complete reciprocity in all actual relations."[10] In addition, sacrificial love is essential even for true self-fulfilment, "for the kind of self-giving which has self-realization as its final result must not have self-realization as its conscious end; otherwise the self by calculating its enlargement will not escape from itself completely enough to be enlarged."[11]

The second concern has to do with the means of salvation. We are enabled to enter into a new relationship with God and to love our neighbour, even more, our enemies, only by the gift of God's grace. This does not come about by any human means, such as the redirection of our natural longings. The proper response to God's gift of love of this kind is trust, gratitude, and obedience. That response is not even appropriately labelled as love.

Third, there is the worry that self-love is pervasive and powerful in sinful humanity. If admitted onto the ground floor of Christian ethics, it would overwhelm the proper focus of love. That proper focus is giving to each person according to the measure of his or her real need and not because of any attractiveness or merit in the needy or of any advantage to the giver. The reality of self-regard must be acknowledged, but it should not be made a virtue. Self-love is not a fire that God needs to fan.

Finally, a quite different concern is held by a distinctive company of Christians who emphasize self-denial. This is the mystic's view; that before the awesome holiness of God and God's love, all egoism is to be renounced: "The human instinct for personal happiness must be killed," and "the satisfactions of the spirit must go the same way as the satisfaction of the senses."[12]

Another formidable list of legitimate concerns! Little wonder that the struggle over the place of self-love in agape has been both intense and prolonged. Two things help us move forward on this important issue. The first is clarifying exactly what is meant by both self-love and self-denial. A contemporary ethicist who has done much to sort out the tangle of this issue has correctly observed that, with such clarification, some of the different viewpoints with their respective concerns turn out to be less contradictory than they first appeared to be. Some may even be reconcilable.[13]

Self-love and self-regard have several possible meanings: *self-worth,* a basic sense of self-identity and value, a centred self, knowing who one is; *self-affirmation,* recognition of the legitimate fundamental needs and interests of the self; *self-assertion,* a more vigorous defence and pursuit of the needs and interests of the self; *self-aggrandizement* or *self-centredness,* marked by a preoccupation with the self's own importance and the priority of its needs and interests.

I suspect there is wide agreement among Christians as to the moral appropriateness of self-worth. This is essential if there is to be any possibility of a person being able to love God or neighbour. The debate centres more on whether this can be acquired by deliberate effort, perhaps by cultivating acceptance from others, or, as I believe, only received as a gift from God. This gift can come through common grace, mediated through the acceptance, affirmation, and love of family and friends. It can come through saving grace, God's accepting and renewing love in Jesus Christ, mediated through the various "means of grace." But I believe that it is only saving grace that can finally secure for one an enduring sense of worth. Thus the good news to those who have little self-esteem and who have been socialized into self-abnegation is the free gift of self-worth and not a discipline of self-assertion, let alone self-aggrandizement, to overcome its lack.

Likewise, there is broad agreement among Christian thinkers that self-aggrandizement is inappropriate in terms of love of God or neighbour. It is the middle two understandings of self-regard, namely, self-affirmation and self-assertion, about which Christians are most divided in terms of their placement within agape. I think it is morally appropriate to lift up self-assertion in the case of members of marginalized or victimized groups, in a way that it would not be for persons of more powerful groups and societies in which assertion hardly requires any further encouragement.

Self-denial and self-sacrifice also encompass various meanings. Self-sacrifice can be understood to mean loss of a centred self or of personal identity, as in self-abnegation or excessive self-abasement. When this is the definition, most of the criticisms against the self-denial approach are valid. But self-denial may mean, not a loss of self-identity, but rather setting aside some of the legitimate interests of self for the sake of others. These interests could include possessions, comfort, prestige, even food, clothing, and shelter. With self-denial defined as such, the virtue of love may well be described as a stable *readiness* to give a second place to oneself, understood as one's legitimate interests, for the sake of the other. Questions remain as to whether such a disposition entails calculating when such putting aside really does achieve good for the other, or rather whether the disposition is marked by a quality of heedless, spontaneous giving.

Distinguishing clearly between love of neighbour as an action guide and as a virtue will also help us move forward on this issue. Love of neighbour as an action guide, as we have seen, includes standards of justice, respect for the self-directed and deliberate choices of others, actions that seek the highest well-being of others, and so forth. Following these norms faithfully will sometimes involve putting one's self-interests, though not self-identity and worth, to one side. Justice may require me to accept a lower income or be taxed more highly or support affirmative action at some risk to my own career opportunities. Caring for a neighbour may call me to go without sleep or may jeopardize my career goals because a child or a parent or a friend is ill and requires my assistance.

On the other hand, in certain circumstances, sacrificing my self-interests for those of another may actually do them harm. It may contribute to serious injustice. Acquiescing in the verbal and physical abuse of a spouse is definitely not fostering the bully's well-being. It certainly violates justice. I agree, then, with those that claim self-affirmation and even self-assertion have a legitimate place in the moral life, but that place is as part of the norm of justice. The self's interests should thus, in certain situations where the norm of justice comes into play, receive equal weight with those of the neighbour, but no more than this.

Love as a virtue is another matter. Based on the model of God's love for humankind, it includes a *readiness* to bear the burdens of others and to place one's self-interests second or even to sacrifice them. However, this readiness should be enacted only when the love of neighbour action-guide (with its various principles) indicates such sacrifice is appropriate, for instance, when it would be truly efficacious of another's essential well-being. It does not entail an *automatic* sacrifice of self-interest or laying down of one's life. In the security of God's love and of the worth God bestows upon us, we should seek to be free of a preoccupation with our own needs and interests, so that we are able to perceive when the norms of love call for this sacrifice and be ready and willing to comply.

In addition, a loving disposition involves persistence in caring for others, even if there is no response from them. It also means readiness to receive the love and care of others. For love of neighbour, both as an action guide and as a virtue, moves us to the communion characteristic of covenant with God, our fellow human beings, and other-than-human nature.

> *Just as my ability to love God is his gift to me, so our ability to love each other is our gift to each other.... My greatest fulfillment is the other-centeredness of love, my greatest human need is for that which creates this possibility — that is, love from others, the acceptance*

> *of me as a person. Similarly, my greatest gift to them is my self-donation to them, because this is also their greatest need.*[14]

The mystery of love and the giving and receiving of it will continue to challenge human understanding.

Hopeful Disposition

Another disposition that is viewed as a central virtue from a Christian perspective is hope. Hope may be defined as "a feeling that what is wanted will happen."[15] Simple desire for some object constitutes a wish, but hope entails "desire accompanied by anticipation or expectation." On the other hand, if what is anticipated or expected is not wanted or desired, the result is dread, not hope. Hope is usually contrasted with despair, one of whose roots is a fatalistic sense that all things and events are predetermined and unalterable. By contrast, "hope lives in the confidence that new possibilities of life exist, that present social systems and patterns of life are not fated by the blind god Necessity, but are susceptible to alteration, to recombination of the elements of life."[16] This feature of hope is essential to moral life in the sense that, without it, human agency, the possibility of humans engaging in meaningful action to affect any kind of change, is not possible. There can be no moral or immoral action by the terms of fatalism. Hope, then, assumes that there is freedom to change both one's life and to some extent the world and society one lives in.

Hope is also necessary to the moral life in that it is the basis of every other virtue. Without hope "that our existence is responsive to moral endeavour ... that the adventure of living virtuously will be worth the risk," it is not possible to acquire other moral virtues or to make the endeavour to live the moral life. In other words, hope is a necessary antidote to cynicism.[17]

"Most of us are not any more consistently hopeful," observes James Gustafson, "than we are consistently loving or courageous." But a person with a hopeful disposition is likely one whose "basis and objects of hope are so sufficient ... that attitudes of despair are the exception, whereas for others the occasions which give rise to hopefulness are more sporadic and episodic."[18]

Christian Ground of Hope. What we hope for (the object of hope) and why we hope for it (the basis for hope) is what gives hope its moral content. Hope, as we have been describing it thus far, is morally neutral, even though, as we have seen, it is essential for human agency and the moral life. However, hoping for the destruction of a particular group of people or even the destruction of the world itself, for example, would hardly be deemed by many as virtuous. What is the appropriate ground and object of hope from a Christian perspective? Once again, it is the gracious God revealed in Jesus Christ. As we have seen, this grace may come partly through the ministrations given to us in the everyday realities of family and community.

The prominent psychoanalyst Eric Erikson identifies the foundation of hope in trust. In turn, he traces its roots to early infancy and the experience of a newborn with a "caretaking person," one who tends to physical and emotional needs. If the experience with the caretaking person is positive, a trusting and hopeful fundamental disposition towards life emerges. Erikson describes hope as "the enduring belief in the attainability of fervent wishes, in spite of the dark urges and rages which mark the beginning of existence."[19] In theological terms, this is a form of common grace.

The experience of love and care from others generates a basic disposition to trust that the world is essentially reliable. As we mature and grow, however, there is the need to find a more focused and enduring basis of hope. We need a basis that sustains us through the vicissitudes of life when our experience seems to contradict the notion that the world is essentially reliable or that our heartfelt desires will be met. Further, growth entails a more discriminating selection of what to hope for, a maturing and even transformation of our desires. And what of those whose early life is marked by abandonment and abuse rather than a reliable and loving caretaking person? The saving grace of God in Jesus Christ as forgiveness and empowerment for new life is, amazingly, glimpsed and trusted by persons from the most shredded families and communities and those facing the most oppressive and tragic conditions.

The enduring foundation for hope is the deep trust that God will be faithful. The resurrection of Jesus Christ testifies to God's reliability in fulfilling his promise of the redemption of each of us and the entire creation. It is Paul's ringing declaration: "For I am convinced that neither death, nor life, nor angels, nor rulers, nor things present, nor things to come, nor powers, nor height, nor depth, nor anything else in all creation, will be able to separate us from the love of God in Christ Jesus our Lord" (Rom. 8:38-39).

This basis for hope, then, is closely tied to a particular object of hope. God's grace is the foundation of hope, the reason we dare to hope at all in face of the sins and tragedies of the world around us and within us. The fulfilment of God's grace is the object of our hope, the realization of God's kingdom of shalom.

There is wide consensus among the various strands of the Christian tradition concerning the foundation or basis of hope and its object as I have stated it in broad terms. The interpretations of this object of hope, however, vary considerably. These are revealed in response to a bewildering array of questions. Does the realization of God's kingdom include all human beings, only certain human beings, other-than-human creation? Is this kingdom for which we hope to be realized within history? At the end of history? Within another realm outside time and space altogether? Or partly now in history but with its completion to take place only at the end or above history? In what ways is God now acting in the world to fulfil God's promise, and will the object of our hope be realized in a gradual unfolding or in an apocalyptic struggle? Will it entail the completion and fulfilment of this world and life? Or its total transformation? Or its restoration to the original state of creation? Or the complete destruction of this present world and a new creation? What is the role of human beings and the Christian community in realizing this hope?

The significance of basic convictions (to be discussed in part 3) leaps out at us. Fortunately, the answers to these questions do not fundamentally alter the ground of a hopeful Christian disposition towards life, the world, and the future. Nevertheless, they do lead to important variations of this disposition and hence the ways in which a person engages the world.

This is dramatically, if somewhat humorously, illustrated by the policy that an airline in the United States formulated a few years ago. The company stated that they could not employ any pilot who, as a Christian, believed in the "rapture"—the sudden apocalyptic destruction of this world as a prelude to the new creation. Such a person might, in an emergency, act in a way detrimental to the life of the passengers. In other words, the particular object of hope of such a person, combined with their belief about how that hope was to be realized, would dispose them to relax rather than respond quickly in a crisis.

Does the Christian basis of hope and its object of hope, the fulfilment of God's kingdom in the future, dispose us to passive indifference towards the conditions in this life? Karl Marx and other critics have claimed that it does. On the contrary, says a group known as "theology of hope" theologians.[20] The "otherworldly" thrust of Christian hope relativizes all present social conditions. This in turn fosters an openness to and readiness for social and political change, in the confidence that God is at work making life more human in accord with God's redemptive purpose.

There are beliefs, however, about the content of hope and the means of its realization that generate a different attitude towards social change. These can be found in particular veins in the Christian tradition. A colony of Christians who belong to a breakaway sect from the Russian Orthodox Church and now reside in northern Alberta provide us with one example. Their life together is characterized by a strict regime of family life, farming, care for the earth, and worship. They are descendants of a Russian group that has lived with powerful hope through all sorts of adversities and persecutions, since the time of Peter the Great. But the hope of the members is in the apocalyptic coming of the kingdom for which they wait with confidence. They feel called to live quietly and patiently and thereby to bear witness to this trust.

This contrasts, for example, with the hope that characterized the Social Gospel movement of the late nineteenth and early twentieth centuries. Its confidence was also in God's grace and the object of hope the coming kingdom. But the kingdom was to be progressively realized in Western democratic societies. Christians were called upon to be one of God's agents in extending the principles of democracy from politics to the economic system.

Regardless of these kinds of variation concerning means, a

hopeful Christian disposition clearly differs from other versions that have a different basis and object. For example, in his book *The Third Wave* , Eric Toffler expresses a hope that appears to be widespread in modern Western societies: "with intelligence and a modicum of luck — the emergent civilization can be made more sane, sensible, and sustainable, more decent and democratic than ever before."[21] A contrasting hope, very differently based, is expressed by Robert K. Thomas, a Cherokee elder:

> *I have stood on top of Klingmans Dome in the Great Smoky Mountains, on the spot where God gave the Cherokees our second law, several centuries before whites appeared on this continent. I felt at that spot a sense of the continuity from the beginning, and a sense of immortality because I was part of the people, the Cherokee people, and I knew that as long as the Cherokee people lasted in the world, I would last in this world, and that when the Cherokee people cease to endure there would be nothing that would endure.*[22]

A hopeful disposition founded on the confidence that God's promises and mercy are "ever faithful, ever sure" fosters clarity of vision. We can dare to look squarely at the limitations of immediate prospects. An inadequate foundation for hope begets illusions. We are pressed to look at immediate prospects through rose-coloured glasses, because only in this way can we avoid falling into despair. The combined virtues of hope and patience are the only true antidotes to cynicism and despair. "Hope without patience results in the illusion of optimism or, more terrifying, the desperation of fanaticism," says Stanley Hauerwas, a specialist in character ethics. "Patience is training in how to wait when there seems no way to resolve our moral conflicts or even when we see no clear way to go on.... Yet patience equally requires hope, for without hope patience too easily accepts the world and the self for what it is rather than what it can or should be."[23]

The basic mistrust that produces hopelessness is also conducive to gluttony. "Gluttony reflects a mistrust of the future.... It focuses on the present moment of need gratification and dares not look beyond this moment." Is fanaticism a more sophisticated expression of gluttony? Another root of gluttony is hoping for the wrong thing and trusting in the wrong ground for realizing that hope. "Indiscriminate hope does not take the real world and its dangers into account, whereas real hope involves the training of expectations so that they are responsive to the real world and not oblivious of its dangers and threats." Sound hope is not foolhardy like gluttony; "it knows how to limit and channel its desires."[24] Both fanaticism and gluttony, therefore, arise in part from an inadequate hope.

Other Virtues and Vices

We have looked briefly at the virtues of love and hope. Clearly, interpretations of these and their relationship to each other are as varied and abundant as interpretations of obligations, values, or rights. Love and hope, along with faith, have long been widely regarded in the Christian community as the central virtues. In the Roman Catholic tradition, they are called "the theological virtues." Which additional dispositions should be assessed as virtues and which as vices? As we have come to expect, a range of answers emerge as Christians through the ages have sought to understand the implications of their faith for moral being.

Prominent in Western moral thought, at least since the time of Plato, are four "cardinal virtues." Prudence or practical wisdom is a virtue of the intellect that has to do with the ability to recognize the good and act upon it in a way that is appropriate to a particular situation. Justice as a virtue is a settled disposition to treat others fairly, a "steady, habitual determination to make space in life for the needs and claims of others."[25] Included as a cardinal virtue is temperance or self-control, the ability to restrain passions and desires so they do not deflect one in carrying out the good. Fortitude or courage enables one to do what prudence and justice require without being deflected by failure. Some virtues are tied closely to roles and institutions. But prudence, courage, and temperance are regarded by some as perennial virtues, appropriate for all times and cultures. "They are perennials, because they are integrally related to the *human capacity to sustain a course of action* based on overarching principles, ideals, plans, or goals."[26]

A proposed alternative to the four cardinal virtues are the "eschatological virtues," claimed to be more scripturally based. These are gratitude-humility, which arises out of recognition of God's goodness and mercy; hope, a disposition that looks to the future and human possibilities for participating in the ongoing creation and redemption; vigilance, a disposition that focuses on the present, seeking to discern present opportunities for following the Lord and giving attention to the small matters of everyday life; serenity and joy, which are gifts of the Spirit and qualities of character that save the individual from useless worry, anxiety, and fear.[27]

Of course, other qualities of character have also been regarded as virtuous in the history of Christian thought. Some of these have been drawn from scripture, such as the list in Galatians 5:22-24. Others are expounded in Christian literature, especially in the period of medieval Catholicism, in the works of Chaucer, Dante, and, much later, in John Bunyan's classic Protestant work *Pilgrim's Progress*. This latter book develops the idea that there are certain virtues and also particular vices associated with different stages of a person's spiritual pilgrimage. This is portrayed, for example, in the vivid story of the person named Christian and his companion Hopeful, who were imprisoned by Giant Despair in Doubting castle. They finally discover that the means of their release is a key called Promise that Christian had in his possession all along! Virtues and vices are more adequately displayed through lives of persons, actual or fictional, than they are in abstract definitions.

There is also the long history in the Christian tradition of the "seven deadly sins." These are dispositions of moral being designated as vices: pride, envy, anger, sloth, greed, gluttony, and lust. They are called deadly because experience indicates that they both manifest sin and underlie other vices. Now take this list of deadly sins and put it together with psychologist Erik Erikson's life stages, stir in the spiritual journey of Bunyan's *Pilgrims Progress*, and add the Beatitudes. The result is an intriguing proposal by author Donald Capps. He establishes a correspondence between each of these vices and a particular "saving" virtue. He further claims that there is a correlation between a particular stage in the life-cycle of human growth and a focus on a specific set of vices and saving virtues. Thus, young adulthood is a time when lust is a prominent temptation and vice, but also a period of growth most appropriate for acquiring the virtue of love. Adulthood is marked by the particular temptation to the vice of apathy, whereas the saving virtue most needed at this stage is the quality of caring.[28]

CHURCH AND CHARACTER

There is increasing awareness of how cultural context and communities affect both which dispositions are valued and how these are acquired. This was vividly displayed for my wife and me when we watched a rodeo with an audience of Papago people. The rodeo announcer was from outside the community. As is usual for such announcers, his task was to contribute to the show by drawing the crowd into the competition of the events, stirring them into cheering support for various competitors. He encountered, instead, a devastating silence. No yelling, no urging favourite contestants on, no cheers for triumphant winners riding prancing horses around the ring. Gentle and polite applause was given, at most. The announcer became increasingly shrill in his efforts to "whip up enthusiasm."

We were later to learn that the unnerving quiet was not because the Papago people were indifferent to the spectacle. They were enjoying it. Nor was it simply the result of the characteristic Papago quiet and modest way of expressing emotion. It was mainly because their culture does not value competition highly or cultivate a competitive disposition in its members. People were not disposed or tuned to the hype of competition. We must look at which dispositions our communities foster in ourselves and our families and how this is done.

For Christians, the church is one of the prime shapers of moral character. Its common narrative tradition, which makes sense of life as a whole and expresses an understanding of the purpose of human life, is what is needed for moral formation, including the selection of virtues and their cultivation. These resources are in scarce supply in liberal, modern societies. The same social context that makes discussions of the common good so difficult also works against any commonly recognized set of virtues, let alone their cultivation.

A recent sociological study of Americans revealed that there is little sense of "a community of memory and a tradition of humane freedom" to which people are freely committed. This, however, is what is needed to define and generate virtuous persons. Instead, they found the socially *unsituated self,* or, put more graphically by a Native friend, they found a bunch of individuals rattling around like stones in a hubcap. People seldom experience any intrinsic meaning in their work or career. A job is simply a way of earning status and a livelihood. Such a lack of calling indicates the absence of a sense of moral meaning. People find little "substantive community," individuals with different views sorting out what are to be their shared goals and values. Instead, the sociologists found "the 'life-style enclave', i.e., groups of the homogeneous, class specific tribal enclaves, reinforcing group bias and prejudices."[29]

Under these social conditions of fragmentation, then, the calling of the church to shape its own life in terms of the story of Jesus and the kingdom assumes a new urgency. Is the church nurturing its children in the posture towards life and the virtues that arise out of this story? Or is it merely sanctioning the moral formation of some secular enclave or acquiescing in the constant inculcation by media, advertising, peer groups, and the like of a confusing plethora of dispositions — many of which are vices? A number of Christian ethicists, led by Stanley Hauerwas, seek to re-call the church to being a distinctive community: in, but not of, the world, in which members, especially children and young persons, might learn to be people of a certain kind. There, they might form a character marked by virtues, such as faith, hope, and love.

Indeed, the church should be concentrating on habits of

behaviour, on moral being, rather than focusing, as it has mistakenly and too often done, only on decisions and dilemmas. Christians may work in the public arena, Hauerwas says, but they cannot expect to make a case that will be persuasive to our fragmented culture regarding the way in which they view and act in the world. "The first task of Christian social ethics, therefore, is not to make the 'world' better or more just, but to help Christian people form their community consistent with their conviction that the story of Christ is a truthful account of our existence."[30]

The simple reality of such communities with their unifying narratives and appropriate virtues is radically counter-cultural in the context of the "stones in a hubcap" individualism of modern societies. Christian communities, therefore, will find themselves to be "an island of one culture in the middle of another, a place where the values of home are reiterated and passed on to the young, a place where the distinctive language and lifestyle of the resident aliens are lovingly nurtured and reinforced."[31]

But is it true that the virtues generated by the Christian story cannot be made intelligible to or be seen as important by those who may not share Christian convictions? We have tapped into a major issue that cannot be pursued here; namely, the relation of Christians to culture and what it means to "be in the world but not of it." Historical differences on this matter between Anabaptists, Calvinists, Catholics, and Lutherans persist to the present.[32]

William F. May, a Roman Catholic ethicist, shares Hauerwas' belief that we need to attend more carefully once again to moral character and the communities that form it. May is also disturbed by the present social conditions and climate. In modern society, he observes, we have come to develop an unhealthy sense of awe and respect for destructive powers and forces. This modern reverence for destructive powers has led to serious distortions in the field of health care and the practice of medicine; for example, in the tendency to overemphasize the image of the healer as a foe of the dark power of disease. Forces that are themselves dangerous and destructive may then be mobilized in such a cause, with terrible side effects. What is needed in health care are the virtues that grow out of belief in a creative and nurturant Ultimate Power.

For May, of course, this is rooted in Christian conviction, but unlike Hauerwas, he believes that this belief and these virtues are readily recognized and sought in health care by others who are not Christian. Nevertheless, the task of relating to the understandings of modern culture without compromising virtues, or indeed any other aspect of the Christian moral life, is much more difficult than liberal Christians are prone to recognize.

How do communities form moral character and cultivate virtues? Moral character formation has come under increasing study in recent years from a variety of disciplines. Studies of human growth by developmental psychologists have brought another dimension to the discussion of virtues. The psychosocial theory of Erik Erikson has already been mentioned. Educational psychologists have attempted to study and describe various stages in the moral development of children. Some Christian ethicists and educators have contributed to this research.

Unfortunately, the work of each of these several disciplines has not as yet been well informed by the others. Thus, with regard to moral development generally, considerable controversy exists as to whether and to what extent the "empirical findings" of the psychologists reflect, not only their own particular school of psychological theory, but also the unacknowledged philosophical presuppositions regarding ethics and other assumptions of their particular worldview that they have brought to the research. In addition, their findings are limited by the culture, class, and gender of the subjects studied.

The ongoing debate about the part played by gender in the way children are morally formed illustrates this. Carol Gilligan, a research psychologist, challenged previous work in this area on the grounds that conclusions about the moral formation of human beings could not legitimately be drawn from studies of boys alone. Her work purports to establish that young girls mature morally in different ways from boys, at least in Western culture. She finds, for example, that a focus on good relationships rather than obedience to rules characterizes the approach of girls to moral behaviour. Two different formations and styles of moral reasoning come from the two gender tracks.[33]

However, important challenges to these claims have arisen. One set of critics question her sharp distinction between norms and relationships, duties and virtues. Such distinctions reflect Gilligan's own operative ethical framework, the categories with which she interprets, as much as it does the actual data itself. Many ethicists and some anthropologists would question these simple dichotomies.[34] Others query her neo-Freudian view of moral development. Another woman psychologist writes, "If women have more often developed maternal thinking, it is because of their self-conscious intellectual development (in the process of raising children), not because of their female gender."[35]

In regard to cultivation of virtues in particular, the matter is further complicated by differing understandings of what constitutes a virtue. Unfortunately, like other features of the moral life, there is no consensus in either philosophical ethics or theological ethics as to exactly how virtues and vices are to be understood, let alone how they can be cultivated. There are important theological matters as well as psychological ones involved in this issue. Are virtues a skill that can be learned by instruction and therefore achieved by practise? Or are they more a habit of the heart that is only "caught" through example and story or received as a fruit of the Spirit? In the tradition of Greek thought, a virtue is that which causes a thing to perform and function well, as in the case of the eye, seeing. In the case of the whole human being, then, virtues are those excellences that enable a person to fulfil his or her true function or to attain the furthest potentialities of his or her nature.

In the New Testament, what we call virtues are often designated as gifts of the Spirit rather than as excellences to be acquired. Thus humility is a gift of grace appropriated in faith. It is a virtue with important implications for political life, since it "combines a fervent devotion to values with a clear recognition that these values are fragmentary in character and tainted by our prejudice."[36] If humility is an acquired virtue, then pride insinuates itself into the achievement of humility itself. We become proud of being humble, as Reinhold Niebuhr observed.

Gilbert Meilander, a contemporary Christian ethicist, believes that virtues are not skills in the sense of a technique or an ability to do things proficiently. They have more to do with the capacity to live life well, and with the inclination to do so. Yet, there is an attribute of every disposition, he claims, that can be cultivated and enhanced by practise. Without regular exercise, the habit of truthfulness, for example, will give way to the contrary inclination of lying.

We need to recall our discussion on God's grace as the foundation of the entire Christian moral life. Thus, cultivating virtues may be done as a form of cooperating with sanctifying grace rather than as an achievement of a self presuming to earn or possess righteousness.

Enough has been said to illustrate the difficulties involved in gaining a more complete understanding of moral development and the lively ongoing discussion of it. As yet, no really satisfactory overall account of character formation and moral development has emerged, though important insights, as we have seen, are beginning to emerge.

Hopefully, these diverse approaches to the study of moral formation will continue to deepen our understanding of how we may nurture both ourselves and our children in the Way of Christ, as we participate in God's sanctifying grace. Meanwhile, it is notable that these various disciplines are united in the conviction that persons are formed in their fundamental disposition to life and in their habits of the heart by the communities in which they grow up and are sustained.

The church engages in moral formation and character development, partly through direct moral teaching, but primarily through retelling the Christian narrative and lifting up the pivotal images of the faith. This is done in its liturgy, Christian education, and sustaining fellowship. The rite of baptism, for example, whether for children or adults, dramatizes the new orientation of the self to Christ. Through this sacrament, persons are incorporated into a new community and a new structure of life. The image of dying to the old Way and rising to the new is a powerful one for the moral life. It signifies that a change in being involves a shift away from the moral life of the world. An example from modern societies is leaving the "world's" celebration of freedom as a maximizing of personal choice and moving to the gospel's celebration of freedom as serving God with praise and thanksgiving.

The new life is nourished by participation in the drama of the

Eucharist. The reenactment of the life, death, and resurrection of Jesus Christ portrays a truth and way of being that stands in judgement of all existing orders and realities in both the church and society. This calls us back from the beguiling standards of the world and the compromising conditions of society to the radical vision of the kingdom. The fruits of human labour represented in bread and wine are received, transformed, and returned for our nourishment, both physical and spiritual. We are thereby reminded that even our broken efforts to serve are used by God for good. This enactment of God's unconditional love fosters a basic stance towards life of praise and thanksgiving and generates loving and patient dispositions. The drama of Christ's death and resurrection engenders a hopeful disposition even in the face of the tragedy and death that surround us.

The church also helps to form and shape our moral character through its Christian education programme and preaching. The basic narratives of the Bible and tradition contain instructive examples of strong moral character and right doing, as well as examples of corruption and failure. The creative rehearsing of this material cultivates the moral imagination and a Christian way of looking on the world. This is also assisted by participation in the social service and action programmes of the church and its ecumenical coalitions. Through the scripture, preaching, prayers, the sacraments, and social action of the church, habits of the heart, such as humility, love, patience, kindness, justice, and joy, are slowly fostered and regularly strengthened in Christians.

The church has the important task in moral formation: to facilitate ethically sound integration of the variety of moral materials that come from the various other social worlds and communities in which Christians participate. "The faith community gives perspective and places to the images, stories, pressures, and events that reign in our lives, whatever their source."[37] In order for persons to maintain moral integrity, the various values, goods, standards, and virtues that are espoused and fostered by the culture must somehow be assessed, those that are appropriate grafted into the Christian tradition, others rejected or resisted. The ongoing task of interaction with society requires a place and a process in the community of faith.

THE PLACE OF CHARACTER IN THE CHRISTIAN MORAL LIFE

Moral character as a way of being in the world is important. God calls us to a new way of being, not only a new way of doing. Christians should cultivate, with God's grace, a character that includes a fundamental stance towards life, together with virtues, suitable for faithfully carrying forward the adventure of walking the Way. Character, however, also profoundly affects moral decisions and actions. Posture and dispositions pervade all aspects of the self and shape the way we relate to each other and the world. Character is the chamber in which new moral experience resonates and is interpreted and known. It provides the tonality of moral consciousness.[38]

The eyes with which we see, the angle of vision from which we view the world and decision-making situations, are significantly shaped by character. A hardened heart, for example, will blind us to certain realities and prevent us from responding. Such was the case in the much-discussed failure of people living in the new suburbs of the 1960s to see the urban poverty through which they travelled daily on their way to work. William F. May suggests that one of the goals of ethics is to provide a "corrective vision" to offset the warped visions of the world, which in turn lead to aberrant behaviour. "Ethical theory may not always eliminate moral quandaries, but it opens up a wider horizon in which they may be seen for what they are and thus become other than they were. It helps correct our perceptions of the world as it appears to the myopia of timidity and the astigmatism of vice."[39]

Character, both as posture towards life and as dispositions, is central to this corrective vision. It allows us to see a context one way rather than another or perhaps even to simply see it at all. A Czech writer, Erazim Kohak, describes the "habits, skills, and attitudes" engendered in his people by forty years of Communist rule in Czechoslovakia. One of the habits that was useful under the old regime was the vice of lying, habitual deception. This vice eventually resulted in a kind of blindness. It created "the inability to distinguish between illusion and reality, between fantasy and truth, between 'for real' and 'just pretending.'"[40]

Character also affects our selection, interpretation, and evaluation of what we see. It shapes our longings and desires, our intentions, the goods and ends we seek, the way we balance norms and standards in situations when they conflict.

As important as character is, however, it cannot adequately replace the other aspects of the moral life or the need to reflect ethically on them. Other sections of the moral orchestra, if ignored, will simple "play on" in one's life, but in discord. Just as there is a danger that exclusive focus on norms and standards will slide into the corruption of legalism, so a single-minded focus on character alone can result in excessive preoccupation with the self and its perfection. In addition, norms and standards and other base points are needed, for while we usually count on morally good persons to perceive what is morally right in any situation, they sometimes have difficulty and are frequently the first to recognize and acknowledge that they do not know what ought to be done."[41] We continue our exploration of the base points for reflecting on the Way, then, by taking up our repeatedly announced inquiry into the basic convictions that lie beneath and inform our interpretation of both norms and character.

Three

Worldview and Basic Convictions: Eyes to See, Ears to Hear

A look at how worldview (the taken-for-granted understanding of reality held by a person in common with his or her people) affects the moral life. This is illustrated by reference to some of the basic convictions that form part of a worldview shaped by the Christian faith. These are beliefs about who we are, where we are, what is wrong with the world, and what the remedy is.

A MODEL FOR ETHICAL REFLECTION

Moral Agent in Community

Basic Commitment

Analysis of Self as Agent

Moral Character

Analysis of the Social Setting

The Context

Worldview and Basic Convictions

- Who Are We?
  - Human Nature
- Where Are We?
  - Creation
- What Is Wrong?
  - Sin and Fall
- What Is the Remedy?
  - Christ and Redemption

Authoritative Sources

Mode

Narratives

Propositions

Doctrines

Creeds

The Situation

Authoritative Sources

Moral Norms and Standards

Resolution

INTRODUCTION

Is the foetus a human being, a neighbour? We know that the answer to this question is crucial in the "abortion debate," which continues to trouble modern Western societies. The significance of the answer, which depends on beliefs about human nature, points to another major facet of the moral life, another base point. This one is less obvious than either norms or character, yet is essential to them both. It is our basic, operative understanding of reality. Often unconsciously held or at least unarticulated, such an understanding is usually taken for granted. This understanding may be called a *worldview*. It becomes most apparent when it is challenged, as in the case of the abortion debate. Cross-cultural experiences also help us become aware of our particular worldview. Cultural minority groups are usually pressed to be more consciously aware of their own worldview, because they are usually surrounded by alien worldviews.

To illustrate, I shall summarize (at the risk of caricature) two contrasting but widely operative worldviews.

One, we are a people by blood relationship, who dwell in a sacred universe inhabited by other creatures, including plants, animals, and seldom-seen spiritual beings. The created harmony between us all is constantly jeopardized by human failure to observe the Creator's law. Dangerous and sometimes devastating results follow. Harmony must be restored by appropriate ceremonies and a return to the Creator's law.

Two, we are individuals who have formed societies. We live in a universe that consists of other beings (plants and animals) who are somewhat like us, but inferior. The rest of the universe consists of arrangements of energy and matter devoid of any purpose except for that which we decide to invent. We are in jeopardy as individuals, as a society, and as a species from internal conflicts and wars and the natural environment, unless we can further develop and use our superior intelligence more rationally and effectively.

These are two very different ways of viewing the self and world. The first still distinguishes, to a large degree, the Aboriginal peoples of North America. The second distinguishes the dominant, modern cultures of the continent. These worldviews are often the unrecognized source of differences in the way each of these groups understands land, sovereignty, justice, liberty, society, rights, and community. They lead to different ways of being and doing.

A worldview, then, contains fundamental beliefs, either simply assumed or consciously held, about the self, the world, and ultimate reality. *Who am I? Where am I? What's wrong? What is the remedy?* These four key questions are addressed one way or another, implicitly or explicitly, in any worldview.[1] I identify these fundamental beliefs contained in a worldview as *basic convictions*. Many of them are so close to the core of a person's psyche that they are referred to by social psychologists as "of course" beliefs. They are key components of a worldview. Their content, whether held consciously or simply taken for granted, determines the distinctive cast of a people's worldview.

A worldview is, so to speak, like the navigation theory and geography required by explorers. These are needed as background for reading maps, interpreting trail markers, and generally making sense of the various kinds of terrain through which a journey may lead. Included is a stated destination and purpose for the trip. Using the orchestra analogy, we could think of a worldview with its basic convictions as the string section. The strings provide the foundation of the moral orchestra.

At its deepest level, a worldview (including basic convictions) is expressed through sacred narrative or story. This may not be verbalized but re-enacted through ritual, dance, and ceremony. A scholar of such narratives states:

> *These stories lie too deep in the consciousness of a people to be directly told: they form consciousness rather than being among the objects of which it is directly aware.... These are stories that orient the life of people through time, their lifetime, their individual and corporate experience and their sense of style, to the great powers that establish the reality of their world.*[2]

People do not sit down and think up or create sacred stories; rather they awaken to them. At a different level, from sacred stories are mundane stories. These are the various narratives of a community that tell about past happenings, real or imagined. "They are told in the effort, never fully successful, to articulate [sacred story]."

The sacred story for Christians is the grand narrative of scripture, which recounts the drama of God's creating, sustaining, and redeeming work. It is told and re-enacted in the liturgy, especially in the Eucharist. People of any culture blend and weave their own particular sacred and mundane stories into the great, sacred Christian story. The Easter celebrations of the Yaqui people (an aboriginal group native to Mexico, with some communities in Arizona) illustrates this vividly. The Yaqui Easter ceremony is a drama enacted throughout Lent. Masked dancers representing various wild spirits of chaos and death slowly take over the village. On Good Friday, they join with the soldiers of Rome and crucify Christ. However, by Easter Sunday these forces are finally overcome by the redemptive power of Christ, working through the deer and other good animal spirits represented by a different set of dancers. These, together with the women and children, vanquish the forces of death and chaos by showering them with rose petals, which symbolize Christ's blood. The world is safe for another year! This liturgy expresses a distinctive worldview. It is a way of apprehending reality.

A worldview may contain a more conscious component in the form of basic convictions. These are often expressed as propositions or doctrines. Further, some of these teachings may be formally declared by a community to be true, embraced with commitment, celebrated, and used as a fundamental guide for action. They become a "creed." Creeds, then, are the firmly held, openly stated basic convictions of a people.[3] They too are a way of expressing answers to the questions: Who are we? Where are we? What is wrong? What is the remedy? In whatever way these convictions are stated, they do not fully articulate a worldview. Dimensions remain imbedded in deeper stories or narratives.

A Christian worldview includes, but is more comprehensive than, the basic convictions expressed in creeds, doctrines, and propositions. Likewise, Christian narrative contains or implies certain concepts about reality or basic convictions but cannot be simply reduced to such.

IMPLICATIONS OF WORLDVIEW AND BASIC CONVICTIONS FOR MORAL BEHAVIOUR

What is the relation of a worldview to moral behaviour? This is a matter of considerable controversy. The influence of worldview on action is indirect, complex, and often subtle, but nonetheless profound.

The Relation Is Indirect and Complex

Modern philosophy may overstate the case in claiming that beliefs about reality (the basic convictions of worldview) are of a quite different kind and order than beliefs about what we ought to do (moral norms). However, it is correct in observing that there is no logical, *necessary* connection between them. A particular understanding of what *is* does not by itself yield a specific, related directive as to what *ought to be* done. The belief that the foetus is my neighbour, for instance, does not by itself logically require a position of no abortion under any circumstances. The call to love our neighbour does not necessarily follow from the belief that God is a loving God. Hence any claim that a specific political action can simply be "read off" from a particular set of basic convictions regarding God, Christ, and human beings is mistaken.

South American liberation theology arises in the context of

peoples struggling for survival and for justice. This influences the way the liberating, saving work of Jesus Christ is understood and experienced. The resulting Christology, in turn, affects understandings of development, economic policies, and political action. A particular economic or political policy, however, cannot be derived solely from a single Christology. There are Christians who have the same beliefs about Christ but who reach different political conclusions. Likewise, there are others who hold a quite different understanding of Christ's saving work, but share the same political agenda as many South American liberation theologians.

Similarly, it is a mistake to conclude that when a particular behaviour or action is wrong, then the basic convictions and perhaps the entire worldview of the agent perpetrating them must *necessarily* be false. This is so even when those convictions are used explicitly by the agent to justify the reprehensible actions. What directed the behaviour may not be the basic convictions, but rather the norms that people held or their applications of those norms or their interpretations of those doctrines or the relation of those doctrines to their perceptions of the context or situation.

Attempts have been made to justify racism, for example, in the name of certain views of Christ, God, and human nature. But studies of white racism in North America clearly demonstrate that almost every conceivable scientific theory and every form of religious doctrine and belief has been bent and used at one time or another to support forms of white racism.[4] This use (we would say misuse) does not necessarily invalidate the truth of these doctrines in themselves. These doctrines are unlikely to be completely mistaken even though the racism they were bent to justify is so terribly wrong.

The Relation Is Very Real

We have recognized that the connection between worldview and moral behaviour is not simple or direct (as it is, for example, with moral norms, since they prescribe actions). Now we need to acknowledge that the connection between actions and a worldview with its basic convictions is nonetheless very real. A Christian philosopher expresses it well when he suggests that our understanding of reality is *action-evoking*, even though not action-prescribing. In addition, actions *bear witness* to a certain understanding of reality, even though those same actions do not require such convictions.[5] It is wise, therefore, to examine what actions and dispositions are evoked by the basic convictions that make up our worldview and to assess our convictions accordingly. Here are two examples.

"Should we give permission for this elaborate programme of costly treatment that will keep our newborn child alive?" ask the troubled parents of a severely malformed baby. They ponder what kind of future their son will have with his chronic condition and the burden of indefinite treatment. Their assumptions about the nature and meaning of suffering by themselves are insufficient for determining in any precise way what they ought to do. However, those who believe that suffering has redemptive possibilities will weigh its effect on their child (and on themselves) differently than those who believe it to be always and only a meaningless burden. This will in turn affect the decision as to whether or not to continue treatment.

"Unreliable." That is how Christians have been described by patriots and revolutionaries alike. Christian refusal to give ultimate allegiance to any particular nation or political cause (or any other human authority) is rooted in the earliest Christian creed, "Jesus is Lord." Those holding a worldview for whom this conviction is integral will regard all nations as being under the judgement and mercy of God in Jesus Christ. This leads to a very different approach to politics than the assumption that the nation state or the revolution can legitimately claim ultimate loyalty. At the same time, the creed "Jesus is Lord" does not give precise directives regarding when the state should be obeyed and when not.[6] Those sharing allegiance to this creed may indeed arrive at quite diverse judgements about particular political policies or actions.

BASIC CONVICTIONS SHAPE OTHER FACETS OF THE MORAL LIFE

If our basic convictions or worldview influence and evoke certain behaviour and understandings of what is the right, the good, and the fitting, but not in a simple or direct way, then how do they do this? They do so by shaping the other elements of the moral life, the other base points.

First, basic convictions provide the ground from which norms or standards for behaviour are interpreted. They influence what moral weight is attached to various norms. The parents pondering the fate of their newborn were trying to find guidance in the norm of seeking the well-being of others. But how we understand well-being depends upon our view of who we are and what the remedy is to what is wrong in the world. In other words, our basic convictions about the quality and true meaning of life will lead to our interpretation of what the well-being is that we should seek for a particular neighbour. We saw in our earlier examination of values how such convictions also shape views of the common good. Convictions having to do with where we are, as well as who we are, form our interpretation of what is entailed in trusteeship of creation. They affect whether or not we acknowledge, for example, such a thing as animal rights.

The second way in which worldview (including basic convictions) influences the moral life has to do with the qualities of character that it calls forth. Both the ground and object of hope, we noted earlier, are found in basic convictions about what is wrong with the world and the remedy for this. The conviction that we are all finite and sinful human beings who stand under the judgement of God, and are at the same time recipients of God's forgiveness and mercy, calls forth, though alas by no means guarantees, a quality of humility. This conviction calls forth humility because it entails a self-understanding that acknowledges the fragmentary nature of our wisdom, admits the limited nature of our power, and confesses that all our virtues are tainted with guilt and inadequacy. On the other hand, a conviction that some person or group has achieved a degree of moral righteousness that warrants absolute religious sanction for any action engenders pride and ruthless fanaticism. Reinhold Niebuhr writes:

> *Only those who have learned the grace of humility can be loving for in a conflict love requires forgiveness and forgiveness is possible only to those who know themselves to be sinners. Moral idealists never forgive their foes. They are too secure in their own virtue to do that. Men forgive their foes only when they feel themselves to be standing under God, with them, and feel that under divine scrutiny all 'our righteousness is as filthy rags.'*[7]

Third, basic convictions about reality affect the eyes with which we see. Hence they influence what we perceive to be going on in the context and the situation. In addition, our interpretation of what we see is affected by worldview. An excellent CBC-TV series on Native land claims and concerns illustrates this point. In one programme, which examined a group of northern Native peoples, the focus was almost entirely on poor housing, especially things like the lack of indoor plumbing. It was as if the cameras were only able to see this one aspect of poverty — lack of certain amenities and consumer goods. They missed entirely the self-identified, major concern of that community: poverty experienced as lack of community self-determination, which in turn makes it almost impossible to maintain its historic relationship with the land.

I suspect that the programme's selected perception reflects the worldview characteristic of modern North American culture. This includes the conviction that the good life consists primarily in the plenitude of consumer goods. This view of who we are and what kind of world we live in led to a particular perception of what was going on among Northern peoples.

Basic convictions about reality also influence analysis and interpretation of context and situation. Estimates of the likely consequences of actions, for instance, reflect such views, even in the case of technical experts making educated predictions. I recall a lengthy and highly technical debate between a biologist and a physicist concerning the likely environmental impact of uranium mining and milling. It finally emerged (after two hours of debate on seemingly technical matters) that the differences in their estimates had less to do with hard scientific data than with their varying interpretations of the future needs of society for additional electric power.

The view of human nature held by one of the scientists led

him to predict that human beings would have increasing needs, almost without limit, for more electric power. The lesser of evils, he thought, was to promote the nuclear generation of such power. He did not distort any hard evidence. He was, however, inclined to be more conservative in his interpretation of the data regarding the environmental effects of uranium mining because nuclear power requires it. The other scientist arrived at the opposite conclusion concerning future power needs, because he had a more optimistic view of human nature. He assumed that if the public were simply better educated, they would restrain their demands for electrical power. He was more inclined to see great danger in the same evidence regarding the effects of uranium mining. Their basic convictions regarding human nature, in other words, shaped their prediction of the likely consequences of particular actions.

To summarize, worldview, including basic convictions, constitutes another major element of moral being and doing. This is true whether it is expressed in narrative form or in the more abstract concepts of doctrines and propositions. Therefore, these basic convictions are an important base point for reflection, as we seek to discern what God is enabling and requiring us to be and do.

What are sound basic convictions from a Christian perspective regarding who we are, where we are, what is wrong with the world, and what is the remedy? The worldview of any Christian community is formed by the foundational Christian narrative. However, it is also partly shaped by the particular peoplehood of its members and by the culture in which it is embedded. This is always easier to see, of course, in churches located in societies other than our own, like the Yaquis already described. Is it possible to delineate the distinguishing marks of a Christian worldview in its central narratives? Or are these always too intertwined with those of a particular culture and era, past or present? Hopefully, through diligent use of the means of grace, we participate in the ongoing, difficult process of "being transformed by the renewal of our minds." In this way, the largely taken-for-granted worldview of our culture, whatever it might be, will continually be reformed and made more congruent with the worldview of God's activity as revealed in the gospel story.

The task of theology is to help us with this transformation. The base point of basic convictions is where Christian theology and doctrine (i.e., the theological understanding of God, Christ's incarnation, cross, and resurrection, and the sacraments) most explicitly bear on Christian ethics. Usually, Christian doctrine has been not only concerned with making Christian truths coherent and intelligible, as contemporary theologian Ellen Charry reminds us, but also with shaping the moral life and enabling believers to walk the Way. She illustrates this in part by reference to three great theologians in Christian history: Calvin, Anselm, and Luther. For all three, wrestling with doctrine is more than a search for truth.

> *It is a practical tool that unpacks the creeds, laying bare the Christian story as a teaching instrument, a vehicle of personal transformation that God has crafted for us. Such explanations aim to turn our heads, reorient and refocus our minds, and cause us to reflect deeply on who we are and what we do with our lives in light of what God does for us.*[8]

Four fundamental questions are pivotal for any worldview: What are we? Where are we? What is wrong with the world? What is the remedy? The answer to each question entails a number of important convictions. We can briefly examine only a sample selection and illustrate a few of their implications for the moral life. In some cases, I have deliberately chosen a Christian conviction that displays tension with a liberal modern conviction. In other cases, I have picked out convictions about which Christians are sharply divided. Altogether, this should give us a feel for the string section and its contribution to the moral orchestra.

Who Are We?

The Christian basic assumption, rooted in sacred narrative and expressed in creed, is that we are creatures of God, called and enabled by Christ to enter a covenant relationship with God, with each other, and with other-than-human creation. In a number of ways, this is at variance with the assumptions about who we are that are characteristic of modern liberal societies. Over the last two hundred years, Christian theology has wrestled with these conflicting points in worldview. Basic convictions regarding the nature of the human self is one of the points of tension. We have already noted how this doctrine has very important implications for each of the other base points examined. This is so foundational that it is worth reviewing again at this point.

One of the deeply ingrained assumptions of liberal modernity, built into the very fabric of a modern society's institutions, is the belief that we are primarily separate individuals and only secondarily in relationship with others as members of a community or society. Canadian political scientist C. B. McPherson summarizes the assumptions of this "creed," which has evolved from the time of the Enlightenment, through the seventeenth and eighteenth centuries, to the present. He calls these the assumptions of "possessive individualism." He lists seven such propositions but the first three will suffice to illustrate our point:

> *(i) What makes a man human is freedom from dependence on the will of others. (ii) Freedom from dependence on others means freedom from any relations with others except those relations which the individual enters voluntarily with a view to his own interest. (iii) The individual is essentially the proprietor of his own person and capacities for which he owes nothing to society.*[9]

This form of individualism contrasts with the modern collectivist view that claims we are simply units in a social whole, and that persons have meaning and purpose only in relation to their usefulness to that whole. Both of these views, however, differ from the Christian tradition. Central to the Christian tradition is the understanding that human beings are basically social creatures, brought into being through relationships and finding fulfilment in community. We are clearly both individuals and members of groups at the same time and not primarily one or the other. The community sustains and fulfils the life of the individual person, yet the individual person is more than simply his or her connection to the community. Noted theologian Karl Barth argues that if we base our thinking on Romans 5:12-21, "we can have nothing to do with either collectivism on the one hand, or individualism on the other."[10]

A number of feminist Christians have been lifting up the truth that to be a strong self is not the same as being a separated self. They remind us that relationship is at the very heart of creation in biblical understanding. According to the doctrine of the Trinity, even God is essentially a relationship of three persons within the unity of the Godhead. To be created in the image of God, therefore, is to be created, not with some special endowment or substance, but rather for relationship in love, as the very being and character God displays. Authentic humanity means being in relationship with God, with one another, and with other-than-human creation.

From the beginning, God created the world that God might enter into relationship with it and, in particular, with human beings. God calls humans into such a relationship through the covenant with Israel and through the universal covenant in Jesus Christ. "The quintessence of the relational understanding of the *imagio Dei* is its underlying presupposition that the human creature is created for relationship, that is, that relatedness-in-love is of our very essence and vocation as creatures of the God who *is* love. We image God in loving."[11]

Each of these views of who we are tends to be connected with a particular understanding of what is wrong with the world. In the case of liberal individualism, what is wrong with the world is all that stifles or inhibits the independence of a separated self. This usually includes most institutions, unchosen relationships, tradition. In the case of a relational understanding of human life, what is wrong with the world is that which violates or breaks right relationships. This includes anything which alienates us from God, from other human beings, and from other-than-human creation.

These two understandings of the self lead in different directions on a number of moral issues. We need to recall, however, that such basic convictions do not in themselves entail precise directives as to how we should behave. Rather they help guide behaviour by shaping other base points. The implications of these views of the self for norms has already been illustrated in connection with our earlier discussion of collective rights and the common good. Some implications for character surfaced when we examined the virtues of love and hope. I will now offer two additional illustrations. One will indicate how such basic convictions concerning human nature affect interpretations of the norm of liberty. The second will show their impact on our perception of what is happening.

From the perspective of an individualistic view of the self, freedom is understood as primarily the absence of external restraint or even internal compulsion. From the perspective of a Christian view of the self as relational, on the other hand, freedom is not mere caprice or license: it is freedom *for* something, the ability to form and carry out a purpose. This entails self-control, self-determination, and self-direction. Ultimately for Christians, of course, this means freedom from the control of sin, freedom for spontaneous loyalty and obedience to God in Jesus Christ. Even apart from such ultimate freedom, however, true deliberate and reflective choices and actions (as distinct from any arbitrary or random ones) involve responsibility to others. "Apart from a context of responsibility — something outside ourselves which is worth responding to — freedom is meaningless."[12]

When defined in terms of autonomy or independence, the principle of liberty establishes a moral burden of proof against all forms of coercion. By "moral burden of proof," I mean that there must always be very good and strong reasons for overriding the directive of the norm, which in this case is respecting another's free choice. This continues when the principle is interpreted in the Christian sense of freedom to be with, for, together. However, with this Christian understanding of the principle of liberty, a moral burden of proof against individualistic anarchism is also established. According to this richer meaning of the norm of liberty, any set of social arrangements must be assessed, not only in terms of whether it gives every citizen the maximum opportunity for making deliberate choices, but also "the best possible training for the use of that opportunity."[13]

A concern for social well-being is thereby built into the principle of liberty itself. It is not in sharp tension with the norm of justice as it is when freedom is understood in individualistic terms. Rather the principle of liberty will itself be violated unless there is responsibility before the community. Genuine freedom entails participation in the "life of society in its multiple dimensions and ... in the common good of society understood in a pluralistic way."[14] Liberty as well as justice presses us, therefore, to seek the civil, political, social, economic, and cultural conditions required to support and protect this kind of participation.

Assumptions about the nature of the human self also affect the eyes with which we see others. They in turn influence our application of norms. For example, individualistic convictions of liberal culture lead to a perception of North American Native peoples primarily as individuals. Consequently, when the norms of liberty and justice are applied to Native people, it is assumed that equal opportunity for Natives to participate as individuals in the dominant culture should be the result. The whole reality of "peoples" and their enduring significance has been obscured in the liberal, individualistic worldview. "Tribalism" is expected to disappear. Societies of freely contracting individuals will replace "peoples" when liberty and justice prevail. From a Native perspective, this is assimilation. It is not the interdependence that they deem to be just.

The relational understanding of human beings, on the other hand, better enables us to see Native people in terms of their understanding of themselves as kinship societies or "peoples." Liberty and justice, properly applied, should produce freedom to continue as such peoples. It should also result in a right relationship between the dominant culture and First Nations, and not simply a relationship with Native individuals.

Where Are We?

Another cluster of basic convictions are assumptions about where we are. What kind of cosmos do we live in? What is the place of human beings within it? Convictions about these matters, whether expressed in narrative or propositional form, once again impact, albeit indirectly, upon moral being and doing. Let me illustrate this by reference to views on the relationship of human beings to other-than-human creation. Paul Santmire, a contemporary theologian, provides a helpful summary of the various motifs in Christian thought regarding this theme.

According to one view that recurs throughout Christian history, described as the "spiritual motif," humans are seen as essentially spiritual beings "rising above and beyond the world of nature, in order to reenter into the communion or union with God who is thought of as pure spirit."[15] Other-than-human creation provides only the backdrop for the main drama of God's creation; namely, the story of humankind's fall and salvation by the grace of God. With the coming of the kingdom, the non-human backdrop will pass away. This motif is seen clearly in the early church (the teachings of Origen), and more ambiguously in the medieval church (Bonaventure and Thomas Aquinas), and it has, with a few important exceptions, shaped much of Protestant thought in the last two hundred years.

A second view, with perhaps stronger biblical roots, also forms a major strand in the history of Christian thought. It affirms that creation is good and bears the imprint of its Maker, but in addition claims that other-than-human creation is included in God's redemptive purpose. Though caught up in the fall of humankind, it too will be transformed along with human beings by God's grace in Jesus Christ. In the kingdom there will be a new earth as well as a new heaven. Paul expresses it this way in Romans 8:

> *For the creation waits with eager longing for the revealing of the children of God; for the creation was subjected to futility, not of its own will but by the will of one who subjected it, in hope that the creation itself will be set free from its bondage to decay and will obtain the freedom of the glory of the children of God. We know that the whole creation has been groaning in labor pains until now; and not only the creation, but we ourselves, who have the first fruits of the Spirit, groan inwardly while we wait for adoption, the redemption of our bodies.*

Human beings, as creatures made in the image of God, are given stewardship or trusteeship over other-than-human creation. This means that their relationship to it is one of limited authority. This authority is to be exercised in accord with God's purpose. The dominion of human beings over the rest of creation, therefore, is not that of total control but is the delegated and limited authority of a trustee, which is a particular kind of servant. It is an authority for which we are accountable to God and for which the object is not exploitation but service in terms of God's providential and redemptive purpose. This was the position I espoused earlier in discussing the norm of trusteeship and again with regard to animal rights.

These views in Christian thought may be contrasted with

two that are widespread in modern Western societies. One of these views would see other-than-human creation as simply matter and energy, as living material that is potentially subject to the total control of human beings. It is open to our use and manipulation for whatever values or ends we deem desirable. The other view that is becoming more popular in these later days of the twilight of modernity is one associated with the new field of ecology. It sees the whole of creation as a web of interdependent life and matter. The human species is simply one species among others belonging to this web, with no particular responsibilities or powers with regard to the rest.

These different convictions affect whether or not the norm of trusteeship of creation is acknowledged. With the first modern view (nature as a resource), trusteeship of creation may, but not necessarily, be accepted as a basic norm. If accepted, the norm is likely to be interpreted as one for wisely conserving the material and life resources that are given to humankind. The Christian view of stewardship, on the other hand, not only entails the principle of trusteeship, but interprets that norm to mean serving and caring for nature in a way that is in accord with God's redemptive purpose for it. Preservation of a species and not simply its conservation as a resource is therefore our concern.

The moral weight ascribed to the norm of trusteeship will differ according to the view of nature. With the "nature-as-a-resource" view, it is likely that the norm will take second place in importance to standards having to do with human well-being. With the stewardship view, the moral weight ascribed to the norm of trusteeship will be greater, though not necessarily overriding the norm of love of neighbour with its principles of justice and well-being.

Needless to say, the four different alternative views outlined above concerning what kind of world we live in and how human beings are related to it will also lead to different perceptions of what is happening. The particular conviction held will affect what things are looked for, what is actually seen in a decision-demanding situation, and the interpretation of what is happening in the wider social context of that decision.

What Is Wrong with the World and What Is the Remedy?

Another set of basic convictions that profoundly shape the moral life are those having to do with what is wrong with the world and what the remedy is.

Some broad comparisons will help us to catch the flavour of what varied understandings of and directions for the moral life are evoked by various convictions on what is wrong and what is the remedy. One example is the belief that the root problem with the world is that humans are caught in the flux of finitude and of nature. The remedy, accordingly, is to escape entrapment in the natural process of things and to transcend it, either through rational or spiritual contemplation. It is easy to imagine the very different thrust given to the moral life by an alternate basic conviction; namely, that the root problem is human ignorance. The solution to everything from sexual misconduct and misuse of power to environmental abuse is simply education. Informed persons will no longer have unwanted pregnancies or over-indulge in alcohol or drugs or pollute the environment!

Contrast both of these with the following Christian perspective: What is wrong with the world is human lack of trust in God and consequent separation from God. This leads to blindness and to disobedience. Human beings become alienated from one another and from the rest of creation. This has reached such a degree that we are all now caught up in the power of sin and death, unable to live the flourishing life that God intended for us. The remedy is God's action in Jesus Christ, which clarifies the purpose God has for human living and for creation. God forgives. This action breaks the power of our distrust and disobedience, namely, sin. It restores the relationship between God and humans. In accepting this, we are empowered to lead a new life and pursue God's purpose, the vision of shalom (justice, harmony, well-being). In other words, Jesus Christ inaugurated the kingdom of shalom, even though it will only be fully realized in God's own time.

Let us now turn to some of the important variations in how the Christian story of sin and redemption is recounted. Bruce Birch and Larry Rasmussen are helpful when they observe that

> *if 'God's story' is that in Christ God is bringing about the divinization of humanity and the transfiguration of all life (the teaching of Eastern Orthodoxy), the understanding of the Christian moral life will line up with this theological claim. If God-in-Christ is the liberator from evil in the hearts and minds of human beings as well as in the structures of human society itself, and human beings are themselves empowered by God as co-participants in the drama of redemption (the teaching of liberation theologies), then the ethical implications will move along lines appropriate to this rendering of 'God's story'. If, by way of contrast, God-in-Christ is the preserver of an immutable moral order reflected in traditional patterns of social arrangements (as in some earlier versions of Christian natural law ethics), then the moral life will have a very different face on it than the liberationist portrayal.*[16]

Christian Convictions Concerning Sin and Redemption. A quick look at three of the disputed aspects of this doctrine so central to a Christian worldview will illustrate different Christian convictions concerning sin. These three aspects are: the constitution of sin, its social dimension, and its persistence in the redeemed. The various beliefs about each of these aspects of sin can only be sketched here in broad brush strokes in order to give the flavour of ongoing discussions. I shall restrict observations about the many implications of such beliefs for other base points or sections of the moral orchestra to only a few illustrations.

First, is sin constituted simply by wrong moral choice? Or is sin a mysterious power larger than the individual human being? Is it a force by which individuals are enslaved and unable to choose rightly even when they would? This long-standing debate about the meaning of sin finds its definitive expression in a controversy dating back to the early part of the fifth century. Pelagius said yes to the first question, and Augustine said yes to the second. Since that time, many theologians struggling with this issue have been at pains to retain Pelagius' insight that somehow human choice and responsibility are involved in sin and wrongdoing. At the same time, they have wished to acknowledge the common human experience to which Augustine referred, that of being caught up in a power that is greater than one's self. Paul describes sin as holding sway or reigning over the world (Rom. 5:21; 6:14) and that this "superpower"[17] enslaves humanity (Rom. 6:6, 17, 20; Gal. 3:22). Likewise, the Johannine literature sees Satan as the "prince of this world" (John 12:21; 14:30; 16:11), so that the whole world is seen as hostile to the work of Christ. Our will seems to be entrapped by the power of sin and becomes, in Martin Luther's vivid term, a "slave-will."[18]

Each of these conceptions of sin has a correspondingly different interpretation of the Christian narrative of the remedy. In theological language, a doctrine of redemption is closely linked to a doctrine of sin and fall. By one view, redemption wrought in Jesus Christ is a form of enlightenment by which people come to realize their wrong choices. They are then persuaded through reason and the example of Jesus to choose rightly. Or, from another view, redemption is the divine mercy and mysterious power in Christ, which breaks the enslaving and demonic dominion of sin over humanity and the cosmos. Though the presence of sin is not yet completely banished, in Christ persons are set free from its entangling web and can freely respond to God's grace and walk the Way. Each view evokes significantly different understandings, for example, of the mission of the church, including its approach to social change.

A strong emphasis on sin as a superpower *may* (remembering that it need not *necessarily*) lead to a social quietism. Persons feel helpless to do much to change conditions with the exception of those who have laid hold of Christ's redemption. Such an emphasis may also provide warrant for giving priority to the principle of order over liberty or justice because of concern, given the power of sin, for the threat of chaos. On the other hand, an emphasis on sin as simply wrong moral choice, with redemption as enlightenment and suasion, may call forth an unrealistic social analysis of the factors preventing greater justice. The resultant approach to social change is likely to be one that trusts in the sufficiency of education and moral suasion to correct or prevent social injustices. Priority will likely be given to the principle of liberty over the principles of justice or order.

This mistaken idea can be seen in conventional analyses of problems regarding sexual behaviour, about which North American dominant societies are so preoccupied and confused. Convictions that "what is wrong" is simply the result of mistaken and ill-informed choice give way to surprise and dismay when education and moral suasion designed to correct wrong choice do not seem to work. They do not greatly reduce let alone eliminate teenage pregnancies, sexual abuse and harassment, AIDS, or other sexually transmitted diseases. The reaction is, too often, as in the case of sexual harassment, to enact Draconian measures of law. These wind up being more restrictive and imposing than the traditional moral restraints and guiding social conventions that were scornfully dismissed in the name of personal liberty! A subsection of a provincial Royal Commission on family law was addressing the question of what legislation should govern artificial insemination. Some who favoured minimal regulation on the grounds of liberty and in the confidence that good information would lead to right choices were shocked when reports from England told about efforts to market the sperm of rock stars to teen admirers. Those with a stronger view of sin were not surprised by such abuses.

Assessment of likely outcomes of actions and policies and selection of strategies for social change are affected, then, by basic convictions regarding sin. Another example of this surfaces with regard to proposals for legalizing the deliberate killing of those who request it, i.e., voluntary euthanasia. Apart from the important questions of whether, and if so, under what conditions, such killing might be morally permissible, what are the likely consequences of legalizing such actions? Given the commercial and hedonistic ethos of our society, would the door be open to major abuse? Could it be easily regulated and monitored? Would this start us down a slippery slope towards killing dysfunctional persons who are very expensive to the public purse in times of escalating health costs? Again, the answer depends to some degree on beliefs regarding sin.

A more multifaceted doctrine of sin that takes some account of both the Pelagian and the Augustinian views is revealed in an interesting comment on income tax. William Temple, who became Archbishop of Canterbury during the Second World War, once said that he personally welcomed income tax as a public policy, because it forced him to do what in his better moments he knew he should and wanted to do. This was, according to the principle of justice, to share his wealth with others less advantaged. He knew himself well enough not to rely on voluntarily making the right choice regularly through acts of charity.

Likewise, Reinhold Niebuhr advocated democratic structures for keeping economic and political power accountable to the general populace and from becoming too concentrated. These structures are necessary, said Niebuhr, because given the power of sin, no one is good enough not to abuse power if given too much. Yet these structures would become dysfunctional if it were not also true that people can and do make right moral choices. In the words of one of his famous aphorisms, "Man's capacity for justice makes democracy possible; but man's inclination to injustice makes democracy necessary."

Second, does sin reside only or primarily in individual persons, or is it also manifest in groups and social systems? Instead of comparing different answers to this question, I will briefly outline only one point of view: that sin does reside in groups. Even a summary of some of the varied insights regarding the ways in which sin shows itself in groups should make clear that convictions concerning this question have important implications for the moral life and Christian ethics.

I recall having Sunday dinner with an American Presbyterian family when the Viet Nam War was at its height. One of their sons, an intelligent and thoughtful Christian in his last year of high school, expected to enlist in the Marines after graduation.

I had been speaking that morning against the war. His family was hoping he would not have to go. Conversation was intense. He was very ambivalent about the war and not keen to enlist, yet he felt strongly that he had an obligation to serve his country, which he rightly believed had been good to him and his family. The tragedy of the likely loss of such a youth, and the harnessing of these noble motives and values for so dubious a cause, haunts me to this day.

This power of group-claims can beguile individuals. Their very best ethical qualities, such as loyalty, fidelity, and courage can be harnessed for unethical ends. This is one way that sin is manifest in groups.[19] Selfishness is writ large in groups that "drift into evil under sinister leadership, or under pressure of need or temptation."[20] Injustices are built into various social institutions and into the structures and organizations of society, becoming preferred patterns of behaviour. For example, the racial prejudice of individuals may be institutionalized in the organizations and their policies that make up a society. Feminist theologians point to another example, the built-in patterns of male dominance that are now embodied in social organizations and institutions. The institutionalizing of war as an instrument of foreign policy was the example cited by Walter Rauschenbusch, acknowledged as the pivotal spokesman for the Social Gospel movement. He called these institutionalized forms of sin "super-personal forces of evil."

The problem is increased when cultural and religious symbols, or the "ideologies" that prevail in a society, are used to legitimate and reinforce the structures and institutions that embody particular forms of human sin.[21] The justification of war as a good and holy thing is but one example of how a particular form of sin is not only accepted but idealized by a society. The results are dismaying. Again, feminists point to the way cultural and religious symbols reinforce a form of patriarchy and legitimate the structures and institutions that express it.

These institutionalized wrongs, legitimated by cultural and religious symbols, in turn play a major role in molding individuals, especially through the socialization of young people. The glorification of war and its legitimization as a way of dealing with international disputes is one example. Thus sin is transmitted from one generation to another. This is what Gregory Baum, a contemporary Canadian theologian, identifies as "false consciousness." Individuals thus socialized into their culture become convinced that the actions, values, and ideologies of their group are good. They therefore freely, if unconsciously, cooperate and "go along with" the structured injustices of a society. Personal sin and these "super-personal forces of evil" interact upon one another. This whole interacting power of evil, which links generation to generation in sin, is called the kingdom of evil by Rauschenbusch. It is the very antithesis of the kingdom of God.

Finally, then, these various distortions of sin become so built-in that policies and actions detrimental to others are routinely made. They are made on behalf of the group, quite likely by well-meaning individuals who are simply unknowingly caught in the web of distorting sin. "I am just trying to do my job," says a conscientious government forester, but he may, through no intention on his part, be participating in a larger policy and practice that encourages corporations to cut more timber than is ecologically sound.

Reinhold Niebuhr probed more deeply into the roots of these forms of sin in groups. There is a fundamental insecurity and anxiety that accompanies human existence, he claims. (His analysis of its cause need not concern us at this point.) Instead of transforming that anxiety into a positive force by trusting in

God, we inevitably seem to fall into unbelief (the root sin). This gives rise to various sinful and destructive ways of handling our fundamental anxiety.

One of these ways is to deny our limited and precarious nature by various forms of pride, which unduly exalt the self and its achievements. Niebuhr claims that groups, such as nations, also exhibit the four varieties of pride found in individuals. They lust after power (pride of power); show contempt of others (a form of intellectual pride); claim disinterested motives and concern solely for ethical values (moral pride and hypocrisy); and make explicit "unconditional claims for their conditioned values" (spiritual pride).[22] It must be noted that these moral and spiritual claims are much more plausible and therefore more powerful and dangerous when made by groups than when made by individuals.

The problem of collective sin increases with the size, power, and complexity of the group, claims Niebuhr. Individuals have a capacity to stand outside themselves, as it were, and look at themselves. This power of self-transcendence is necessary for the self-criticism essential to true moral action. Yet it is virtually impossible for large groups to achieve any degree of critical self-transcendence. Leaders seldom provide it. They tend to be sentimental idealists, unaware of the ethical complexities and ambiguities involved in their group's actions. Or else they are realists who have become cynical because of their understanding. Within a large group, a minority that has enough critical distance to perceive the false claims and unethical behaviour of the collective is of some assistance, says Niebuhr. However, in the case of nations, for example, "self-criticism is a kind of inner disunity, which the feeble mind of the nation finds difficulty in distinguishing from dangerous forms of inner conflict."[23] One potential vantage point for perceiving the collective pride of groups and nations and opposing their self-glorification is found in religions like Christianity and Judaism. This vantage point is the majesty of God, who challenges all earthly claims of unconditioned value.

The problem is heightened by the fact that these prideful methods for overcoming human anxiety have the opposite effect of increasing anxiety. Security sought at the expense of others creates fear and resistance in those others. They in turn pose an even greater threat. This drives humans, both as individuals and collectives, into more desperate and flagrant sin and the whole revolves in tragic futility.

How do these convictions regarding sin in groups impact on the moral life? For one, they affect the interpretation given to other important basic convictions. For example, they will likely lead to a view that Christians in their pursuit of justice are called to attend, not only to individual needs, but also to the systemic aspects of the way we organize and govern our collective life. Christians are called to work to reform structures and systems so that they are more just and harmonious, in accord with the kingdom. This contrasts with the view that the church is called to attend only to personal and interpersonal relations. Thus a variety of Roman Catholic ethicists and theologians speak of "social conversion," which, together with "personal conversion," is entailed in participating in God's redemptive activity. It involves moving from division, disunity, and conflict within the self, between persons, and between groups to a "solidarity," the overcoming of division, injustice, and disharmony.[24]

The conviction that sin and redemption have a societal dimension also affects our analysis of what is happening and our strategy of response. If sin is regarded as mainly a personal distortion (whether understood as wrong choice or as being caught up in deeper and wider forces), then the focus of analysis will be on the individual. Poverty, racism, sexism, crime, violence will be judged as grounded in wrong and inadequate personal belief and response. The strategy for both evangelism and social action will be to convert or change individuals in the confidence that better social structures and institutions will follow accordingly.

On the other hand, if sin is interpreted as having a societal dimension, then the analysis of these problems will likely take into account systemic, institutional, and organizational factors. A different set of questions is generated. What is it about the way we organize and govern our lives that makes it difficult to trust God and to walk the Way? To be healthy families? To have justice and harmony between men and women? For diverse groups to live together in mutual respect? What is it about the fashioning of our economic structures that leaves a disturbingly large group unemployed or dependent on food banks? That fosters greed and envy? That invites lying and stealing? The bumper-sticker type of easy answers that are often given to these difficult questions ought not to invalidate the importance of the questions themselves.

I have lifted up basic convictions concerning the societal dimension of sin and pointed to a few of their many implications for the moral life. We need to remember, however, that the neglect of personal sin and redemption leads to a one-sided focus on systemic and organizational matters. An analysis that places the root of all problems in faulty economic or political systems and corrupt organizations generates a utopian expectation. We think that if we just get the right social system, then human beings will be fine. The temptation to blame everything but ourselves is itself a manifestation of sin!

Third, to what extent does sin persist in redeemed individuals and renewed or transformed social structures? How complete is the freeing from sin and the transformation of individuals and social structures through the redemptive power of Christ? It will hardly come as a surprise to hear that Christians vary in their answers to this key question! The answer profoundly affects what kinds of claims are made for particular movements, for new structures and systems, how the issue of political and economic power is handled, the means chosen, and the cost justified in social change.

It is helpful here to make use of a distinction made in Christian theology between two aspects of God's grace. One is grace as "justification." The other is grace as the power of "sanctification." Justifying grace is God's free gift of forgiveness and mercy that accepts us as we are and bears the cost of disobedience and distrust. This is the grace of God by which we are all-known and all-forgiven. God's sanctifying grace refers to the empowerment of the Holy Spirit to remake us as new creatures, to transform us so that we might become what we have been recognized to be; namely, true children of God. It is God's sanctifying grace we call upon to help us to both discern the right moral life and to lead it.

Various Christian traditions share the basic conviction that both of these forms of grace are real and operative, but differ regarding the relationship between the two. Again, I will only sketch these differences in broad brush strokes for purposes of illustration and then restrict my comments about the implications of these convictions for the moral life to their effect on the issue of power.

Some Christians adhere to the belief that acknowledgement and reception of God's forgiveness in Jesus Christ (justifying grace) is followed by the empowerment of God's Spirit, which progressively transforms the person into the new creature God intended (sanctifying grace). Not only is the power of sin thus broken, but all of its distorting effects are progressively diminished. The remedy to the world's troubles, of course, remains God's free gift of grace. However, this becomes actual in relatively sin-free individuals and communities. This set of assumptions has tended to evoke the notion that the way to deal with the problem of power in society is to ensure that power is placed in the hands of the redeemed, who will use it wisely to govern in accord with God's purposes.

This approach was characteristic of the liberal Social Gospel in general and Walter Rauschenbusch in particular. Grace as sanctification (God's transforming love) is emphasized more than grace as justification (God's forgiveness and mercy). Regeneration of the individual is the process of developing the person's ethical potential for love, service, and the like. It is brought about by human moral effort in cooperation with God's Spirit. Similarly, social structures and institutions are to be transformed. Rauschenbusch's writings convey a sense of exhilaration and hope that humankind is about to burst into an unprecedented era of prosperity, freedom, and justice. World War I shook, but failed to shatter, this belief. Rauschenbusch dared to hope that "the long slow climb may be ending."

An alternative view of the relation of justification and sanctification places the prime emphasis on God's grace as mercy, with a relatively low expectation of transformation in this life. We will be made into new creatures only at the end of history or in the life to come. High value is placed on social order, because not even those redeemed are sufficiently free from sin in this life to use freedom wisely and for the benefit of humankind. The threat of chaos is ever-present. Fortunately, God has provided the structures of government and authority to preserve us in some kind of decency in our fallen condition.

A third approach to the relation of justification and sanctification sees a balanced, ongoing interaction between the two. Acknowledgement of God's free gift of mercy in Jesus Christ is followed by empowerment to lead new lives, as outlined in the first position. There are no *a priori* limits as to how thoroughly human beings may be transformed by this sanctifying grace and thereby enabled to pursue the moral life and achieve justice and freedom. Nevertheless, these changes, even in the redeemed, remain not only incomplete but to some degree distorted by the power of sin. Therefore we are both continually and ultimately dependent upon God's grace as mercy and forgiveness. No individual and no group, then, is good enough to trust with much power over others. Consequently, we need to attend carefully to both the distribution of power and to the structures that keep it accountable to those over whom it is exercised. Good social analysis will include a study of who controls whom and by what mechanisms.

Reinhold Niebuhr, who espoused a view along these lines, expressed it this way: "Life in history must be recognized as filled with indeterminate possibilities," yet at the same time, "every effort and pretension to complete life, whether in collective or individual terms ... must be disavowed."[25] Sin appears in every level of life and human achievement. The difference between good and evil, truth and error, as they appear either within the person or in social structures and systems, is always relative. This relative difference, however, is a vitally important one. Once freed of the illusion of finding absolute solutions, humans are better able to find proximate solutions to insoluble social problems. The peace that is given to the Christian is "never purely the contentment of achievement, but is largely that which comes from the assurance of forgiveness."

I think Niebuhr is sound on this point of the persistence of sin in the redeemed, whether in personal or collective life. The distorting twist of sin remains, not only alongside new good social orders, but to some degree in the new structures and systems themselves. Hopefully, it remains to a lesser degree than in previous unjust ones. However, the point to be raised here is that basic convictions concerning the persistence of sin and the question of grace as justification and sanctification affect at least four important matters concerning social ethics.

The first concerns the human cost that people are willing to pay or judge as appropriate to achieve new, more just institutions and structures. If one believes that the new system will be relatively, if not completely, free of sin, then it may be worth sacrificing a whole generation to achieve that for the sake of one's grandchildren. However, if one believes along with Niebuhr that these new structures will have their own distortions and forms of sin, the equation of cost and benefit will not be so easy to arrive at.

Second, these basic convictions will affect the designing of new structures and systems. If one expects both structures and persons to be relatively free of sin as the result of reform or revolution, then the checks and balances needed to safeguard against new forms of injustice and tyranny are less apt to be built into the proposed new order. The conviction that sin persists, not simply alongside the redeemed (however defined), but within them, grounds the assumption that such protections are essential.

Third, beliefs about the persistence of sin in the redeemed affect the way we judge past systems of human collective life. When the difference between the just and the unjust, the redeemed and the unredeemed, is not seen as a complete and sharp contrast, we are more likely to perceive some of the good in the old and not only the harm. Further, we are more apt to seek in a new order that which is worth preserving from the old, even as we strive to overcome its injustices.

Finally, convictions about sin and its persistence even in the redeemed and their programmes affect the attitude we hold towards those who oppose our righteous causes. It also affects the treatment they are likely to receive from us. A conviction that regards our struggles for more just social orders as being between the righteous and the unrighteous, the forces of God's kingdom and the forces of evil, is apt to "shut the gates of mercy against the foe." Whereas a conviction, such as Niebuhr's, that the differences between such human causes are very important but morally only relative and not absolute, is more likely to issue in mercy and compassion towards the enemy.

SUMMARY

We have been examining the string section, the essential core of the moral orchestra. This section is another base point for ethically reflecting on the moral life. It consists of a worldview that includes basic convictions regarding who we are, where we are, what is wrong and what the remedy is. These are variously expressed in narrative, creeds, and doctrines. I have illustrated this by pointing to examples of Christian basic convictions, using points of conflict between these and those that prevail in the dominant cultures of North America. In some cases, I have noted points of differing interpretations among Christians themselves. The main value of these glimpses into Christian beliefs and varying interpretations thereof has been to illustrate the significance of such basic convictions for the moral life, even though their impact on it is oblique rather than simple and direct.

Four

Situation and Context: Stand at the Crossroads and Look

A look at how an understanding of what is happening, both in a specific situation and in the wider world, affects the moral life. The main factors entailed in understanding what is taking place are explored. These include selectivity regarding what we see and pay attention to, analysis of why things are happening the way they are, and assessment of their meaning and significance. The effect of the observer's social location and beliefs on each of these factors is noted.

A MODEL FOR ETHICAL REFLECTION

Moral Agent in Community

Basic Commitment

Authoritative Sources

Analysis of Self as Agent

Moral Character

Worldview and Basic Convictions

Moral Norms and Standards

Analysis of the Social Setting

(What Is Happening?)

The Context

- Economic, political, cultural, religious
  - Information and Facts
    - Gathering most reliable data
  - Social Analysis
    - Discerning underlying patterns and causes
  - Assessing the Significance
    - Discerning the "signs of the times" in terms of God's redemptive purpose

The Situation

- Information and Facts
  - What, Why, How,
  - Who, Where, When
- Alternative Courses of Action
  - Actually feasible
  - Probable consequences of each

Mode

Narratives

Statistics

Propositions

Hypotheses

Authoritative Sources

Resolution

INTRODUCTION

In the early 1970s, a fourteen-year-old boy, a friend of my family, took arsenic to end his life. Our whole community was devastated. He was the son of sensitive, caring parents, active Christians who were tireless workers in the civil rights movement and the anti-Viet Nam War movement. A colleague of mine was able to talk with the boy before he died. Arsenic takes a while to work its lethal effect, though nothing can be done to stop it after a certain point. Why did he commit suicide? The boy said that he saw no possibility of correcting the ills of the world that surrounded and overpowered him. This action seemed the logical thing to do. In the language we have been using, he felt that walking the Way was impossible.

We never fully understand things like this boy's death. I have since often reflected on the importance of cultivating, not only the virtues of caring, compassion, and justice in our young people, but also hope. Otherwise, their very caring may drive them to despair. How can we foster a climate of common grace but also point to God's saving grace in Christ, which sustains hope? Evidently another factor in this boy's decision was a certain *perception of what was going on in the world.* One wonders if the church and the school had been so preoccupied with heavy issues that they inadvertently presented to the young what Canadian novelist W. G. Hardy calls "pathological realism," portraying only the sick and distorted side of life. Clearly, our understanding of what is going on in the world around us affects what we think we should and can do.

Another aspect of walking the Way, then, another base point for reflecting ethically on the moral life, is awareness of the terrain through which we are travelling. We have been focusing on developing a discerning eye and navigational skills for discovering the Way. These are ineffective, however, if we do not look around us. What is happening both in the immediate situation and in the wider social context are crucial elements in shaping our moral being and doing. To use our other analogy, this is another section of the moral orchestra, the percussion. It sets the rhythm and measure of our playing.

The Gospel of Mark portrays Jesus' disciples as continually making mistakes because they did not perceive what was really going on in the actions and sayings of Jesus. Perception of the situation, and analysis of the context, then, entail not only information about the "facts" of the circumstances but also the way we "discern the signs of the times."

Our perception of the needs of our era, society, and culture will bear upon the qualities of character that we think should be cultivated. In other words, our comprehension of what is happening also affects what we think we should be. Do we need, for example, to emphasize virtues of self-restraint, temperance, and moderation in our current North American society or qualities of joyous abandon, carefree giving, and exuberant living?

In the model sketched on page 188, I distinguish between situation and context, though they both have to do with what is going on in the world around us. One may think of adjusting a camera lens. When the focus is on the immediate environs, I use the term *situation*. When wide-angle is used, and the national and even global scene comes into view, I use the term *context*. Awareness and analysis of the economic, political, cultural, and religious dimensions of our social context help us to discover the various pressures and influences upon our lives. Then we can assess which of these are and which are not congruent with God's will and purpose in Jesus Christ.

It is useful to distinguish three aspects of the art of discerning what is going on. The first has to do with awareness of events, gathering information and clarifying facts. The second pertains to social analysis or the attempt to discover underlying patterns and causes of a social situation. The third concerns the assessment of the significance of what we perceive to be happening in terms of some larger frame of meaning. For Christians, of course, this means the signs of the times in terms of God's creative and redemptive purpose. Let us briefly examine these three aspects.

INFORMATION AND FACTS

The first aspect of discerning what is going on, gathering relevant information and clarifying facts, can be seen clearly in decisions made by hospital ethics committees. Take for example the decision as to whether or not to treat a severely malformed newborn whose life prognosis is short at best.

First of all, the committee is pressed into an almost full-scale medical review of the particular case. Exactly what treatment is at issue? Why is withholding it being proposed, and when would this happen? Where will the baby be if the treatment is withheld or initiated: at home with parents or in the hospital? Who is already involved in making this decision? Have the parents and other members of the family been consulted? What is their wish? Have they understood in clear layperson's language what is entailed, especially if English is their second language? What are the likely consequences of initiating the treatment or withholding it? Data relevant to these questions is provided by a variety of experts from different fields of medicine, including the nurses who are actively tending the newborn and can see the effects at first hand. Are there any viable alternatives that are more acceptable than stopping treatment?

The questions I have posed here — what, why, how, who, where, when, what are the foreseeable effects, and what are the existent viable alternatives — are called reality-revealing questions.[1] They help us discern what is going on in a particular decision-demanding situation. They are not always of equal moral pertinence. Neither, of course, will answers to them provide moral direction. But they do yield information that is vital in ascertaining what it means to care for the well-being of our neighbour in a particular circumstance. There is no substitute for careful homework in gathering accurate information.

Though obviously important, this task is not as straightforward as it may first appear. What facts are to be attended to or pursued? Ascertaining even so-called technical facts may prove difficult, because facts are slippery things. "What is a fact can sometimes depend upon personal interpretation, as anyone who tries to resolve a quarrel between two people soon finds out."[2]

The eyes with which we see influence what sort of information is sought, what facts are gathered, attended to, and emphasized. These, as we noted earlier, are in turn affected by the basic convictions, qualities of character, and the norms that people hold. In the case of the newborn, should one pursue with diligence the question of whether both parents of the child are aware of the consequences of withholding treatment? Are the wishes of both parents known, or is one parent's response sufficient? Is the information provided by the hospital social worker (that the child comes from a large family, currently experiencing a lot of difficulty) pertinent information, or is it irrelevant to the moral decision?

The other base points that we have been considering also influence the way even experts understand and interpret the facts that are being gathered. This is especially true when a medical or any other kind of expert is making educated guesses concerning the likely outcomes or the viability of alternatives. Further, it is important to distinguish between the authority properly accorded to an expert's knowledge of certain empirical data and that given to value judgements about which the expert is likely no more of an expert than other participants in the decision-making process. There is a tendency to carry over the respect and prestige associated with the first to opinions regarding the second. Experts frequently declare that a certain procedure (in environmental, medical, or other fields) is "safe" or entails an "acceptable risk." Reliable knowledge about facts is thereby combined with certain convictions about values (safe, acceptable) that we may appropriately call into question.

The difficulties in gathering information are obvious enough in the case of immediate and relatively well defined situations, such as the medical decision described. These difficulties are even more apparent and troublesome when one attempts to assess a wider context in which the interaction of groups is entailed. Thus, in policy decisions about economic development, for example, obtaining necessary information is both difficult and expensive. What are the many possible impacts of certain kinds of land alteration? What are the ecological ramifications likely to be, the social effects on populations involved? In cases of large-scale developments, there are often no clear boundaries as to who will be affected. Worldviews, norms, vested interests, the histories of various groups and parties entailed in such projects all influence, not only the final decision, but even the perception of what is going on.

Organizations like churches or ecumenical movements intentionally involved in social issues typically have conflicting opinions among their members regarding the issues on which they are attempting to act. They can progress more effectively towards decisions, observes Canadian ethicist Roger Hutchinson, when they distinguish their disagreement about facts from those having to do with moral evaluation. "There is a place for the rigorous empirical testing of particular claims about the facts."[3] A further gain is made when, in matters of fact, empirical data can be distinguished from differences about selection and interpretation of that data.

Gathering reliable information and data concerning a moral decision requires, then, as objective and exact a science as the subject permits. The inquirer needs to be aware of his or her own convictions, standards, and dispositions. It then necessitates the inquirer making allowances for the way in which these things affect the selection, interpretation, and assessment of the information. No easy task!

SOCIAL ANALYSIS

The second aspect of discerning what is going on concerns the uncovering of the patterns and causes behind a particular social problem and its context. This is done by probing more deeply into the history of the problem and the prevailing structural arrangements. For instance, how should we respond to the problem of high unemployment? The answer will depend, of course, on our norms, dispositions, and convictions. It will also, however, be significantly shaped by our analysis of the underlying pattern and cause of unemployment. Is it due to excessive government regulation of the economy, to unrealistic labour demands, or to unwise government policy and management of the economy? Or do we see it as but another phase of the ongoing struggle between the working class and those classes that exploit them? Perhaps some other social analysis will be made. An operative analysis of why things are happening the way they are is either explicit or implicit in moral decisions. This is particularly true when confronting political and economic questions or the interaction of large groups.

The social sciences, especially sociology, anthropology, political science and economics, provide helpful tools and some useful theories for discerning what is going on. There are various schools of thought within social science disciplines; each employs a different theory of society and social change. One of the major differences between various Christian political and economic ethics has to do with the particular social theory each adopts and uses in analyzing what is going on. Simplified and packaged versions of these social theories are embraced, often without much thought, by various movements both within and without the Christian church. Divisions among Christians on social issues often have less to do with commitment to social justice (or even the church's role in pursuing this) than they do with social analysis. The implicit social theory operative in analyzing what is causing a present injustice, and thereby pointing to a needed corrective, is the unnamed contentious factor.

Most theories are buttressed by an impressive array of empirical data. Nevertheless, it is important to realize what is frequently overlooked: that every theory is also shaped by particular presuppositions and reflects its originator's own commitments, values, and loyalties. A theory is after all only a mental construct that attempts to make sense of the reality we experience. The selection and use of these theories in Christian ethics is a crucial, but alas, little-studied matter. Those involved in the discipline of Christian ethics have only begun to think more carefully and thoroughly about what is entailed in the selection and use of the varied social theories that continue to emerge from the social sciences. Here is a brief "tourists' guide" to a few of the more prevalent social theories that inform most of us, knowingly or unknowingly.

Some Sample Social Theories

One social theory from the discipline of sociology likens a society to a living body: the various structures of society are similar to the organs of the body, each with its own function. Indeed, the theory is called *functionalism*.[4] Societies, like living organisms, operate to assure their own growth and survival. When one part is disrupted or injured, the rest of the body adapts and attempts to restore harmony. The various institutions of a society (its organs) are integrated by a cultural "glue."

This consists of the sum of basic symbols, ritual actions, beliefs, values, and worldview of a society's members. These are internalized through socialization from birth onward.

This theory assumes that the threat of chaos is the chief problem of human existence. All problems of society are interpreted as some form of disintegration. It may be the failure of a particular existing structure to fulfil its functions. If so, the corrective is to replace or reform the malfunctioning part. It may be that the cultural "glue" has begun to disintegrate. Much empirical research has gone into showing how religious systems and moral codes play an enormously important role in stabilizing communities in the face of such a threat.

A very different social theory comes to us from political science. It has been labelled *pluralist*. Society is seen as an agreement between a variety of groups and institutions. The agreement may have grown out of relationship or of historical accident or be an explicit contract. The relationship is not, as in the functionalist view, an interdependence of need and shared allegiance to common values. A pluralist society can contain a great variety of cultures, values, worldviews, and even political loyalties. Each of the various institutions and groups is presumed to have a particular self-interest that it seeks to advance by the acquisition of power. Society is seen as "a continual process of conflict among changing interest groups."[5]

Threats to this process of continuous conflict resolution are the most dangerous kind for the pluralistic society. What is essential, say pluralists, is some kind of *public* forum in which representatives from different interest groups and institutions can resolve their differences, at least temporarily, through persuasion, negotiation, vote, and compromise.

Another cluster of social theories is called *dualist*, so called because society is viewed as a complex system marked by a fundamental conflict between two opposed groups. A "conservative dualist" theory is espoused by fascism and certain proponents of apartheid in South Africa. The fundamental conflict is seen as rooted in nature and is between a superior or higher race or class and a lower or inferior one. Eliminating the conflict is either impossible or undesirable and ways must be found to live with it.

The "radical dualist" theories, on the other hand, view the fundamental conflict as one between oppressor and oppressed, or between an elite and the masses. Karl Marx is the major figure in this radical form of dualism. The conflict is not rooted in nature but has come about through the two groups' respective positions with regard to economic production under the institutions and structures of industrial capitalism. However, the structures of capitalism are historical human constructs, which can therefore be overcome by revolutionary struggle. Radical dualists seek to overcome the inequality and the conflict between the two groups.

For the dualists, it is the economic institutions, then, that are the core of society's weal or woe, rather than the political ones, as it is for pluralists, or cultural, as it is for functionalists. Marx regarded ideas and values as fundamentally shaped, if not absolutely determined, by the economic or material conditions of various groups. Worldviews, values and ideas, therefore, function mainly to express and justify the material interests of a class. The fundamental contradictions between oppressor and oppressed that emerge in a society can only be overcome by altering the basic material conditions or economic structures of that society and not by new agreements or by compromise or by altering cultural values and visions. Thus radical dualists advocate total revolution rather than political or piecemeal reform.

A more recent variation of radical dualism, called *neo-Marx-*

ist theory, develops a different understanding of the relation of ideas and values to social change. The domination of the powerful is in part exercised by convincing the underclasses that the moral, political, and cultural values, indeed the entire worldview of the powerful, is the one true understanding of reality.

Social change, then, entails not only shifting economic power but also a struggle for moral and intellectual leadership in the sphere of civil society. The political parties, universities, and organizations of intellectuals (and for Christian thinkers who espouse this position, the church) are all possible institutional locations for alternate views of reality, with different values and political visions. For example, some Afro-American exponents emphasize that their people must no longer allow themselves to be dominated by the ideas of white supremacy and the cultural linguistic roots in which these ideas are grounded.[6] Some feminist Christian exponents like the Cornwall Collective include the control by males of the "power to name reality" in their very definition of sexism.[7]

Other social theories and further variations of those mentioned could readily be added to this sampling. Hopefully, we have "heard" enough snatches of how these theories "sound" to provide some sense of this part of the moral orchestra. The significance of which social theory is used in analysis should be readily apparent from the quite different directions to which they point.

However, for all their diversity, these contemporary theories share a common, modern worldview. The conviction that societies are merely human constructs, objects of scientific study, understanding, and manipulation is one example. Their common anti-metaphysical bias is another. This blocks them from viewing religion, ritual, and magic in any terms other than as functions subservient to economic, political, or cultural factors, or apart from their usefulness for social survival. These theories are inadequate for comprehending nonmodern societies whose cultures operate on different assumptions; religion for them deals with objective and real phenomena that have their own significance for society.[8]

The modern worldview assumed by social theorists is itself undergoing change. Some learned observers are saying that it is rapidly being replaced by a "postmodern era." This kind of analysis is vitally important for understanding what is happening. It is not expressed as another "scientific" social theory, because, in part, it is claiming the very basis for such is of doubtful validity and is probably disappearing. In what follows, I will attempt to give some indication of the features of this recent viewpoint.

Postmodern Analysis

Is the modern world as we experience it in the West undergoing such fundamental change that it is legitimate to speak of an emerging postmodern world? A growing number of social analysts say yes. They are responding to a variety of important changes taking place over the last two decades. These include economic and political shifts, such as the internationalization of capital and the growth of transnational organizations, the collapse of command economies and the entire Soviet empire, the political renaissance of "peoples." These changes also include the alarming deterioration of the earth's natural environment. In intellectual circles, there is a decline of confidence in some universal reason or form of knowledge that can be used to solve all human problems, including the provision of a common ground for moral standards. Relativism, the belief that there is no Truth or Good that can be known, only various opinions that are equally valid, is on the rise. The "postmodern analysts," as I have labelled them, discern a pattern underlying these changes; namely, the decline of the modern world. They are a provocative and varied assortment of critics.

"Modern" is a notoriously ambiguous term. It has disputed meanings and various uses in different disciplines of study, from architecture to literature, art, science, and theology. But for most of this polyglot group of postmodernists, the term refers broadly to the culture and worldview that has accompanied technologically induced industrialization characteristic of the Western world since the seventeenth century. Stephen Toulmin describes this worldview as a "cosmopolis": a particular understanding of the cosmos marked by the assumptions of Newtonian science combined with a particular view of the political order characterized by the nation state.[9]

"Postmodern" is also a slippery term. It can be misused to legitimate dismissal of "older" ideas or to give credibility to some favoured set of beliefs or ideology. But the varied analyses that are more appropriately designated by this term have at least two things in common. First, they share the view that the "modern" world, in both its liberal capitalist and Marxist socialist forms, is breaking down, though they differ as to the rate of decline and as to what stage we are in now.

Second, this decline in modernity is attributed, as noted, not to some external force but to fundamental flaws within modernity itself. The postmodern analysts draw upon a long line of critics of modernity from previous centuries, as well as from recent scholars.[10] The distinctive postmodern claim is that some of the earlier identified fault lines have now combined with new ones to bring about the actual demise of modernity. This is a marked shift from the previous self-confidence of Western societies in modernity as the fixed and progressive path of history, when the only debate was over which rendition should and would endure.

Apart from the above commonalties, the postmodern theorists display a great variety of analyses. They differ as to whether the changes we are experiencing, such as the emergence of a new world economic order, are symptomatic of the collapse of modernity or signs of the emerging new postmodern age. Thus, American sociologist Daniel Bell and French sociologist Alain Touraine agree that we are moving towards "post-industrial society." Economically there is a shift from labour intensive production to automation, with an increasing investment of capital in services, new technology, and management. Both sociologists point to the emerging new "knowledge class" — technical experts, engineers, and managers. Bell heralds this emerging condition as a new classless society that has moved beyond the old class conflict between owners and workers and the ideological debate that marked that struggle. Touraine, on the other hand, perceives a continuing social struggle, but one between the ruling technocratic bureaucracies and various social movements seeking to achieve particular goals, such as the emancipation of women and ecological balance.[11]

Bell and Touraine, as we have seen, are concerned with shifts in the economic sphere. Other postmodernists are concerned with what has happened to the political life of modern societies. Earlier sections in our discussion of the communitarian-liberal debate drew upon this material, especially that concerned with individualism, impoverished understandings of freedom, and the decline of public life.[12]

Another whole cluster of postmodern analysts focus on changes in our relationship with the natural environment and shifts in human understanding of the cosmos. One of the hallmarks of Enlightenment modernity is its rejection of a "sacred universe" that is alive and has purpose. Instead, the cosmos came to be seen as an object, similar to a machine, subject to mathematical laws and open to infinite manipulation by human beings. This disenchantment of the cosmos was accompanied by a growing dominance of "instrumental reason," meaning "the kind of rationality we draw on when we calculate the most economical application of means to a given end."[13] The combination greatly increased human control over nature and brought many advantages to humankind. But it also brought a dark side that has ultimately led to the deterioration of the natural environment, now at a point verging on disaster. Postmodernists see this as a symptom of the decline of modernity.

However, an earlier move in science away from Newton's mechanistic model to one characterized by Max Planck's quanta theory and Albert Einstein's theory of relativity (ironically called "modern science") has opened the way to a new understanding of the cosmos. This is beginning to make its appearance in the growth of the ecology movement and in the many and varied efforts to relate differently to the natural environment. Some analysts are beginning to speak of "the re-enchantment of the world."[14]

"The collapse of the modern mentality" is the subject of scrutiny by yet another group of postmodern analysts. This concerns the demonstrable lessening of confidence in Enlightenment reason by the intellectual world of the West. Modern thought proclaimed the goodness of rational human beings and the purely liberating power of scientific knowledge. It believed reason to be a universal basis for morality and human progress.

Now, instead of a universal reason and a single ground of knowledge, there is a pluralism of worldviews. Indeed, what passes as knowledge, say some philosophers, does not correspond to any given reality. Every view of reality is regarded as simply a particular point of view, representing the signs and symbols of a particular group. The line between truth and fiction is no longer clearly drawn.[15] "What is clear beyond question," writes a literary critic, is "the extreme unlikelihood that the people of the West shall ever again be presented with any great over-arching [meaning] that subdues all the entanglements of modern intellectual life and integrates the various fields of culture...."[16] One result of this is the growth of moral relativism. All of this is heralded by some as the beginning of a new, more liberated, postmodern era. By others, it is viewed as simply the death throes of modernity.

Finally, postmodern analysts disagree in their diagnosis of the root of this collapse and therefore on what corrective measures are needed. One view is that the breakdown is ensuing because we are "becoming too much what we have been." The central features of Enlightenment modernity that set it apart from previous traditional societies, "affirmation of freedom, equality, radical new beginnings, control over nature, democratic self-rule," have all been carried too far, too fast. The implication is that "the most successful modern societies are those that have a mixture of the traditional, those that somehow avoid getting too far down the road to modernity." Thus, moderation or slowness is the key to survival.[17] Another analysis claims that the breakdown of modernity is caused by "our inability to realize [its] goods in an authentic form. Our agenda will then no longer be defined as limiting or slowing down the progress of modern values, but rather as finding a way to rescue them in their integrity as against the distortions and perversions that have developed in modern history."[18]

We have taken a taste of postmodern analysis and a light sampling of some social theories, but have made no attempt to evaluate them. The purpose of this is to help us recognize the flavour of social analysis. In addition, we may be better able to pick out the particular social theory (or fragment of it) that informs a current ideology, social movement, or political creed. It should also assist us in identifying what social theory (or at least portions of its analysis) we use intentionally or otherwise. The theory can then be critically assessed in light of a commitment to Christ. Social analysis is one important component, then, of ascertaining what is going on in the context and situation.

Selection of an Appropriate Social Theory

How are Christians to select an appropriate social theory for a sound analysis of underlying patterns and causes in the social context? Some liberation theologians and political ethicists have been examining this matter, but on the whole, the relation of Christian ethics to different theories of the social sciences is one of the less satisfactorily developed areas in the discipline of Christian ethics. It is further complicated by the postmodern challenge. The question is, of course, part of the ongoing task of relating the gospel to the different worldviews discussed in the previous chapter. The matter is a complex and important one.

I will make a couple of preliminary observations regarding the selection and use of social theories in analyzing what is happening. My own approach is one in which we learn from and use social theories, but keep them in dialogue with Christian theology. They should be subservient to the basic concerns and truths of the gospel. This contrasts both with an approach that would adopt one particular social theory as most congruent with Christian truth and with an approach that rejects all secular social theory in favour of a strictly theological analysis.[19]

Clearly, when we attempt to understand the deeper patterns and causes of a particular social context, we carry assumptions about society and how it works. Such assumptions are likely to be embedded in our worldview. One important function of this base point on social analysis is to bring these assumptions into the open. They can then be critically examined in the light of Christian faith.

There is widespread agreement that any social theory is just that, a theory, and not an exact science. In the past, those drawn to Marxist social understanding have often claimed that its analysis of society represented the scientific truth about the "laws" of history. Few would now subscribe to that view, especially in light of the collapse of the Soviet empire and the new understandings of knowledge emerging with postmodernism. No social theory approaches the certitude usually ascribed, at least by modern thought, to scientific data about the nonhuman world. Given the interpretive nature of all social theories and the absence of scientific truth about the "laws" of history or the interaction of institutions, we need "epistemological vigilance." We should be modest concerning our capacity to know reality or analyze social conditions. Honest analysis will involve "deliberate and on-going self-critique,"[20] or, as another writer has called it, "humane uncertainty."

Robert K. Thomas, a Cherokee anthropologist, is concerned with another barrier to clear perception of social conditions, let alone the deeper analysis of their underlying patterns. This is the tendency that he sees, particularly in North America, for people to mistake the abstract categories of social theories, concepts developed to help us name and reflect on certain realities, with reality itself.

In a hard-hitting article, he warns his fellow Native Americans against adopting the definition of themselves as a "standard racial minority of American society." In other words, he fears that Native people are beginning to let themselves be defined according to the abstract categories of some particular social theory as if those categories were real. They are even taking on "all of the emotional problems that come with viewing one's self and group as a racial minority of a larger society — concerns about rank, negative definitions, social acceptance, subtle discrimination, etc."[21]

As a result of this, Thomas continues, tribal governments erect elaborate buildings to house their offices, and tribal leaders appear in public in expensive three-piece suits. "Indian history is cleaned up to meet middle class white standards — whites really were the ones who introduced scalping to North America, and the Indians never killed white women and children in battle; Indian religions are just good modern ecological practice spelled backwards, etc." All of these efforts, he claims, spring from a desire to be accepted by whites. Thus, some Indians accept the definitions assigned to them and the analysis of their situation according to some social theory. Theories may be more or less true or useful, but they are reflections on reality — abstractions and generalizations — and are not to be confused with actual human experience itself.

ASSESSING SIGNIFICANCE: DISCERNING THE SIGNS OF THE TIMES

Another enterprise integral to perceiving what is going on in any particular situation or wider context is the task of *assessing the significance* of what is happening. From a Christian perspective, such evaluation is done in terms of God's creative and redemptive purpose. This is the crucial and prophetic task of discerning the signs of the times.

Present issues regarding the natural environment provide an illustration of this. It is claimed that we are headed for ecological disaster. Is this *what* is really happening? We can seek the most accurate information possible from various sciences, recognizing the limits and ambiguities surrounding even informed forecasts. Predictably, analyses as to *why* environmental deterioration is happening vary according to the social theories upon which they are based, for example, the economics of capitalism or unimaginative bureaucratic regulations or the denigration of nature by world religions or the addiction to new technologies and methods of production, and so forth.

However, there is still the question of the *significance* of what is happening to the earth. Is it, on the whole, in accord with or contrary to the purposes of God? What is a theological interpretation of what is happening and why? Is this ecological crisis, assuming we are satisfied that there really is such, a matter of little concern to the work of the kingdom, or is it a working out of human sin or a sign of the end times? Whatever appraisal is made, it will have major implications for specific moral decisions regarding everything from personal consumption habits to public policy.

The other base points, especially basic convictions, largely determine what significance and meaning is attributed to events. Yet social theories often become involved in shaping this appraisal. Presumably designed to probe underlying patterns and causes, they also include, sometimes openly, sometimes covertly, an assessment of what is wrong and a preferred remedy. In doing so, they display previously obscure commitments to selected values and loyalties to particular groups and interests.

We have already noted how the values and convictions embedded in a theory's interpretive framework and method affect its analysis. These also spill over into the assessment of the significance of what is happening. We are pressed again, therefore, to recognize the care needed in selecting and using social theory.

Can a social theory be used for its insights into a situation without necessarily adopting its whole framework of meaning? Do we have to buy the whole package? Some liberation theologians and Christian ethicists would maintain that one can take elements from different social theories current in the social sciences and use them for social analysis without subscribing to their whole framework.[22] Others think it is not possible. Jose Comblin, a liberation theologian from Latin America, is concerned about the so-called Marxism of some Latin American Christians on these grounds. He argues that "the Marxist categories, in interpreting social justice issues, use the whole system and cannot be separated from it."[23]

Clearly there are risks involved. We saw, for example, that the modernist understanding of reality informing most of the social sciences rules out, in advance, the existence of any sacred or divine realm and certainly rules out the possibility of any reliable knowledge about such. Uncritical adoption of social theories based on this understanding limits perception. Its framework may come so to dominate that it is used to analyze and assess, not only the significance of events, but even the Christian gospel, rather than the other way around.

In summary, a sound perception of what is happening is an essential aspect of the moral life. Accurate information, penetrating analysis of underlying patterns and causes, and solid assessment of the significance of what is going on are all necessary elements for such perception. These in turn, however, require the careful selection and use of social theories. I shall conclude this chapter, therefore, with two final suggestions concerning such selection and use.

We can test any social theory and analysis of social conditions partly by whether it uncovers and illuminates the matters to which Christian norms and standards direct us. Thus the norm of love of neighbour as interpreted in terms of God's strategic concentration on the poor leads us to ask whether a particular social theory illuminates conditions from the perspective of this group. Does it reveal things from that angle of vision? Does it provide the information, ask the right questions, search for causes in terms of the needs of such people to find a truly just place within the global community? A number of liberation theologians and Christian political ethicists opt for some variation of a radical dualist social theory on the grounds that it seems to fit this criteria better than the functionalist approach. The latter tends to view society more from above, as it were.

We should also ask of any social theory whether it helps us to comprehend the real identity of those communities and peoples who have less power and are victims of injustice, rather than merely slotting them into abstract categories the theory has constructed. A Papago man from Arizona was puzzled by the categories that had been used to define his identity. "I am not poor," he said. "I am a Papago, but one who happens to have little cash."

One of the inadequacies of the radical dualistic or Marxist approach, even in some of its more recent versions, is that it does not take account of how many in the world understand and perceive themselves as peoples or kinship societies. The assumption of most dualist social theories is that the centre of meaningful reality for human beings is economic; political considerations and all other relationships merely reflect the fundamental economic and political dynamics of life. This has prevented nearly all social theories, both Marxist and liberal ones (albeit for different reasons), from correctly analyzing the enduring strength or legitimacy of peoplehoods. This failing, observed several Soviet experts with surprising foresight some years ago, would contribute to the eventual break-up of the Soviet Union, as we are witnessing in this decade.[24]

We can also test social theories in terms of their congruency with a Christian understanding of human nature and the relation of humans to the sacred and to other-than-human creation. Most social theories propounded by the social sciences are found wanting in terms of these theological criteria. I earlier criticized the inadequate understanding of human relationships and society found in conventional liberal theories of society. They reflect an individualism that does not do justice to several important facets of the human experience.

Social theories that view understandings of the sacred as completely subservient to, or as mere functions of, some other central reality are also inadequate in terms of the Christian experience and, indeed, the experience of much of the world. A Latin American theologian, who himself uses a partial and modified view of Marxist analysis, warns of its weakness in this respect. Its sometimes insightful, but on balance inadequate, understanding of religion leads to condescending perceptions of those poor who maintain their religious faith. They are regarded as mere victims of an illusion.

A few years ago in Arizona, a university wanted to obtain a sizeable tract of land from the Papago Indian people to build a cyclotron for research work in nuclear physics. A group of scientists and economists came to speak to the Papago tribal council about this. They outlined, with charts and graphs and overhead projectors, why this programme was necessary, what it would accomplish, the economic benefits to Native people, and so on. The Papago listened politely, but when the presentation was over, an elder got up and asked the pivotal question from the Papago point of view: "But does God want you to do this with the land?"

The presenters, nonplussed, could only repeat their litany of the economic benefits. Operating with a (no doubt, unexamined) social theory that held that economic concerns are always primary, they were totally unprepared to take the religious question seriously or to understand its significance for the Papago. The result was that the Papago were unconvinced and rejected the project.

None of this means that different social theories are not extremely helpful to good social analysis done from a Christian perspective. Important insights are found in different social theories. It is particularly instructive for Christians to see how Christianity and the church is seen to function, intentionally or not, in support of unjust systems. There are attempts to combine the insights of several theories into a model of social analysis that will be useful for groups and peoples struggling to effect social change towards greater justice.[25] This is a step in the right direction. It is a helpful approach that combines a kind of openness to different social theories with some understanding of their individual strengths and weaknesses.

Five

Authoritative Sources: Where the Good Way Lies

A look at where we turn with confidence to discover which particular norms and standards, qualities of character, and basic convictions should inform our moral life and guide us in the Way. For Christians, an authoritative source is one which is a vehicle of God's self-revelation. These are the Bible, the Christian tradition, reason, and experience. We explore how these are understood and used.

A MODEL FOR ETHICAL REFLECTION

Moral Agent in Community

Basic Commitment

Analysis of Self as Agent

Moral Character

Analysis of the Social Setting

The Context

Worldview and Basic Convictions

The Situation

Authoritative Sources
- Scripture
- Tradition
- Reason
  - Natural Law
- Experience ("taking in")
  - A way of knowing
  - A special segment of life

Moral Norms and Standards

Authoritative Sources
- Experience - especially of those most affected
- Science
- History
- Law

Resolution

INTRODUCTION

We have been examining facets of the moral life: moral standards or norms; character; worldview, which entails basic convictions; and perception of what is happening. These are base points for ethically reflecting on the moral life. I have described them as resources for discerning and walking the Way and likened them to the sections of an orchestra. But what should the *content* of each of these base points be? What are the particular markers, the internal antenna, what is the map we should follow on our journey? What music should the orchestra be playing? The answer will depend on our fundamental commitment.

From a Christian perspective, the content should be that which is in accord with God's will and purpose. This is what designates a particular norm and standard as one that should guide us; or a basic conviction about human beings that should illuminate and inform our deliberations; or an attitude and disposition that is to be deemed virtuous. Indeed, for Christians the main object in reflecting on moral being and doing is that we might cooperate with God's sanctifying grace and be transformed by the renewal of our minds. This means that we must attempt to bring the content of each of these aspects into accord with God's Word, rather than simply letting the content be that of the culture in which we were socialized and thereby conform to this passing age.

FOUR SOURCES OF GOD'S REVELATION

The crucial question now needing to be addressed is, therefore, where is God's will and purpose most reliably disclosed? What form does it take? These matters compose the classic theological question of God's revelation. There is broad agreement among Christians that human knowledge of God is possible only because of God's self-revelation. Regrettably, there is no divine oracle to which we can turn for a definitive answer as to what the content of each of the base points should be. God's self-disclosure is always mediated to us through some finite and imperfect medium, including ourselves. Nevertheless, four key sources have emerged in Christian thought, where God's self-disclosure is reliably mediated and attested to. These are: the Bible, the tradition of the Christian churches, reason, and human experience.

The Bible

The Bible is claimed by the church as its scripture and thereby declared as normative for the faith and life of the church. There are divergent views as to what it means to claim the Bible as scripture, what the grounding of this special authority is, how it relates to other sources of God's self-disclosure, and how it is to be understood and interpreted. I will comment on these shortly. But however Christians may differ on these many points, the Bible remains as "the single necessary reference point," the "constant source to which the church refers." It is "to be taken seriously in *all* ethical reflection within the church."[1] Further, it is clear what we are referring to when we talk about the Bible as a source, even though there are disputes between Protestant, Eastern Orthodox, and Roman Catholic churches over the inclusion of the books of the Apocrypha.

Tradition

In its broadest sense, tradition refers to "something handed down from generation to generation" and the mode of that transmission.[2] In Christian thought, tradition refers to the faith, theology, and practice of the community of faith as it has been transmitted. One understanding of this tradition is broad. It includes the story of the people of faith, their way of life, the "historical identity and self-understanding of the religious community, which is formed by the Scriptures, and which continues to inform its present and future."[3] The multiple traditions of the various churches are viewed as the "residue of corporate experience of earlier Christian communities."[4]

Another formulation of this expansive view of Christian tradition is found in contemporary discussions. It is said to be "the history of that environment of grace in and by which all Christians live, which is the continuance through time and space of God's self-giving love in Jesus Christ." However,

Christian tradition may also be interpreted in a more restricted sense as referring to the dogma and moral teachings formally approved by a church through its own recognized polity. These may be expressed in the form of doctrinal statements, moral and social teachings, liturgies, and basic statements of faith.

Reason

Reason as a source of God's self-disclosure of will and purpose is also variously understood. One way in which reason is appealed to by Christian thinkers is as a way of making sense of divine teachings, rather than as a source of God's revelation itself. Reason is that which makes basic convictions about God creditable and communicable, a way of bringing "clarity and a verifiability" to moral standards. Reason does not supply the materials for the base points so much as bring them to coherence and consistency. Revelation may well transcend the scope of reason, but "since all truth is from God, efforts to discern the connections between revelation and reason, faith and science, grace and nature, are useful endeavors in developing credible and communicable doctrine."

A second use of reason in Christian thought is more disputed. It is viewed as a distinctive source of truth about reality, human life, and God's will and purpose. Most moral philosophies since the Enlightenment go much further. They claim complete "autonomy of reason" as a source of moral wisdom, independent of any revelation. In this approach, reason is viewed as the only valid moral authority for mature human beings. Moral norms and standards, for example, that purport to be based in religious "revelation" are acceptable only insofar as they commend themselves to reason, which has its own capacity to discover ethical principles that are true.[5]

In some Christian thought, this kind of appeal to reason as an independent source of ethical wisdom is interpreted as part of God's general revelation. This means that human beings, created in "the image of God," are able to know by "right reason" something of God's will and purpose. In practice, this most commonly entails adopting a philosophical account of what is essential or ideal humanity, i.e., "what is to be valued and promoted in human existence, or what is fulfilling for humanity."[6] A variety of such philosophies have been embraced at different times by those Christian ethicists who draw upon reason as a prime source for ethical wisdom. The most vigorous and long-term commitment to this approach to ethical wisdom is found in the Roman Catholic tradition. There it has been expressed in what is called the *natural law* tradition.

Natural Law Tradition. Central to the concept of natural law is the belief that there is a moral order integral to the universe and that human beings can discern this by the exercise of their reason. The term "natural law" is itself somewhat misleading. In a sense, it "is neither 'natural' nor is it 'law'. It is not 'natural' in the sense that the natural *moral* law cannot be identified with physical, chemical, or biological laws of nature which try to express the way nature works. It is not 'law' in the sense that it is not a written code of precepts which carry public sanctions from the legislator."[7]

All natural law theories, however, do claim to derive moral norms and standards from a reasoned understanding of human nature. In Christian terms, the purpose of God is reflected in God's creation. One aspect of this is the God-given capacity of human beings to use their reason to discern that purpose. Christians, then, can find ethical wisdom and knowledge, not only in scripture and tradition of the church, but also in human nature as understood by human reason.

Protestant thinkers generally agree with the notion that God's purpose is implanted, so to speak, in creation and that there is a moral order. But they are dubious regarding the capacity of "unaided" human reason to rightly discern this. The power of sin is believed to be so strong in a fallen creation that human reason is distorted and unable to discern, except very dimly, this moral purpose. The transforming power of the Holy Spirit and the guidance of "special revelation" are required. Otherwise, what are purportedly the objective standards reason discerns in human nature tend to turn out to be the biases and interests of a particular group and culture.

The natural law tradition has a long, rich, and varied history in Greek, Roman, medieval, and Enlightenment times. Thomas Aquinas, the great Medieval theologian, achieved a formulation of it that has definitively shaped much of Roman Catholic ethical thought. Natural law is understood as the tendency of humans to move towards their fulfilment as authentic persons. Various natural inclinations that are part of that tendency will yield us guidance as to how we ought to live. For example, all created reality, including human beings, has a tendency to persevere in existing. From this fact, we may deduce that preserving and protecting life is a basic good or value that should guide our actions.

Recently, Catholic moral thought has been marked by new interpretations of Aquinas' multifaceted thought. The earlier approach that still informs moral statements by the hierarchy, especially in matters of sexuality and medicine, draws on one side of Aquinas' view of human nature. The emphasis is on physical and biological nature, those aspects that are common to humans and animals alike. Moral obligations are derived from what nature requires in order to fulfil its maker's inherent design. Thus, the reproductive faculty is for producing life, and the faculty of speech is for truth telling. An action that is contrary to nature in this sense is deemed morally evil. "Speaking falsely frustrates the faculty of speech which is oriented to telling the truth, and contraception or sterilization frustrates the reproductive faculties which is oriented to the giving of life." Approaches to natural law with this emphasis are called "physicalist."

A more recent approach is called "personalist." It draws on the other side of Aquinas' view of human nature. The focus is on those qualities that are distinctively human, inclinations that "extend beyond the physical and biological to include the social, spiritual and psychological dimension as well." An example is the human tendency towards cooperating with one another in a social existence. From this, the norms and standards of justice are derived.

In addition, contemporary Catholic understandings of natural law recognize that human "nature" is not a static thing. It is continually evolving and changing. This means that our understanding of what is morally good needs to change in order to be kept in accord with it. Morality continues to be objectively based on reason's discernment of human nature. It is not merely a matter of human whim. However, since the nature of human beings changes, "what has built up human well-being in the past may, or may not, continue to do so in the present or future."

The reflection by human reason on human experience continues, then, to be a key source for moral truth in the Catholic tradition. The understanding of reason itself has been enriched to include "observation and research, intuition, affection, commonsense, and an aesthetic sense in an effort to know human reality in all its aspects. In short, whatever resources we can use to understand the meaning of being human." Even more significant from a Protestant point of view is the growing acknowledgement that reason, even in this broad sense, is always limited and partial.

Experience

Experience is the fourth major source for human reception of God's self-disclosure. Regrettably, there is little clarity or consistency in the way in which it is identified and used. This is frustrating, especially since experience is increasingly appealed to in some Christian circles.[8]

Root Meaning. It is helpful to remind ourselves of the basic meaning of the word "experience." It has to do with the "taking in," the coming through to the self of objects or events, "an immense sensibility." Experience in this root sense of the term is not merely one source of God's revelation alongside of others, it is rather "the medium through which the sources 'speak' to us, through which we can receive them."[9] I can only know what I "take in." It is the way we "receive whatever is" or "the point at which we feel the *touch* of life."[10] In other words, we cannot appeal to any source or any thing that cannot be experienced.

What is meant when "experience" is named as one source among several for Christian ethics or Christian theology? The various and often confusing answers given may be clustered into two broad types.

First Type of Use. In the first and most ancient and persistent of these interpretations in the history of Christian thought, experience means a particular *kind* of appropriation of God's revelation through whatever sources. It is something we take to ourselves based on participation in the spiritual realities, a direct, or as some would say, "existential" encounter with God. The United Methodist Book of Discipline observes that there is a radical distinction between intellectual assent to the message of the Bible and the doctrines of the Creed, and "the personal experience of God's pardoning and healing love."[11] Thus, experience means the direct encounter with God and God's love and participation in the new life in Christ. This brings a new posture towards the world and illumines one's understanding of God and creation. In this sense, experience entails direct participation through the active risking of one's self. This is in contrast to a detached, purely cognitive knowledge about God and God's will and purpose. This understanding of experience is true to the root meaning of the term, a medium through which other sources are mediated.

Second Type of Use. The second type of usage of the word "experience" in connection with sources of God's revelation is quite different. It is used to identify a particular area of reality or *segment* of life (distinct from scripture or tradition) in which God's revelation can be apprehended. For example, for some this special area of life is an "inner experience." It is "the experience of one's self, one's body, one's emotions and feelings, the flow of one's awareness or consciousness."[12] This provides a different "field of evidence" for God's revelation and hence a source for the content of base points for ethical reflection. Confusion arises partly because this is a very different use of the word than that included in its root meaning.

Confusion is compounded, however, because such a variety of things are called "experience" without further stipulation. Thus, in addition to the inner self, "experience" is used to refer to a more explicitly "religious" or mystic moment, a stirring of the heart. Participating with the poor in their struggles for justice is claimed by many liberation theologians as an area of "experience" in which God is revealed and encountered. For others, virtually the whole gamut of human living mediates divine revelation.[13]

An important variation of this second use of experience (designating a special segment of reality) is in reference to empirical studies. These are studies, done particularly in the social sciences, that attempt to describe what actually takes place in human lives and society. They are seen by some as an important source for ethical wisdom. "One reason that the empirical sciences are important for Christian ethics," writes Lisa Cahill, a contemporary Christian ethicist, "is that they undergird critical perspectives on the other sources of ethics. They provide standards by which to test the adequacy of the latter to human reality and history."[14] Such studies may help us discover, for example, that the consequences of certain actions are different than might have been assumed in biblical times. Empirical studies may also yield findings regarding human emotional needs or gender qualities that challenge some notions of the normatively human adopted by the use of reason as a source. Such findings have a bearing even on the natural law as it is understood, for they help us understand "the total complexity of human reality and all its relationships."

The difficulty in relying on this kind of "experience" as a source of ethical wisdom is that the social sciences are susceptible to the values, beliefs, and loyalties of their designers and interpreters. As we saw in our discussion of social theories, different frameworks yield dissimilar "empirical" results. Lisa Cahill recognizes this. Perhaps that is why she sees this form of "experience" less as an independent source of ethical wisdom and more as a critical corrective used in interaction with other sources. Acknowledging the discrepancies and uncertainties of empirical findings, she suggests that "perhaps the best advice for the ethicist is to recognize her or his own presuppositions and implicit hypotheses, and so consider most seriously the impact that evidence unfavorable to them would have on his or her agenda."

There is yet another significant variation of this second use of the term experience. It refers to a particular field of evidence or segment of life in which God's self-disclosure is found. This is the accumulated findings of humankind on what has proven, over time, to be worthy and what has not. It is what Tillich labels "experiential verification," the long-term, obscure, and complex way in which "experience in the comprehensive sense" confirms or disconfirms theological claims and ethical wisdom.[15]

As Christians, we would look particularly to "the believing community's reflection on human experience and on the personal aftermath of that experience." What sort of behaviour have Christians found in the long term to be conducive to either spiritual thriving or withering? A particularly powerful verification regarding the ethical wisdom of norms that prohibit certain actions, and the naming of certain dispositions as vices, "comes from those who have made a life out of these kinds of behaviour and then looked back on it with dismay."[16] "Experience" used in this sense, then, comes very close to meaning the same thing as tradition.

This second main use of the term experience in all its variations is not, then, the process of "taking in," nor a way of apprehending reality, but rather a particular part of life that is claimed as a place of God's self disclosure, directly or indirectly. Experience in this sense has become increasingly appealed to as a source of ethical wisdom and the content of the base points. Paul Tillich's 1950 description of the theological climate of the time also depicts well the current ethos of much of liberal mainstream Protestantism:

> *The encounter with great non-Christian religions, the evolutionary scheme of thought, the openness for the new which characterizes the pragmatic method, have had the consequence that experience has become not only the main source of systematic theology but an inexhaustible source out of which new truths can be taken continually. Being open for new experiences which might even pass beyond the confines of Christian experience is now the proper attitude of the theologian.*[17]

Now few, if any, Christian traditions or Christian thinkers would deny the possibility and the reality that God is revealed through areas of life and reality other than scripture or Christian tradition. There is little doubt, then, that theological truth and ethical wisdom regarding God's will and purpose are to be found in many different places. The disputes centre on this: Do the revelations that come from the presence of the Spirit in the various fields of reality that we experience bring new and additional truth about God's will and purpose? If so, this could lead to different norms and standards and an alternative selection of what is called a virtue or a vice. Or do they instead testify in various fresh and relevant ways to the definitive revelation of God found in Jesus Christ and the biblical message? If so, the likely result would be clarification, nuanced interpretation, and reaffirmation of Christian moral standards and qualities of character.

This brings us to a crucial question. How are we to recognize whether or not something is of God? What are the criteria by which we can ascertain, in all the varied phenomena that we "take in," which of it reveals God's will and purpose? This is the keystone matter of determining which source is most *authoritative* for ascertaining God's will and purpose. It is difficult to see how experience, in any of the meanings so far enumerated, could provide such criteria. Rather, I strongly concur with Tillich's claim that the unique event of Jesus the Christ is "the criterion of every religious experience. This event is given to experience and not derived from it. Therefore, experience receives and does not produce." However, by making this confession, I have anticipated our discussion of the relationship of the various sources to each other and their relative authority.

Before proceeding, let us review the line of thinking I have followed in what I have said so far about sources.

Summary

The Bible, Christian tradition, reason, and experience are sources or mediums for God's self-revelation. Therefore, they are given authority by Christians for ascertaining the appropriate content of the base points entailed in ethically reflecting on the moral life. From these sources we learn about the music each section of the orchestra is to play. Put differently, we look to these four sources as authoritative grounds for *ethical wisdom*; that is, what should go into moral deliberation. It is important to note that they are *not* being claimed here as authoritative sources for *moral decisions* themselves. We should not turn to scripture, for example, for precise directives in answer to a moral dilemma that quite likely arises in a situation not anticipated anywhere in the Bible. Rather we should look to the Bible for deeper knowledge of God's will and purpose. Such understanding informs all aspects of moral life, the base points for ethical reflection. From these, we can make a faithful decision.

THE RELATIONSHIP OF THE SOURCES

Which of these authoritative sources should be given primacy when they conflict? Which of the dissimilar versions of tradition, reason, and experience should be accepted? Answering these questions continues to be one of the most vexing and divisive issues facing Western Christians. For instance, Roman Catholic ethics has characteristically relied heavily on human reason and its capacity to discern natural law. Protestants, on the other hand, have given primacy to God's self-disclosure in scripture or experience understood as a particular way of knowing. We have already noted the typical Protestant suspicion of reason and natural law. Liberal versions of Protestantism have emphasized experience, meaning some special segment of life where God is to be encountered, and are uneasy about tradition.

Christian thinkers from many traditions are coming to see a more balanced relationship between these four sources. This has been assisted by the Protestant realization that, in its own ethical tradition, "reason" has and continues to have a significant, even if different, place as a source. It has also been enhanced by the more modest claims for reason and natural law made by many Roman Catholic thinkers as described earlier. A fine example of this more integrated use of the four sources is Lisa Cahill's approach, which both specifies exactly what each source entails and employs all of them as mutually corrective to one another.[18] Of course, we can have most confidence in those norms and standards (or the content of any other base point) on which scripture, tradition, reason, and experience agree.

Another advance in sorting out the use and priority of sources is made, I think, when we distinguish between the various base points and ask which source is crucial for each.

What we are looking for will affect the selection of which source is to be regarded as primary. This is most obvious in the difference between asking, on the one hand, about what is happening in the situation or context and, on the other hand, inquiring about norms, character, or convictions. I believe the most authoritative source for determining what is happening in a situation is the experience of those most affected by the events under scrutiny and, secondarily, the empirical studies of those events. Nevertheless, all experience (what we "take in") is first filtered and then interpreted partly in accordance with our stance towards life, our dispositions and convictions, as we observed earlier. Therefore, the other three sources, related more to the remaining base points, should also play a testing and corrective role.

When asking what norms or standards of behaviour, basic convictions, and moral character are in accord with God's purpose, I believe the most authoritative source is the Bible. The other sources serve to assist in interpreting scripture; they also corroborate and complement it. They may challenge conventional understandings of scripture and press us towards new and deeper comprehension.

The Bible as Primary Authority

The need to grant the highest authority to one source unavoidably persists, even after recognition of the interrelatedness of the sources. God's will and purpose and the ethical wisdom grounded therein is revealed in a variety of ways, represented by all four sources. Nevertheless, to repeat our earlier concern, it is essential to distinguish between the matter of *where* God's will and purpose is revealed from the inescapable question of how is it to be *recognized* as truly that of God. In other words, what is the definitive revelation of God? How are we to distinguish between the demonic and the Holy Spirit? I share the Christian belief that Jesus as the Christ is that definitive revelation.

The Bible is granted prime authority as a source of God's self-disclosure, because it is indispensable for understanding Jesus as the Christ. It is a very human document or set of documents drawn together over a period of approximately 3,000 years from oral traditions and various writings. It was edited into collections, amalgamated and re-edited into larger collections, and finally formed into the "canon" as we have it.

The Bible's diverse literature contains a tremendous variety of witnesses both to God's grace and to human responses to that grace. Our knowledge of Jesus Christ, however, is dependent on the words through which he and the events connected with him have been made known to us. It is dependent upon words that embody the understanding of those who witnessed them or who participated in them. It is similar to a multitude of witnesses at a trial: they may differ from one another, even contradict one another, but taken together they give the only rendering we have of the characters and events of whom and which they speak.[19] Yet, "to understand Jesus requires not only the diverse witnesses of the New Testament to his life and work, but also the rich heritage of the Old Testament, which provided foundation and content for Jesus' own understanding and proclamation of the good news that God had acted to redeem the world."[20]

Thus, through the prism of these peoples of the Bible, through their strange and sometimes repugnant, other times magnificent, practices and morality, through their frequently alien customs and thought forms and tortured history, the light of God is refracted. This "means of grace," provided by God, has given the church its identity. Here we find "the determinative clue to the character and activity of the One whose purpose is the final meaning of history."[21]

We may well receive insight regarding God's will and purpose and derive ethical wisdom regarding norms and standards or basic convictions, for example, from some philosophical view of the normatively human (reason). Or we may receive it from the long tradition of Christians seeking to be faithful as they live in the world (tradition). Or we may receive it from new understandings of human needs and struggles (experience). However, these are to be assessed, finally, as appropriate or inappropriate from a Christian perspective, in terms of whether or not they are in accord with Jesus Christ as understood in the light of the entire Bible. This is the approach that I have attempted to use in our examination of justice, liberty, hope, understanding of human nature, and the like.

Difficulties arise, however, when we try to understand and interpret scripture and thereby apprehend this definitive revelation of God. History is replete with the tragic consequences of the misuse of the Bible. It has been used to sanction destructive directives and practices not in accord with Christ. This has been done both through selective literalist readings and through slippery interpretative methods that accommodate its teachings to fit the worldview, values, and interests of a particular culture or group. Even the devil quotes Scripture!

The fallibility of our understanding and interpretation is one strong reason why we cannot look to scripture as an oracle for ethics, let alone for precise directives for particular moral decisions. The other three authoritative sources are essential for balancing and correcting our perception, understanding, and interpretation of scripture. This interpretive function, however, constitutes their relation to scripture; "they are not independent counterbalancing sources of authority."[22]

Understanding and Interpreting Scripture

The interpretation of scripture is a storm centre for Western Christians immersed in a modern worldview. What can be said, short of writing another book? Let me venture instead a few guidelines for approaching scripture. The object is to apprehend as faithfully as possible the will and purpose of God in terms of ethical understanding.

The Community of Faith. This is the appropriate location for engaging scripture for ethical purposes. The angle of vision from which scripture is viewed affects the questions brought to it and the manner of comprehension. Therefore, this angle influences what is likely to be found. However, the angle of vision itself is profoundly affected by the social location of the viewer — his or her culture, historical era, economic class, age, gender. What a difference this makes when we examine the Bible with regard to such matters as violence, divorce, civil disobedience, the relation of men and women, and the like!

There has been much discussion as to whether or not there is a privileged place to stand that better enables us to ask and discern truly. Some say that to stand with the poor or oppressed is to find such a location. As stated earlier in our discussion of justice, I doubt if any "place" is free from its own form of the limitations of finitude and sin. Locations do vary, however, in the particular temptation and distortion they engender. The church catholic, i.e., universal, which is currently worldwide, also includes many different strands of tradition down through time. By entering into conversation with this wider church tradition, we are entering into conversation with a great diversity of persons and communities from different historical eras, classes, cultures, gender, and the like. This is a marvellous help in correcting the limitations of any single social location.

The teachings and creeds of the churches are the vehicle for such an ongoing conversation with the Christians of the past who similarly struggled. Like us, they sought to discern rightly the word of God in scripture and be faithful to it under many kinds of circumstances. The conversations help us to see the peculiarities of our own circumstances. The biases, prejudices, and limitations of our own era and culture come into view. When these conversations reveal a strong difference between our own interpretations of a text and those of the historical or present wider church, we are pressed to ask whether we have understood correctly or whether we are blinded by our own needs and self-interests. Have we really understood what other interpreters mean? Have we probed to the deeper meaning of that text?

However, our experience in the context of a culture and particular group is also a legitimately different angle of vision that leads to asking new questions of scripture. These may respectfully challenge other interpretations or throw new light upon them. In this way, both tradition and experience (understood in the sense of a segment of life) function as resources for understanding scripture, rather than as independent sources of, or rival authorities regarding, God's self-revelation. As part of the community that struggles to discern God's will and purpose, "we open ourselves continually to Scripture, always in company with our fellow disciples of this and former ages and in the context of the struggle for obedience; and we constantly find in it fresh insights into the character and purpose of the one who is 'rendered' for us in its pages."[23]

Social location affects not only the angle of vision of the interpreter; more significantly, it carries a worldview. Earlier we discussed basic convictions that are included in a worldview. Here, I am interested in those taken-for-granted presuppositions about what knowledge is and how it is to be obtained. These presuppositions can be called a "plausibility structure." We observed previously that, since the Enlightenment, Western modern thought has assumed that its plausibility structure is universally valid. Its view of what constitutes real knowledge is the only basis for assessing all other claims to truth.

The great struggle by Western Christian thinkers for the last two hundred years has been to understand, in terms of modernity's plausibility structure, the Bible's very different way of knowing. Many of the claims to understanding scripture in its own terms have actually been efforts to understand it in terms of the rational tradition of modernity. Now that rational tradition itself is called into question, as we noted in our survey of the postmodern challenge.

Accepting the primacy of scripture as the authoritative source of God's self-revelation entails letting its plausibility structure call that of modern Western culture into question. This claim is convincingly made by Lesslie Newbigin, former bishop in the Church of South India and prominent leader in the ecumenical movement. The location best suited for this is the Christian community which has made scripture normative for its life. Those who inhabit such a community enter into a different plausibility structure from that of their contemporaries. "Things that are myths or illusion for others are real for them. God's power active in world history is not a mythical way of speaking for them, but an account of reality. But it is so only in the context of an active engagement with current events that corresponds to and continually renews this experience."[24] This community itself will need to be continually challenged and tested by the revelation in scripture. Entering into this different biblical tradition of rationality is part of the meaning of conversion. It is an act of faith, an act that is also required by those who adopt the assumptions and axioms belonging to the plausibility structure of modern Western culture.

Commitment to God. This is a second guideline for approaching scripture. Knowledge of God is not like knowledge of things or objects. It is more like knowledge of persons. Just as we only really get to know a person when we actively commit ourselves in trust to them, "knowledge of the will of God *follows* the community's submission and transformation."[25] If an understanding of God's will and purpose is to be rendered to us by the Bible, then we must join the struggle that we see in scripture. This is "the struggle to understand and deal with the events of our time in the faith that the God revealed is in fact the agent whose purpose created and sustained all that is, and will bring it to its proper end."[26]

Letting the Texts Have Their Say. An essential task in the faithful reading of scripture is what New Testament scholar Richard Hays calls the "descriptive task." This is the exegetical enterprise that forgoes all attempts to prematurely find unity or harmony in the message of the texts. Here, reason has important contributions to make. Indeed, the particular rational tradition of Western thought has gifts to offer in interpreting scripture, providing it does not finally dominate and control.

The historical-critical study of scripture, developed and honed over a hundred years, is an example. This discipline, known as exegesis, assists in letting the text speak. The tools and techniques of exegesis help us to examine the many different literary styles used in recording the relationship of God to a variety of communities found in the Bible, and aid in the difficulty of translating these styles into another language. The text is probed by exploring the kind of literary style and organization that both it and any parallel passages represent. What form or genre of writing and tradition is it: a prayer, oracle of judgement, parable, or something else? The historical context of both the experience described in the text and that of the audience or group to which the passage is addressed is investigated. This kind of probing also seeks to discern the theological meaning of the text: what it is saying about the human story or about the rest of creation in relationship to God and God's purpose.

Seeing the place of the theme and the message of the text in relation to the entire canon, and to similar themes and messages found throughout, is likewise important. Such a thoroughgoing analysis can be of great assistance to the community of faith, as it seeks to understand how it is being addressed by God and how God is revealed anew for our time and place.

The shift to the plausibility structure of the Bible, therefore, does not require complete rejection of the different rational tradition of Western culture — the modern scientific worldview — for, argues Newbigin, "from within the plausibility structure that is shaped by the Bible, it is perfectly possible to acknowledge and cherish the insights of our culture." The difference is that these insights are now seen with different eyes. The worldview of scripture is no longer viewed as one totally discontinuous with that of modernity. The gap between them is no longer almost impossible to bridge.

Respecting the Mode in Which a Text Speaks. When we look to scripture to supply or test the content for the various base points or aspects of the moral life, it is vital to turn to those texts that speak in the same mode as the base point. For instance, we may be asking what dispositions or habits of the heart are in accord with God's will and purpose. If so, we should look to those texts that either explicitly speak of such or else lift up desirable qualities through story.

Likewise, if we seek for theological understanding of human fallenness, or of God's providence, we should turn to passages that deal with these matters, for example, Romans 1:19-32 and Matthew 5:43-48. Richard Hays, who forcefully makes this point, criticizes the widespread tendency to mix these modes, turning "narratives into law (for instance, by arguing that Acts 2:44-45 requires Christians to own all things in common) or rules into principles (for example, by suggesting that the commandment to sell possessions and give alms [Luke 12:33] is not meant literally but that it points to the principle of inner detachment from our wealth)."[27]

Discerning Moral Themes and Concerns. This aspect of interpretation requires care since there is such diversity and plurality of perspectives in scripture. So many past efforts to harmonize or unify the messages have resulted in distortions. Again following Hays, the recommended steps are, first, to confront the full range of canonical witnesses, including passages that may stand against your views and interests and not just favourite or congenial texts. In addition, do not force harmony through abstractions. One example Hays gives of this last temptation is the attempt to reconcile the very different assessments of the state found in Romans 13 and Revelation 13 by claiming they are complimentary expressions of a single view. "Let the tensions stand," declares Hays.

Tracing trajectories of moral instruction (as described in the discussion of the Ten Commandments) is one example of discerning moral themes in scripture. Hays himself proposes three "governing images" that predominate in the New Testament. These images provide a framework for further interpretation: the church as a counter-cultural community of discipleship; Jesus' death on the cross as the exemplar of faithfulness to God; the new creation which already appears but is not yet here in fullness.

To summarize, I believe we should look to scripture as the prime source for the definitive revelation of God in Jesus Christ. I do not believe, however, that the Bible is the exclusive source of God's self-disclosure. We can look to scripture for an understanding of God's will and purpose that brings ethical wisdom in the form of basic imperatives (norms and standards), formation of a perspective on life and dispositions or habits of the heart (moral character), and basic convictions about the human story and the rest of creation in relation to God. These in turn will lead to additional imperatives. They will shape our interpretation of what is happening today in the world around us. To let scripture inform us in this way, however, means a disciplined and ongoing study of it by a community of faith in conversation with the entire Christian tradition.

THE CHURCH AS BEARER OF SCRIPTURE AND TRADITION

Faithful ethical reflection on the Way or the moral life from a Christian perspective, then, depends ultimately on the church functioning as a bearer of the scriptures and the teachings that have formed its identity. When I was a pastor in a congregation, I recall being asked to start an adult study group on Christian ethics because members wanted to know how to relate their faith to difficult moral decisions they were facing. After two or three sessions the members of the group quickly realized they were unable to do serious moral deliberation from a Christian perspective because they felt so ignorant about the scripture and the faith tradition of their church. The group became an adult Bible study group. Later, they went on to explore the doctrines and creeds of the church. As a result of this study, they were then able to reflect ethically in significant ways on the moral questions and dilemmas that members brought to the group. Neither scripture nor the faith tradition provided ready-made answers, of course, to the moral questions raised, but they were essential for grounding the substance of the ethical base points. These in turn allowed them to creatively engage the moral issues from the perspective of their faith.

Being a good steward of scripture and the tradition is not an easy task. To be able to truly hand these on entails a living engagement with them. We have seen that both scripture and the teachings of the church contain diverse strands. Real engagement with them involves a "continuous sense making, and appropriation," a sorting and assessing.

The process is similar, suggests Lesslie Newbigin, to that described by Michael Polanyi regarding the scientific community's approach to tradition in its pursuit of truth. Scientists are free to differ with each other, and to argue, but they still operate within a tradition that embodies the findings of the past members of the community of science. "The tradition is not infallible or incorrigible. On the contrary it is constantly being modified by new discoveries. But it nevertheless provides a firm framework for scientific research." To be a member of the scientific community requires "a long apprenticeship to the tradition." Certain standards must be respected in research, and long-established views are not cast out or set aside without a great deal of testing in public forums over a period of time. Differences of opinion "are the subject of debate, argument, testing, and fresh research until either one view prevails over the other as more true, or else some fresh way of seeing things enables the two views to be reconciled as two ways of seeing one reality."[28]

The church is called to be a faithful bearer of scripture and tradition, including the moral teachings and actions of those who have preceded us, not only because these are essential ingredients for the base points, but because this stewardship is needed to provide a "framework of accountability." The tradition

> *mediates the claims of others upon us and we upon them.... in a certain way, I am responsible to Abraham and Sarah and their lot. I am part of the fulfillment of the story that was theirs, is mine, and will be that of those who come after me. They bequeathed a legacy and vocation to me. The legacy and vocation continue, and I am responsible to the ancestors through the heritage placed in my hands.*[29]

Likewise, our accountability continues into the future. We are responsible to coming generations.

Six

The Art of Discerning the Way: An Undivided Heart

A look at the relationship between norms, character, worldview, understanding of what is happening, and authoritative sources. How are these five base points combined in their use for moral guidance? This is the question of ethical method. An illustrative sampling of different ethical methods is followed by an explanation of the particular one in this book. The requirements for sound moral deliberation and ethical reflection in the church are listed.

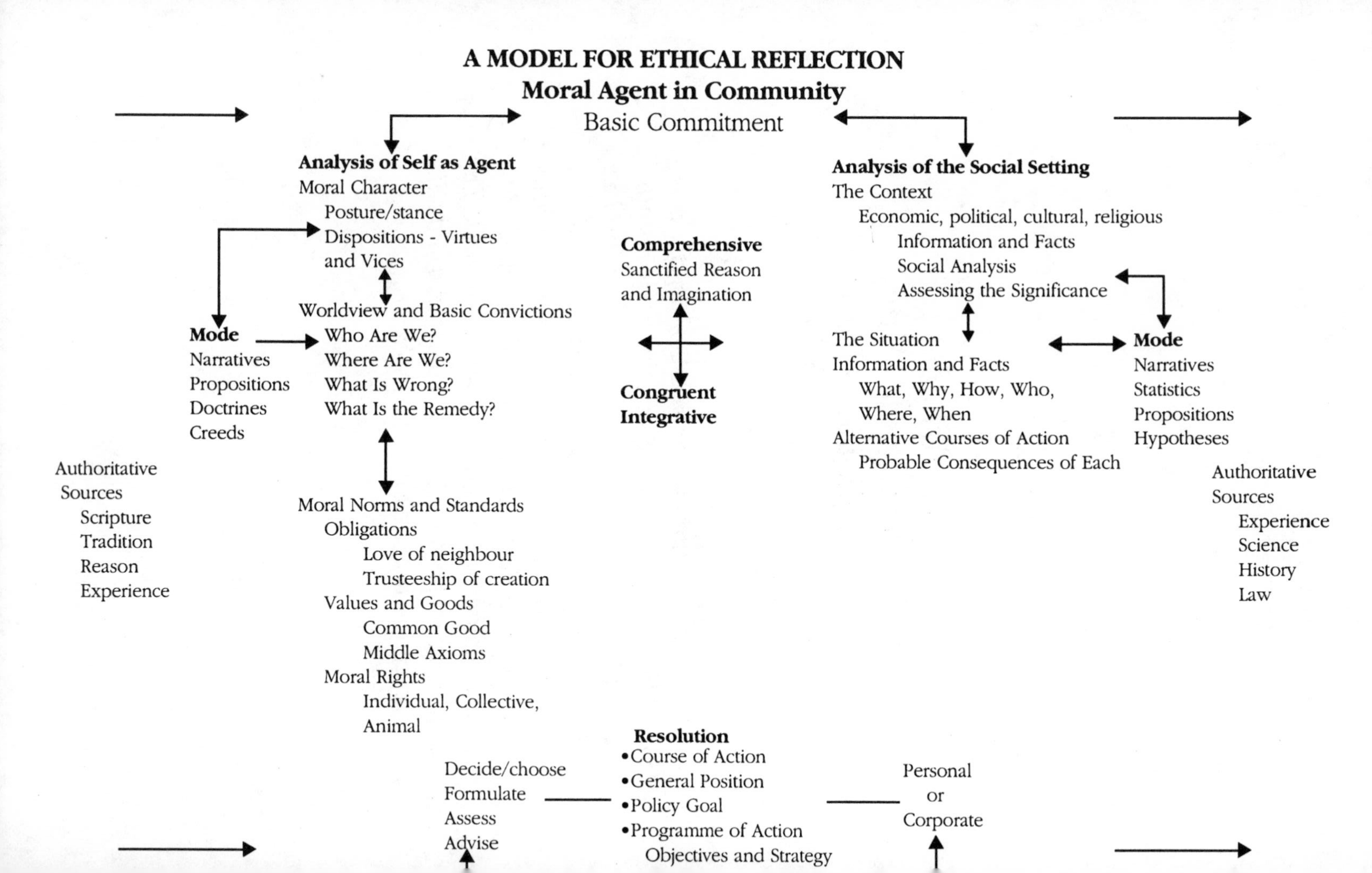
A MODEL FOR ETHICAL REFLECTION
Moral Agent in Community
Basic Commitment
Analysis of Self as Agent
Moral Character
Posture/stance
Dispositions - Virtues and Vices
Worldview and Basic Convictions
Who Are We?
Where Are We?
What Is Wrong?
What Is the Remedy?
Mode
Narratives
Propositions
Doctrines
Creeds
Authoritative Sources
Scripture
Tradition
Reason
Experience
Moral Norms and Standards
Obligations
Love of neighbour
Trusteeship of creation
Values and Goods
Common Good
Middle Axioms
Moral Rights
Individual, Collective, Animal
Comprehensive
Sanctified Reason and Imagination
Congruent
Integrative
Analysis of the Social Setting
The Context
Economic, political, cultural, religious
Information and Facts
Social Analysis
Assessing the Significance
The Situation
Information and Facts
What, Why, How, Who, Where, When
Alternative Courses of Action
Probable Consequences of Each
Mode
Narratives
Statistics
Propositions
Hypotheses
Authoritative Sources
Experience
Science
History
Law
Decide/choose
Formulate
Assess
Advise
Resolution
•Course of Action
•General Position
•Policy Goal
•Programme of Action
Objectives and Strategy
Personal
or
Corporate

INTRODUCTION

Why is it when you try to do something about mosquitoes in Florida, you wind up with deadly chemicals in mammals in the Arctic? Why is it when one clarinet is out of tune, the entire orchestra sounds "off"? The answer is obvious: both the environment and the orchestra are integrated wholes. They are intricate webs of related, living entities. Start looking at one aspect and it leads you to another that turns out to be connected to many more. The leg bone is connected to the thigh bone, the thigh bone is connected to the hip bone, and so on. The moral life, which entails both the good being and the right doing of human beings, is such an integrated whole.

This book has been exploring Christian ethics as a discipline concerned with reflecting upon the moral life from the perspective of Christian faith. The objective is to work with the Holy Spirit to bring all aspects of this integrated whole into accord with the new creation inaugurated in Christ. In doing so, we begin to discern more clearly the Way God intends for us. We may also be empowered to walk in this Way.

Different aspects of the moral life have been identified as five "base points" for ethical reflection. I have likened them to different sections of a "moral orchestra." These are norms and standards; moral character; worldview and basic convictions; what is happening, both in a specific situation and the wider social context in which moral living and decisions take place; and the authoritative sources from which comes the content for each of these facets of the moral life.

One question now remains: How are these various aspects or ingredients related? Should all of them bear with equal weight upon questions concerning the Way?

PERCEIVING THE LINKS: ETHICAL THEORIES AND METHODS

The use of the base points in reflecting on the moral life brings us to the issue of ethical method. What considerations go into making a moral decision? Should norms be the only factor that guides us, or should we rely on our dispositions? How should the various considerations relate to each other? Maybe some should count for more than others. The answers provide a good indicator of a person's ethical method.

Behind each method lie assumptions about the nature of the moral life itself. Does it consist only of habits of the heart or does it also include standards of behaviour? How are these different aspects related to each other? We are now opening up the issue of ethical theory. In other words, how you apply something reveals some particular understanding of what that thing is. This book is not about ethical theories. However, of necessity it reveals a particular theory about the moral life. I have been claiming that the moral life is an integrated whole, that it consists of norms, character, and so on. We have yet to see what relationship between these different aspects of the moral life is accorded by this theory. This will now become apparent in the following discussion about method and we should also begin to get some idea as to how this theory and method are distinguished from others.

Let us begin by glancing at a few different ethical methods. One method places a strong emphasis on norms and standards, with some attention to the situation; the orchestra of the moral life is limited, more like a brass and percussion band. However, there are different emphases within this approach. Thus, one answer to the question What am I to do? is that we should look only to obligation types of norms (principles, rules, and guidelines). These are then applied to the particular situation and moral duty is thereby determined in terms of what actions are intrinsically right or wrong. (In philosophy, this is labelled "deontology."[1])

A different answer, but one that nonetheless still relies almost completely on norms and standards, says that we should look to values and goods. In this approach, the likely consequences of a given action are analyzed in order to determine which goods and values would be achieved. The question asked is, Which action in any given situation will produce the greatest amount of "utility" (variously defined) for the largest number of persons? This "bottom line" question characterizes "act utilitarianism," a method widely operative in modern, liberal cultures.

A much older, alternative variation of this consequentialist method, common in Roman Catholic moral theology, is called "teleology." It focuses on the ultimate end or purpose of human life, namely, union with God. The key question to be answered from this perspective is, What action will be most conducive to achieving values and goods that in turn will lead to this ultimate end?

A more recent approach called "proportionalism" retains the focus on the ultimate end of human life and the values and goods appropriate to achieving it.[2] However, it is more sophisticated in its understanding of the complexity of human relations and thus the range of goods and evils likely to result from any proposed action. The method looks at intentions and intrinsic features of the actions themselves. It also takes into consideration the likely effects on the complex of human relationships that are involved. In light of all this, the question asked is, Which alternative course of action would not intend wrong and would result in a proportionally greater amount of good over evil? This method, then, like most contemporary Protestant ethics, attempts to take into account all types of moral norms and standards having to do with both actions themselves and their likely consequences. The full orchestral range of brass and percussion are sounding out.

Yet another ethical method places basic convictions at the centre, together with an analysis of the situation and context. The moral orchestra becomes a string ensemble with percussion. Proponents differ as to which basic convictions are judged to be central and in how to move from such convictions to particular moral decisions. For instance, some place a strong emphasis on an understanding of God's creative and redemptive purpose and activity. From there they attempt to move, in an almost intuitive way, to what God is now requiring us to do in a particular situation.

Recently there has been a revival of "virtue ethics." This has happened partly as a corrective to prevailing methods that are perceived to have concentrated on dilemmas that arise at the boundaries of life (thus the term "quandary ethics"). The enduring qualities of moral being seem to be neglected. Moral character, both of a community as a whole and of individuals, becomes the centre of an ethical method. The moral orchestra has dwindled to a woodwind ensemble.

RELATIONAL-RESPONSIBILITY METHOD

The ethical method that I operate with is a particular variation of an approach labelled "relational-responsibility."[3] I did not originally come to this approach through any of the noted Christian ethicists who developed it, even though I have since learned so much from them. Rather, I began nearly thirty years ago to draft a very rough version of the diagram we have been using, which represents the view of ethical reflection I offer here. This was in an effort to describe the factors that appeared to me to be operative in the ethical reflection of my mentors (Reinhold Niebuhr, John Bennett, and William Temple). Needless to say, this diagram has been further hammered out and refined as a result of my struggles over the years in various social and personal issues and from knowledge garnered from the ethicists who espouse this approach.

From the relational-responsibility point of view, the foundation of moral life and ethics is response to God's grace, as stated in the introduction. The moral life is characterized primarily by multiple relationships. Central to ethical reflection, therefore, is proper attention to these relationships with God, neighbour, the world (including other-than-human creation), and self. In this book I have made, without supporting argument, other assertions that are in accord with the relational-responsibility ethical theory. A key one is the claim that the five kinds of considerations or base points named correspond to different facets of the actual moral life of persons. They are therefore operative in one way or another in human moral life, whether or not they are acknowledged. Related to this premise is the view that ethical method should be comprehensive, congruent, and integrative. The first two of these characteristics require only brief comment since they simply make explicit what has been implicit throughout earlier chapters. The integrative quality requires more extensive exploration.

Comprehensive

A sound ethical method should attend explicitly to all facets of the moral life and therefore to the base points that attempt to delineate them. In many other theories of ethics only some of these facets are acknowledged, and in the corresponding methods, as we just saw, are therefore not considered. Yet whatever the theory or method, it is very difficult in actual practice to ignore entirely the facets of the moral life that the theory neglects. Thus, those methods that attend primarily to norms and standards must operate at least implicitly with assumptions about human well-being. Those that attempt to rely only on convictions frequently appeal to principles they, in theory, reject.

If this is true, then it makes sense to openly examine those factors that are actually operative. "The bane of ethics," says Daniel Maguire, "is incompleteness."[4] He is referring particularly to the need for careful, even exhaustive, analysis of all the factors involved in the situation when a moral decision must be made. However, I think it applies equally to the importance of considering the full orb of the moral life. The full orchestra of the moral life is there. We should, in our ethical reflection, attend to all of it.

Congruent

A second feature of a sound method of ethical reflection suggested here is congruency. There should be internal consistency within a particular facet or base point. For example, dispositions we hold to be virtuous should not be in fact mutually contradictory: aggressiveness is hardly congruent with patience. We also need to seek congruency between the various aspects of the moral life so that our basic convictions, dispositions, and norms are in harmony. If the full orchestra of the moral life is called upon, we must be sure that the same music is being played so we hear harmony rather than discord.

This follows from yet another kind of congruency; namely, the accord of all the facets of the moral life with what we know of God's will and purpose through Jesus Christ. Christians are concerned with the transformation of the total self. They should therefore seek to bring all facets of the moral life into harmony with the new life in Christ. Each aspect of the moral life, conceptualized as a base point and thereby available for reflection, is to be scrutinized in light of the gospel, and its content changed as needed to bring it into accord. Our habits of the heart; our convictions about God, creation, human nature and redemption; and our moral standards: the more these are in harmony with what we perceive God's will and purpose to be, the more congruent they will be with each other. We will then be more able to discern rightly what God is willing us and enabling us to be and do.

In any given situation, the prescriptions of a principle (such as respecting the self-directed choices of others) may conflict with one of our inclinations (such as the need to protect). We then need to test to see whether there really is an incongruity and, if so, whether it resides in the fact that we have not yet brought one or both into harmony with Jesus Christ. Likewise, if it appears that one particular virtue (for example, the virtue of justice, which entails a certain impartiality) is in conflict with another virtue (for example, the virtue of caring, which is sensitive to the exceptional needs of some persons), we then need to probe for a deeper interpretation of them. In light of a commitment to Christ and a proper understanding of love of neighbour, it may well be that the apparent conflict between such virtues is only incidental and not fundamental.[5]

Integrative

Ethical reflection according to the relational-responsibility method should not only be comprehensive and congruent but also integrative. This means bringing all the various base points or aspects of the moral life to bear on whatever question regarding the moral life is under consideration and giving each aspect appropriate weight. Let us see how this works out with moral decisions.

One step in any decision-making situation is to examine what is happening and to consider possible alternative courses of action. We have seen that basic convictions, character, and standards are integral to such an assessment. Another step is to ask which of the actual action alternatives available is most in accord with an integrated set of virtues, basic convictions, and norms and standards. If these have been thought through in light of a commitment to Christ, then the norms and virtues will be congruent with basic convictions. Thus we can focus on norms and virtues and still be comprehensive.

Next we can ask the following questions about each possible course of action: Does it yield the best consequences in terms of our standards of goods and values? Is it in accord with the various principles of love of neighbour and trusteeship of creation? We should also ask, Which course of action is most in accord with the dispositions of myself and my community that we deem to be virtuous? What habits of the heart does it reflect and will it foster? Together these steps bring all the base points to bear on the decision in an integrated way. They will provide us with reasons for or against each of the competing courses of action. Usually one particular action is indicated and our moral decision is made.

Bringing all the base points to bear on a moral decision, however, can result in conflicting guidance. Sometimes, for example, the principles seem to point to a course of action that is different from the direction commended by the dispositions of our hearts. What are we to do in such cases? We may be pressed to re-do our homework. First, we can check to see if indeed there are any other possible courses of action that would avoid these conflicts. Second, we can see if the conflicts are only apparent or if they are real. A closer examination and interpretation of both the principles and virtues involved in light of basic convictions may resolve the matter. But if the conflict is real and persistent, then we have a genuine moral dilemma.

We live within complex sets of human relationships, each with its own kind of obligation. Consequently, we are sometimes faced with a multiplicity of claims, all of which cannot be met. This results in moral dilemmas. Sometimes we are faced with alternative courses of action, all of which violate one or more aspects of the moral life. Each viable alternative contravenes a basic norm or is contrary to a fundamental disposition or flies in the face of a particular basic conviction. Again, the result is a moral dilemma.

Such "hard cases" throw the question of what moral "weight" is to be granted to different base points, or to various components within a base point, into sharp relief. This tests the mettle of all ethical methods and is where differences between them become most apparent. For example, one way of resolving such conflicts is to appeal to a pre-established priority, say, of norms over virtues. As we saw earlier, certain kinds of consequentionalists would give priority to goods and values over obligations. Therefore, the action that generates the greatest good for the greatest number should be chosen. Deontologists would argue that obligation-type principles should receive priority over goods and values. Even then, however, the problem remains as to which obligations should take priority over others. Should fidelity to promises always take precedence over truth-telling or vice versa? A set of standards for appropriately weighting standards is required.

The comprehensive and integrative features of a relational-responsibility method show us the importance of giving "due weight" to all the base points. The goal is to attend to all the different facets of the moral life and find the action that seems most in harmony with them. There must be, according to this method, "good reasons" for overriding or setting aside any of them. This is the point at which some of the weaknesses of this method emerge. The wholistic balancing seems complex, time-consuming, and rather vague, at least in the face of urgent moral decisions.

One such instance of this involved a difficult case concerning abortion, under discussion by an ecumenical class at a Roman Catholic seminary. Needless to say, the engagement was heated. I was attempting to teach this version of a relational-responsibility method to the class. Finally one of the students said in exasperation, "The trouble is, by the time you weighed all these factors, nine months would be up, and she would have had her baby!" Fortunately, most moral decisions are not intractable dilemmas that require exhaustive ethical reflection. But critics are correct in observing its lack of precision or clear formulas for arriving at decisions. It requires a refined moral sensitivity developed over time more so than those methods that rely primarily on moral standards. One critical commentator has said, "To caricature this method's weakness one could say that it raises 'muddling through' to the undeserved heights of ethical sophistication.... Anyone who follows this method must learn to live with ambiguity and an uneasy conscience and be ready to revise one's judgment as the evidence changes."[6]

Can some of these weaknesses be overcome without losing the profound insights into the moral life that are the great strength of this approach? There are three things, I think, that can help us in the hard cases. First, important gains in clarity and rigour can be made by spelling out more carefully what the "due weight" is that is supposed to be given to all the base points. My own view is that while giving due weight to all the base points and the elements in them is essential, it does not properly mean giving them equal weight. Not all of the moral claims found in the base points should have equal force upon us; a stronger moral claim should not be surrendered for a weaker one. It is appropriate to attach greater moral weight to certain moral standards over others. However, it is important to note that this is quite different than assigning a fixed priority. For example, I think that principles of obligation should count for more in a moral decision than goods and values used to assess consequences. Again, this is not an absolute prioritizing of one set over the other but a relative weighing between them.

I assign greater weight to obligations for two reasons. One is the basic conviction stated earlier: the world as God has created it is basically relational. Human beings are created for relationship with God, with one another, and with other-than-human creation. The obligations that are integral to right relationships, therefore, should receive greater weight or attention than other types of norms. Second, we can never be very certain or clear as to the likely consequences of our actions, even upon those most immediately affected, let alone the wider or longer term implications of such actions. The ramifications are usually many and not entirely predictable. Therefore I think we should focus more heavily on right relationships than we do on outcomes. This does not mean, of course, that consequences should not be weighed or that they are unimportant in any ethical reflection. It means, rather, that they are not given as much weight in a decision-making situation as is given to the obligations that bind us to one another and to God. In summary, all moral standards and virtues congruent with a basic commitment to Christ should count in ethical reflection, but some should count more than others.

A second thing that will help us in the hard cases is clarity about what should count as "good reasons" for overriding some moral considerations in favour of others, in situations where all of them cannot be realized. As Christians we recognize a variety of norms, each of which represents a prime obligation. The philosopher's word for them is *prima facie,* meaning, on first appearance. There have to be very good reasons for overriding any of these or setting them aside. However, in hard case circumstances, we may be forced to. You may promise your children that you will take them on a particular outing. They have been looking forward to it. But on the way home from work, you witness an accident. A person's life is in jeopardy, and your immediate assistance is needed. The *prima facie* duty to care for the person who is threatened with death will likely override the *prima facie* duty to keep your promise to your children.

Or take the example of an economic situation in which, for the sake of achieving efficient production and thereby increasing the amount available to all, it may be wise to pay more for some kinds of work or demand less tax on certain kinds of investments. Goods would thereby be distributed less equally. In these instances, a *prima facie* responsibility, such as promise keeping, or a value, such as equal distribution, should not be overridden lightly but only for good reasons. What kind of reasons should count?

The answer once again varies according to ethical method. I suggest that a *prima facie* norm may legitimately be overridden when all available courses of action will otherwise entail *(a)* transgressing a norm or virtue which is appropriately regarded as more fundamental; *(b)* transgressing other norms and virtues that together weigh more heavily; or *(c)* when setting aside a particular norm or virtue will in the long term justify and uphold it.[7]

A third means of assistance for helping with hard cases is of more limited use. This is the comparison of cases. The first step is to find a similar case to the one which puzzles us, choosing one in which we can make a firm moral judgement. Then we assess by analogy. Since clearly such-and-such should be done in the nonpuzzle case, then we should do the same thing in the puzzle case, provided that there are not morally relevant differences between them.[8] But the case comparison method has a major drawback. It is often hard to find parallel cases in which there are no morally relevant differences.

A proportionate weighing of norms, clear reasons for setting aside some primary responsibilities in favour of others, and case comparison — all three can assist this variation of a relational-responsibility ethical method in reflecting on hard case moral decisions. In the final analysis, however, integrating all of the base points and bringing them to bear upon a moral decision requires a kind of sanctified imagination.

As nearly all Christian ethicists and moral philosophers have recognized, there is, finally, an intuitive element in moral decisions. Illumination by the Holy Spirit is vital, not as a substitute for our ethical reflection, but as a source of empowerment and illumination of that reflection. There is a need, in other words, not only for careful reasoning, drawing on all the base points, but also for creative and sanctified imagination: imagination that helps us to see new alternative forms of action that might be less violating of one or more of our convictions and principles; imagination that helps us finally fit together the various elements of all the base points in a way that is in keeping with our relationship with God, other human beings, and creation.

This method requires "a 'sympathetic' sense or a 'fine feeling' of what fits the relational context. The method recognizes that making a moral decision is more an art than a science. As such, it requires a mode of thinking which is grounded in a *well-ordered heart*."[9] Such a heart is formed and nurtured by all the "means of grace." It is strengthened by regular prayer, which is attention to the presence of God. In the terms we used earlier, it entails an ongoing process of sanctification by grace.

We have been using hard cases to explain and test the relational-responsibility method. However, an ethical method is not a neat technique for making moral decisions but is rather a process for thinking about the moral life in general. It should be helpful preparation for moral decision making, which is only one aspect of the Way.

This was my response to the student engaged in the abortion debate, who complained about a nine-month decision process. The test of an ethical method is not whether it provides a handy instrument that we can simply apply to solve urgent dilemmas. The test is whether it allows us to examine the various aspects of the moral life so that we can bring them more into accord with Christ. It should assist us in making our habitual way of being and acting more faithful. Then, when we are confronted by difficult moral decisions, we will be ready.

The hope is that, increasingly, each of us will approach any dilemma as an integrated person shaped by the spirit of Christ. Our eyes will be opened so we can perceive what is really happening and what the central moral question is. Our ears will be educated to pick out the distinctive "sounds" of various aspects of the moral life most at issue. Our minds will be trained to weigh and apply various moral considerations quickly. Our sensitivities, dispositions, and imaginations will be cultivated so that our final moral decision is likely to be more, rather than less, faithful to God's Way. In short, we will have that "well-ordered heart."

We have been engaged in such preparation on this journey. We have begun the work of Christian ethics. We have been practising our scales, so to speak. We have been rehearsing the different sections of the moral orchestra, balancing the sound, honing technique, in preparation. We know, however, that when we finally perform a work, whether it is familiar or something new, an additional, intangible element will need to be present if it is to be truly artistic. The players and conductor must have music in their souls as well as technical expertise.

Much of the time, it is true, most of us do not function at this level of moral virtuosity. But it is important to know that all the aspects of the moral life, the base points, the sections of the orchestra, continue to be operative in us. They are there in a simplified, more packaged form. We travel on automatic pilot. The daily demands of complex, changing relationships and conditions demand some such simplification. One form this takes, especially in more stable societies, is morality and behaviour according to custom or code. But another form it takes in modern societies is ideology. Because this has such a powerful, motivating, and guiding force, we should look at ideology more closely before concluding our exploration.

IDEOLOGY: THE NECESSARY BUT DANGEROUS SIMPLIFIER

What Is Ideology?

The term "ideology" has a number of different meanings. In its broadest sense it refers to any set of beliefs or ideas about social reality. But in the sense in which I mean it here, ideology is an idea system that relates beliefs and ethics to political goals and strategies. Ideologies of this kind attempt to unite ideas, behaviour, and character. "They demand a hardening of commitment."[10] They are an amalgam "of information, ideas, purposes, and emotional tones."[11] Thus we speak of a socialist ideology or a liberal ideology or a conservative ideology or, more recently, a "green" or "feminist" ideology. Each has its own particular set of moral values, standards, social analysis, and policy formation. I believe that ideologies, in this sense, are really packaged and simplified formulations of the ethical base points that we have been examining.

Consider this: Any typical ideology includes a certain posture towards life, a set of dispositions that it regards as virtuous and others that it regards as vices. It has underlying convictions combined with certain norms and standards that are affixed to a particular social theory and analysis. From all this comes a set of formulated responses for action in the present social realm. Roger Shinn, a contemporary Christian ethicist, observes that "usually ideology takes shape in slogans, not necessarily consistent. The slogans are sources of comfort and are often weapons." He cites some familiar ones, such as "one person, one vote," "sexual equality," "self-determination," "small is beautiful," "minority rights," and so on.[12]

The advantage of ideologies of this kind, then, is that by such selection and fixing of the base points, they enable us to be comprehensive in the sense of including all the various aspects of the moral life. This is done in a simplified way that helps us move practically to policies and decisions. In comparison, the complexity and web of relationships in life, together with the myriad possibilities for the content of each base point, tends to be overwhelming. In short, ideologies serve as a kind of fighting creed that gives us clear direction and helps us deal with the variety of issues that confront us.

The Dark Side of Ideology

The problem is that ideologies of this kind can also be dangerous. They have a dark side. The convenient packaging can easily become fixed, closed, and thereby resistant to any experience or empirical data that does not fit its "box." The selectivity and simplification that can lead to "sharpened perception and creative action" can also easily lead to "purposeful ignorance, distortion of information, and destruction." As Julius Lester, a black American leader in the sixties, complained, asking an ideologue a question is like putting the correct change in a Coke machine: the response is totally predictable.

This dark side of ideologies is what lies behind Karl Marx's critical analysis of ideology and the rather negative connotation the term has generally had in much of modern thought. This is expressed in the common epithet used to dismiss some position as "merely ideological." Marx was concerned that these idea systems that link ideals and moral vision to practical issues and problems tend to function as masks. They often hide the vested interests of privileged groups behind lofty sounding rationales. Ideologies can, without the intention or awareness of their believers, easily function to distort reality, to stereotype persons, to justify or obscure particular interests and power realities.

Reinhold Niebuhr saw another masking function of ideologies. Besides cloaking the interest of a group, they can also cloak an uneasy conscience. Ideologies can "obscure the deep tension between the individual conscience and the moral realities of man's collective life ... a reminder to individual man of the moral ambiguity of all human virtue."[13]

Further, ideologies can quickly become religious substitutes. In such cases, a person's identity may be formed and sustained by the ideology. Such a person is likely to cling to the formulated perceptions of reality of their particular ideology rather than risk the threat of change by acknowledging the existence of new conditions or fresh social analysis. The terrible fanaticisms that can be generated by this kind of idolatry of an ideology have been all too apparent in fascism and Marxist-Leninism. Some of the major divisions among Christians today are as much around ideological packages as around particular theological disputes.

Christians and Ideology

In light of these both positive and negative functions, how are Christians to relate to ideology? Is there a way of holding on to the positive function of ideologies without slipping into their dark side? The task is very difficult, but there are possibilities of at least mitigating the negative features of ideologies.

Acknowledging Ideology. One important step is the acknowledgement that, in modern societies at least, all persons inevitably operate with an ideology. It is necessary to bring such ideologies to awareness if they are to be kept under critical scrutiny. The more people and groups ignore or deny having an ideology, the more powerful the ideology becomes and the more it is apt to function negatively.

During the sixties, some social scientists and some proponents of secular theology observed the decline of older ideologies. They promptly proclaimed a new era free of ideologies. Ideologies would be replaced by a new, flexible, pragmatic approach to politics, oriented to empirical analysis by experts, free from grand theories and ideals. Indeed, this vision has since become espoused in many parts of the globe.

Whatever the merits or lackings of this pragmatism, it does not avoid the problems of ideology. On the contrary, it is itself an ideology. For example, the vaunted criteria for testing public policy is, "Will it work?" But this must contain assumptions about worthy ends, namely, "Work for what?" Its proponents assume this new secular society and the "end-of-ideology" era will embody such values as basic human rights, a measure of freedom, equality, and justice. It will include, along with a "religiously neutral" state, a pluralistic culture, a mixed economy, and welfare social system. That this is an ideology becomes clear when it is challenged by rival ideologies. Thus its exponents want it to prevail over both communism and traditional cultures in the developing world.[14]

The point to be made here is that refusal to acknowledge this as an ideology makes it more difficult to safeguard against the dangers of closed dogmatism and masking of interests. Thus, nonmodern societies experience this pragmatism as masking the cultural and industrial imperialism of modern nations. Those concerned with the environment discover its resistance to changing what one early critic discerned: namely, its hidden, assumed compulsion to economic growth.[15] Ironically, these were the very problems the supporters of this secular "pragmatism" sought to avoid in the first place.

Relativizing Ideology. Another way of mitigating the dangers of ideology is to avoid granting it a high degree of religious sanction. Such legitimation only increases the tendency to absolutism.

How, then, should the Christian faith be related to ideologies? Important insights concerning this can be gained by noting the various ways in which the Christian faith was connected in practice to an assortment of socialist ideologies by a range of Christian thinkers, from the mid-nineteenth to the mid-twentieth century. Their own reflections on this relationship are also illuminating.[16] Two main types of relationship between faith and ideology, each with its own variations, are found among their writings.

The first type makes a lofty religious claim for an ideology, in this case, socialism. One can label this approach as "Christians, therefore socialists" (or some other ideology). If one is a Christian, it follows from the very nature of the faith that he or she must be a socialist. Conversely, if he or she is a socialist, one is either implicitly a Christian or very close to the faith, even if not aware of this fact. In one variation of this, the Christian faith was reduced to an ethical idealism and then combined with Leninist socialism to create a new "mature" Christian religion. In a more plausible variation, the Christian faith retained a transcendent element, and socialism was viewed as the necessary economic and political basis for the kingdom of God on earth. In my judgement, the claim that any ideology is the true essence of the Christian faith or even the political expression of Christianity, the basis of the kingdom, is unwarranted. It simply provides the religious sanction that enhances all the dangers of ideology.

A second type of relationship between the Christian faith and ideology sees only a provisional, not a necessary, relationship between the two. This may be labelled "Christians *and* socialists" (or some other ideology). In one variation, socialism was regarded as the temporary, imperfect vessel of God's judgement and grace in history. Christian alliance with it was regarded as an imperative for a particular moment in history, but not necessarily in the future. In another variation, socialism was regarded as simply the tool for the next step in social justice. The relationship between Christianity and an ideology was seen in practical, ethical terms rather than religious ones.

The experience of Christian socialism demonstrates that this more pragmatic and relative type of relationship between the Christian faith and a political ideology reduces, though it does not eliminate, both the masking function of ideologies and their tendency to become closed, rigid, and dogmatic. The acceptance of the relativity of any ideology is a major factor in keeping it open to change in the light of experience and altered conditions.

It is important to note, however, that even more modest claims for ideologies do not entirely eliminate their dark side. The recognition by the "Christians and socialists" group of the relative nature of all ideals and programmes did not eliminate the masking function of the ideology they espoused. "The Christian politics of a moralist socialism," Niebuhr observed in retrospect, "hid the power realities of a collectivist state behind the concept of 'cooperation' interpreted as Christian love."[17] The ideology of the Christian and secular left, whatever modest claims were made for it, also "tended to obscure moral perplexities in man's social life which are perennial and not merely the fruit of capitalism or any other form of social organization." The recognition of persistent dangers with ideologies is a vital, though again inadequate, safeguard.[18]

Critical Scrutiny of Ideology. The enterprise of Christian ethics as critical reflection can provide yet another check against the hazards of ideology. One of the tasks of Christian ethics in relation to ideology is to keep ideologues as aware as possible of the dangers and urge them to keep it open to change in light of shifting realities. This is not, however, an easy task, since ideology, including its dark side, becomes intertwined in ethics itself. In addition, such a critical enterprise is resisted by strong ideologues. This resistance is similar to that of moralists: both become so convinced that they are right that careful thought about the Way seems a waste of time, if not subversive. As for sanctification, it simply means being more vigorous in support of the ideology. The Christian ethical enterprise is seen by them as either superfluous, since the Way is obvious and unambiguous, or else it is resented as disloyal.

Nevertheless, an ethic should be able to provide some critical analysis of ideology. It can do this if it is an ethic that recognizes its own ideological factors; if it is grounded in a basic commitment to Christ; and further, if it is disciplined in being comprehensive, congruent, and integrative in its use of the base points. Such an ethic can challenge the particular interpretation of those same base points, which so often become simplified to the point of distortion and congealed in any ideology. Be warned: such scrutiny should include the ideology espoused by the ethical reflector! All political programmes and policies and all ideologies surrounding them are found wanting under the measuring rod of God's love and justice, as Niebuhr reminds us. None warrant our absolute loyalty. That loyalty belongs to God alone.

There are important relative differences between rival ideologies. Some are more in accord with God's purpose and action in a given context than others. Christians may critically support such an ideology as the next step to higher justice. Their commitment, however, should be only provisional, with knowledge of both the moral ambiguity of all ideologies and the imperfect justice that will be actually achieved. Christians must be sensitive to the fact that even this relative acknowledgement of merit for an ideology will help it to function as a cloak for group interests and as a mask for an uneasy conscience.

The kind of ethical reflection that keeps ideology, including its own, under critical scrutiny is most feasible in the context of the ecumenical community of faith, which spans many eras, cultures, classes, and the like. In such a company, one's own ideology is most likely to be revealed and challenged in light of a common commitment to Christ. This brings us to the role of the church in moral deliberation.

THE CHURCH AND MORAL DELIBERATION

We have seen that the Christian church is involved in the moral life as a community that helps to form moral character and as a bearer of the Christian moral tradition. It is also, of course, continually involved in moral action. It is involved in such action, first of all, as a *gathered community,* in terms of the way in which it organizes and governs its collective life and in the way members treat each other. The gathered community is also usually involved in activities within the greater society in which it is set. This takes the form of social service, such as developing housing for lower income groups or the elderly, in providing hospitals to serve those in remote areas, and in a whole range of caring for human beings. It also takes the form of social action in which the church, through its agencies and officials, may advocate certain public policies or join with ecumenical coalitions or secular alliances to promote selected policies and programmes. It often engages in educational enterprises to raise the awareness of people about particular social issues.

The main way in which the church is involved in moral activity, however, is through its members and their actions in the place where they live and work. This is the *dispersed community,* and it constitutes the major way Christians are involved in the world.

These activities entail a wide variety of moral tasks for both groups and individuals: *choosing* a course of action; *formulating* a general moral position on certain matters, such as euthanasia; *assessing* public policy goals or the actions of other groups, for example, with regards to unemployment; *advising* each other on particular programmes of action or strategy; *admonishing* each other concerning important personal and societal moral behaviour.

The basic moral question — What is God enabling and requiring us to be and do? — takes many different forms. Ethical reflection from a Christian perspective on these various moral tasks is demanding, as we have seen, especially if it is to be comprehensive, congruent, and integrative. It is imperative, therefore, for the church to relate to the moral life in yet one more way. It must be a community of moral and ethical deliberation.

By deliberation I mean much more than speculation, discussion, or even debate. I mean, with regard to significant moral tasks, a disciplined process of ethical reflection: gathering data, consulting, reflecting on the data, making a proposal, entertaining counter-proposals, doing more research, testing these in light of scripture and the Christian tradition.

The kind of moral deliberation that I am claiming the churches should be engaged in is well illustrated by several different hospital ethics committees in which I participate. They function as communities of moral deliberation when they discuss what action to recommend in a particular case or when they seek to formulate a more general policy. Members come from diverse backgrounds and hold differing convictions, but they share a common commitment and loyalty to certain fundamental moral principles related to health care. In light of these principles, we are able to discuss, argue, and debate the moral appropriateness of various alternative courses of action. Since the issues before us are usually matters of life and death, the discussion is often emotionally intense. Yet mutual respect enables it to be civil and productive.

I am always surprised at how frequently a consensus is reached by the group, though it often requires considerable time and discussion. In any case, comprehensiveness in ethical reflection is made more possible and likely by such a group discussion than if left to any one of us alone. The range of expertise available in the group brings out the full facts of the case, with all the problematics of diagnosis and prognosis. Various perspectives on the patient emerge in the discussion, as do some of the implicit operating assumptions of those involved, which can then be identified and challenged. The application of the norms and standards that guide our moral decisions is well tested.

This kind of careful, civil moral deliberation can, should, and occasionally does take place within the churches. There need to be more opportunities for working through together what God is enabling and requiring us to be and do, given the confusing times in which we live.

There is also an increasing need for deliberation in the

churches about what should go into such moral consultation. What should the content be of the ethical base points themselves that are used to reflect on moral questions? We have looked at some of the important differences and disputes regarding these. How do Christians take counsel together about these matters? This might be designated as ethical deliberation.

The issue of homosexuality, which has been before most mainline Protestant churches in the last decade, illustrates this point. When discussing or deliberating on the important moral question of the acceptance of and care for persons of homosexual orientation, the matter is one of bringing the familiar moral norms and standards, basic convictions, virtues, and all the base points that we have been discussing to bear on the question. However, when the churches are asked to formulate a general position on what, from a Christian perspective, is the appropriate way to live out a homosexual orientation, another level of deliberation emerges. It is called into play by the challenge to the familiar rules and guidelines that Christians have used for governing sexual behaviour, including the goods and values to be sought in sexual union. This in turn raises questions around the basic convictions concerning the meaning and purpose of sexuality in God's creative and redemptive purpose.

Not just the application of ethical base points to a particular moral question is at issue, then. Rather the content of some of those base points themselves becomes a matter of dispute. This in turn drives us back to a more careful examination of the authoritative sources we use for formulating the content of ethical bases — the place of scripture, tradition, reason, experience. Proposed changes in basic convictions, and the norms that express them, have far-reaching implications not only for sexuality but for other areas of human behaviour. This is one of the reasons that the question of homosexual behaviour has been so vexing and controversial in the church. Many Protestant denominations are ill equipped to publicly deliberate in a systematic, disciplined, and responsible way on ethical matters (what should go into moral decisions) as distinct from moral questions (what should we be and do).

A number of factors are essential if the church is to engage in faithful moral and ethical deliberation. The first is that "the community and its leaders need to be able to delineate some *moral tradition* in which they stand."[19] This connects to our earlier discussion of authoritative sources for understanding God's will and to the church's role as bearer of moral tradition. Second, an *ethical framework* is needed, i.e., identification of the kinds of considerations that do and should go into making faithful moral decisions from the Christian perspective. This includes an ethical method for testing and applying them. James Gustafson suggests that the minister might well be the ethical resource person for this key ingredient of moral deliberation.

A third essential factor is some kind of common *moral language,* known and understood by participants. Much of the language used by church members is therapeutic; that is, "the language of salvation, self-fulfillment, relief from guilt and anxiety, in short, the language of what religion can do for you (i.e., your self-interest)." But a good portion of biblical language, and that of Western religious tradition, is "religious-moral" language: "the language of command, obedience, of responsibility, of good and evil, of right and wrong, better and worse." This language, as we have already seen, need not only be concerned with moral norms but also may point to morally exemplary persons and actions through parable or through narrative and story.

Fourth, there must be *forums* in the church where moral and ethical deliberation can take place. Regrettably, there seem to be few such opportunities in most churches. In the course of my work, I conduct workshops on ethics for many different groups of people in the secular workplace — health care, business, social action movements. Invariably, after the workshop a number of people identify themselves as fellow Christians and ask longingly where they might find communities in which they may relate their faith to the difficult issues before them as workers and professionals. When I suggest they try their own congregation, the usual response is a look of shocked disbelief. Many have said forthrightly that that is the last place they would take a moral dilemma for scrutiny and discussion! Yet the need for such opportunities grows in proportion to the increasing pluralism of our culture and the church's minority status. Such forums of moral deliberation will not, of course, resolve all the uncertainties or the conflicts besetting the church. They will not guarantee that the right decisions are made. They may, however, help us to see more clearly where and why we differ and encourage us to move forward to more faithful decisions.

Fifth, appropriate *processes* is another requirement for good moral and ethical deliberation. Parliamentary procedure is the usual method for assemblies in Protestant churches. As a contemporary theologian observes, however, the parliamentary model, with its mechanistic paradigm of parts exerting pressure on one another, tends to excessively politicize the process of decision making. It is not conducive to responsible deliberation.

In a typical parliamentary procedure, "representatives of particular interest groups bargain with one another in order to achieve a majority, even a slim one, and thus to vanquish their opponents."[20] Important differences in moral viewpoints in this system tend, like other conflicts, to be regarded as merely conflicting interests. The object of rival interest groups then becomes winning as much of its way as possible by skilful parliamentary debate and manipulation. Resolution of continuing conflict takes the form of negotiating some form of compromise between factions. This is very different from respectfully listening to differing views (which is not simply the same as listening with pastoral concern), and seeking through discussion and argument to hold these differing viewpoints "under the scrutiny of word of God." This means testing varying perceptions in the light of a common reference. Community discernment and decision making regarding matters of faith and morals requires an atmosphere of communal seeking, rather than a partisan mood of adversarial debate.

Sixth, a *style of discourse* appropriate for inquiry that facilitates exploring, pondering, testing, persuading is needed for good community moral deliberation. The atmosphere of real deliberation on faith and morals "is one of communal seeking, not of debate. The purpose is not that one 'party' prevail, but that all discover the actual word of God to the whole community. One is not a representative of a faction, but a member of the community seeking ... to find God together in a specific corporate decision."[21] This requires a different style of discourse than that which is used to declare, exhort, convict, inspire and admonish, a style that is perhaps more familiar in the churches.

Let me give an example of what is meant by style or mode of discourse. At a recent international consultation on new forms of racism, representatives from various continents described the situation of racism now facing them. The British representative used a mode of discourse that invited scholarly debate but inhibited a broader kind of deliberation. The lone American was an Afro-American woman. She gave a powerful speech reciting her own experience and hurled angry "prophetic" anathemas regarding sexism at her listeners. When she finished, there were virtually no questions and no comments, unlike those following other presentations. This upset her even more. She was followed by a Mohawk woman, who also shared her own experience of racism and sexism, and who was equally full of anger and frustration. But her talk evoked a lively and illuminating discussion.

The American's presentation brought closure by its mode, style, and tone. There were only two options left to listeners: agree totally, confess, and repent; or turn away in anger or sorrow. The second invited us, through all the subtleties of style and tone, to struggle with the presenter in analyzing both the complex causes of these things and what to do about them. It was conducive to deliberation and appropriate to an event of consultation. The mode of discourse employed by the Afro-American was appropriate to certain kinds of preaching and political rallies, but not to consultations.

Seventh, good moral and ethical deliberation in and by a community of faith is sufficiently demanding that it requires the full range of the *variety of gifts* found in the church. The insight of persons who are most directly involved in the issue under discussion, who will be affected by decisions pertaining to it, are, as we have seen, invaluable, especially in discerning injustice and in describing the situation. The community of faith has rich resources of this kind, sometimes in the local congregation, but almost always in the church worldwide, past or present. Further, in its membership, the church has persons whose training, work, and experience in environmental, biomedical, economic, business, and politics brings special knowledge to bear on issues. Such persons can offer an assessment of likely outcomes, alternative courses of action, and insight into the whole base point of social situation and context. A bountiful variety of gifts, knowledge, and wisdom pertinent to other base points of ethical reflection is also to be found in the wider church. One small portion of these resources consists of Bible scholars, theologians, and even ethicists! Taken together, these assets provide promising potential for faithful moral and ethical deliberation in the churches. This deliberation, to be responsible, cannot be left to "experts" of any kind; it requires the full variety of gifts given to the church.

A CONCLUDING WORD

"... and grace will lead me home."

There is a Way of being and doing founded in God's will and purpose as revealed in Jesus Christ. We are moved by God's forgiving grace to participate in the transforming sanctification of the Holy Spirit, and thus to be ever more adept at discerning the Way and ever more empowered to live the Way. Christian ethics, as the enterprise of systematically reflecting on the Way, participates in this sanctification process. It attempts to discover and conceptualize the various facets of the moral life in order that we can work with the Holy Spirit to bring these facets within ourselves into greater congruency with God's will in Christ.

Christian ethics, however, is no cure for sin! Our discernment of the Way, let alone our ability to follow it in the midst of a fallen world, remains at best partial and distorted. Our journey may readily become a wandering. Even with the best of ethical reflection, our moral decisions may be wrong, and we may miss the Way. Christian ethics, like any other human enterprise, is subject to sin. It is sometimes used simply as propaganda for a cause. Or as a weapon to attack and demean others. Or as a tool for self-justification.

In the final analysis, our salvation is dependent upon God's mercy. Fortunately it is assured through the grace of forgiveness granted in Jesus Christ. Awareness of the deep power of sin, and trust in the even greater strength of God's gracious mercy, is foundational for engaging the confusions of our society. They help us to name and address the human experience of the gap between what we, in our more lucid moments, know we ought to be and do and our actual practice. Without resources of grace there is a strong tendency to deal with this gap by reducing moral standards and qualities of character to match common practice. This is all too obvious in modern societies and to some degree in churches that reflect these. The temptation is not to face the harsh realities that confront us but to pretend that things are better than the facts actually warrant. We are even inclined to call dubious conditions and behaviour good, making a "virtue of necessity." The workings of God's forgiving, transforming, and again, finally, merciful grace are described vividly and, for me, persuasively by theologian Ellen Charry:

> *Awareness of God's care comforts as it stimulates gratitude. God directs and prods us (who in Calvin's eyes are, according to Psalm 32:9, a cross between a horse that needs to be bridled and a mule that needs to be goaded) to become the person God intends us to be, dependent yet responsible, humble yet active, awestruck yet exuberant, morally culpable yet safe and defended.*[22]

We are given "the means of grace" — prayer, scripture, the sacraments, the fellowship of the community of faith. By diligent use of these means we may walk what Augustine called the narrow way between the pinnacle of pride, which assumes we know perfectly the moral truth and can live it, and the chasm of sloth, which despairs of righteous relationships and living.

NOTES

THE WAY: AN INTRODUCTION

1. Martin Luther, "Treatise on Christian Liberty," *Works of Martin Luther* (Philadelphia: Muhlenberg Press, 1943), 337.
2. Stanley Hauerwas and W. H. Willimon, *Resident Aliens* (Nashville: Abingdon Press, 1989), 92.
3. James Gustafson, *Can Ethics Be Christian?* (Chicago: University of Chicago Press, 1975), 156-7.
4. James Gustafson employs this term and it is now widely used in Christian ethics. See *Theology and Christian Ethics* (Philadelphia: Pilgrim Press, 1974), chap. 5.

I. MORAL NORMS AND STANDARDS

1. G. P. Horsefly, *A History of the True People: The Cherokee Indians* (Detroit: Oral History Publication by Rick Smith, 1979), 13.
2. Robert Horsefly, *A Fork in our Road* (unpublished manuscript), 43.
3. For development of this theme, see T. W. Ogletree, *The Use of the Bible in Christian Ethics* (Philadelphia: Fortress Press, 1983), 23.
4. Immanuel Kant, *Groundwork of the Metaphysic of Morals* (1785), trans. H. J. Paton (New York: Harper and Row, 1964).
5. Anders Nygren, *Agape* (Philadelphia: Westminster Press, 1953). This surveys the history of Christian thought in terms of how love has been variously understood.
6. The following owes much to Gene Outka, *Agape: An Ethical Analysis* (New Haven: Yale University Press, 1972), especially 9ff., and J. L. Allen, *Love and Conflict* (Nashville: Abingdon Press, 1984), 65ff.
7. Karl Barth, *Dogmatics*, IV, 2 (Edinburgh: T. & T. Clark, 1958), 745.
8. John Burnaby, in *The Westminster Dictionary of Christian Ethics* (Philadelphia: Westminster Press, 1986), 357.
9. For a good summary of this issue, see Outka, chap. 4.
10. Patrick D. Miller, Jr., "The Place of the Decalogue in the Old Testament and Its Law," *Interpretation*, XLIII/3 (July 1989), 232ff.
11. See J. W. McClendon, Jr., *Ethics: Systematic Theology, Vol. 1* (Nashville: Abingdon Press, 1986), 177ff.
12. Miller, 238.
13. For a more extensive treatment see Walter Harrelson, *The Ten Commandments and Human Rights* (Philadelphia: Fortress Press, 1980), chap. 5, 6; and T. W. Ogletree, *The Use of the Bible in Christian Ethics* (Philadelphia: Fortress Press, 1983), 53ff.
14. The following discussion draws mainly on J. M. Lochman, *Signposts to Freedom* (Minneapolis: Augsburg, 1982), 87ff. and Harrelson, 107-122.
15. See John Calvin, *Institutes*, II (London: SCM Press, 1960), 39; and *Book of Concord: The Symbols of the Evangelical Lutheran Church* (St. Louis: Concordia Publishing House, 1957), 181f.
16. The phrase is from Karen Lebacqz, *Six Theories of Justice* (Minneapolis: Augsburg, 1986), 14.

17. J. M. Mays, "Justice: Perspectives from the Prophetic Tradition," *Interpretation*, XXXVII (1983), 8.
18. *Ibid.*, 11.
19. *Ibid.*, 16.
20. Ismael Garcia, *Justice in Latin American Theology of Liberation* (Atlanta: John Knox, 1987), 94.
21. J. C. Bennett, *The Radical Imperative* (Philadelphia: Westminster, 1975), 13-4. Italics mine.
22. R. L. Mouw, "Jesus and the Poor," *Mid-Stream*, 20/4 (Oct. 1981), 411.
23. Reinhold Niebuhr, *Moral Man and Immoral Society* (New York: Charles Scribner's Sons, 1960), chap. 5, 6.
24. Mouw, 416.
25. Reinhold Niebuhr, *Nature and Destiny of Man* (New York: Charles Scribner's Sons, 1949), Vol. 2, 265 ff.
26. Robert Nozick, *Anarchy, State, and Utopia* (New York: Basic Books, 1974). Karen Lebacqz provides a helpful summary and analysis of Nozick's theory in *Six Theories of Justice*.
27. T. L. Beauchamp and J. E. Childress, *Principles of Biomedical Ethics* (New York: Oxford University Press, 1983), 187.
28. The above is taken from Allen, 165-167.
29. John Rawles, *A Theory of Justice* (Cambridge, Mass.: Harvard University Press, 1971), 15. His theory of justice, however, is found wanting from a Christian perspective.
30. William Temple, *Christianity and Social Order* (Harmondsworth: Penguin Books, 1942), 44.
31. These are outlined in Frithjof Bergmann, *On Being Free* (Notre Dame: University of Notre Dame Press, 1977), chap. 2.
32. Bergmann, 37.
33. *Ibid.*
34. Daniel Callahan, "Minimalist Ethics," *Hasting Center Report*, Vol. 11, No. 5 (Oct. 1981), 19.
35. Joseph Sittler, *Gravity and Grace* (Minneapolis: Augsburg, 1986), 13. Joseph Sittler was one of the pioneers in contemporary theology of Christian concern for nature.
36. *Ibid.*, 21.
37. D. J. Hall, *The Steward: A Biblical Symbol Come of Age* (Grand Rapids, Michigan: W. B. Eerdmans, 1990), 32.
38. *Ibid.*, 29.
39. Sittler, 18; see also Hall, 210.
40. Sittler, 14.
41. R. M. Gula, *Reason Informed by Faith* (New York: Paulist Press, 1989), 44.
42. Other terms used are "nonmoral" or "ontic" goods or evils.
43. Outka, 263ff.
44. Walter Rauschenbusch, *Christianizing the Social Order* (New York: MacMillan Co., 1912), 329.
45. David Hollenbach, S.J., "The Common Good Revisited," *Theological Studies*, 50 (1989), 71.
46. Douglas Sturm, *Community and Alienation* (Notre Dame, Indiana: University of Notre Dame Press, 1988), 75ff.
47. *Ibid.*, 86.
48. Hollenbach, 87.
49. Reprinted in Gregory Paul and Duncan Cameron, *Ethics and Economics* (Toronto: James Lorimer & Co., 1984), 3ff.
50. J. C. Bennett, *Christian Ethics and Social Policy* (New York: Charles Scribner's Sons, 1950), 76.

51. J. H. Oldham coined the term in J. H. Oldham and W. A. Vissert Hooft, *The Church and its Function in Society*, the preparatory volume for that conference.
52. Ronald H. Preston, *Church and Society in the Late Twentieth Century*, (London: SCM Press, 1983), 149.
53. *Ibid.*, 154.
54. Joseph L. Allen, "Catholic and Protestant Theories of Human Rights," *Religious Studies Review*, 14/4 (Oct. 1988), 347.
55. Max L. Stackhouse, *Creeds, Society, and Human Rights* (Grand Rapids: W. B. Eerdmans, 1984), 1.
56. Allen, 348.
57. Stackhouse, 36.
58. Stephen C. Mott, *Biblical Ethics and Social Change* (New York: Oxford Press, 1982), 52.
59. Allen, 350.
60. David Hollenbach, *Claims in Conflict* (New York: Paulist Press, 1979), 204-5.
61. Michael McDonald, "Indian Status: Colonialism or Sexism?", *The Canadian Community Law Journal*, 1986, 36ff.; and "Should Communities Have Rights? Reflections on Liberal Individualism," *Canadian Journal of Law and Jurisprudence*, IV/2 (July 1991), 224.
62. *Ibid.*, 235.
63. *Ibid.*, 236.
64. Andrew Linzey, *Christianity and the Rights of Animals* (London: S.P.C.K., 1987).
65. Jeremy Waldron, ed., *Nonsense Upon Stilts* (London: Methuen, 1987), 195.
66. Examples are J. Raz, Jeremy Waldron, and David Hollenbach.
67. Waldron, 187.

II. MORAL CHARACTER

1. Alasdair MacIntyre, *After Virtue* (Notre Dame: University of Notre Dame Press, 1981), cited in John Coleman, "Values and Virtues in Advanced Modern Societies," in D. Mieth and J. Pohier, eds., *Changing Values and Virtues* (Edinburgh: T. & T. Clark Ltd., 1987), 8.
2. Abraham J. Heschel, *I Asked For Wonder* (New York: Crossroad, 1987), vii.
3. J. Gustafson, *Christ and the Moral Life* (New York: Harper & Row, 1968), 244.
4. *Ibid.*, 240.
5. Carol McMillan, *Women, Reason and Nature* (Princeton: Princeton University Press, 1982), 151.
6. D. D. Williams, *The Spirit and Forms of Love* (New York: Washington: University Press of America, 1981), 37. Italics mine.
7. Reinhold Niebuhr, *Moral Man and Immoral Society* (New York: Charles Scribner's, 1932), 262.
8. See, for example, Catherine Keller, *From A Broken Web: Separation, Sexism, and Self* (Boston: Beacon Press, 1986).
9. Stephen Post, "Communion and True Self-Love," *Journal of Religious Ethics*, 16 (Fall 1988), 355.
10. Reinhold Niebuhr, *Faith and History* (New York: Charles Scribner's Sons, 1949), 185.
11. Reinhold Niebuhr, *Christian Realism and Political Problems* (New York: Charles Scribner's Sons, 1953), 141.
12. Evelyn Underhill, *Mysticism* (New York: E. P. Dutton, 1978), 400, 176.
13. Gene Outka, *Agape* (New Haven: Yale University Press, 1972), 55ff.
14. Richard A. McCormick, S.J., *How Brave a New World? Dilemmas in Bioethics* (Washington: Georgetown University Press, 1981), 42-3.

15. Donald Capps, *Deadly Sins and Saving Virtues* (Philadelphia: Fortress Press, 1987), 2, 76.
16. James Gustafson, *Christian Ethics and the Community* (Philadelphia: Pilgrim Press, 1971), 206.
17. Stanley Hauerwas, *A Community of Character* (Notre Dame: University of Notre Dame Press, 1981), 127.
18. Gustafson, 208.
19. Erik Erikson, *Insight and Responsibility* (New York: W. W. Norton and Co., 1964), 118.
20. Jurgen Moltmann, *Theology of Hope* (London: SCM Press, 1967).
21. Eric Toffler, *The Third Wave* (London: Pan Books, 1981), 19.
22. R. K. Thomas, *The Chosen of the Land* (forthcoming).
23. Hauerwas, 127-8.
24. Capps, 79.
25. Gilbert Meilander, "Virtue in Contemporary Religious Thought," in R. J. Neuhaus, ed., *Virtue — Public and Private* (Grand Rapids: W. B. Eerdmans, 1986), 8.
26. Jean Porter, "Perennial and Timely Virtues: Practical Wisdom, Courage and Temperance," in Mieth and Pohier, 61.
27. Bernard Haring, *Free and Faithful in Christ*, vol. 2 (New York: Seabury Press, 1979).
28. Capps, 142.
29. The study is reported in Bellah, et al., *Habits of the Heart*. I have paraphrased a summary of it by John Coleman, "Values and Vices in Advanced Modern Societies," in Meith and Pohier, 9-10.
30. Hauerwas, 10.
31. Stanley Hauerwas and W. H. Willimon, *Resident Aliens* (Nashville: Abingdon Press, 1989), 12.
32. See, for example, Richard Mouw and John Howard Yoder, "Evangelical Ethics and the Anabaptist-Reformed Dialogue," *Journal of Religious Ethics*, 17/2 (Fall 1989), 121.
33. Carol Gilligan, *In a Different Voice* (Cambridge, Mass.: Harvard University Press, 1983).
34. Claudia Card, "Gender and Moral Luck," in Owen Flanagan and A. O. Porty, eds., *Identity, Character, and Morality* (Cambridge, Mass.: M.I.T., 1990), 207. Mary Ellen Ross, "Feminism and the Problem of Moral Character," *Journal of Feminist Studies in Religion* 5 (1989), 57. See also Owen Flanagan, *Varieties of Moral Personality* (Cambridge, Mass.: Harvard University Press, 1991), 196-252.
35. Sidney Callahan, *In Good Conscience* (San Francisco: Harper Collins, 1991), 233. See also 196.
36. Gordon Harland, *The Thought of Reinhold Niebuhr* (New York: Oxford University Press, 1960), 135.
37. B. C. Birch & L. L. Rasmussen, *Bible Ethics in the Christian Life* (Minneapolis: Augsburg, revised and expanded edition, 1989), 126.
38. D. C. Maguire, *The Moral Choice* (Garden City: Doubleday & Company, 1978).
39. W. F. May, *The Physician's Covenant* (Philadelphia: Westminster Press, 1983), 15.
40. Erazim Kohak, "Ashes, Ashes ... Central Europe After Forty Years," *Harper's* (June 1992), 16.
41. For a helpful discussion of this see T. L. Beauchamp and James F. Childress, *Principles of Biomedical Ethics* (New York: Oxford University Press, 3rd ed., 1989), 379 ff.

III. WORLDVIEW AND BASIC CONVICTIONS

1. I have been helped in this section by Richard J. Mouw, *The God Who Commands* (Notre Dame, Indiana: University of Notre Dame Press, 1990), chap. 2. The questions were formulated by Brian J. Walsh and J. Richard Middleton, *The Transforming Vision: Shaping a Christian World View* (Downers Grove, Ill.: InterVarsity Press, 1984).
2. Stephen Crites, "The Narrative Quality of Experience," in S. Hauerwas and L. G. Jones, eds., *Why Narrative?* (Grand Rapids: W. B. Eerdmans, 1989), 69-70.
3. Max Stackhouse, *Creeds, Society, and Human Rights* (Grand Rapids: W. B. Eerdmans, 1984), 2.
4. See for example Winthrop D. Jordan, *White Over Black* (Baltimore: Penguin Books, 1968).
5. Oliver O'Donovan, "How Can Theology Be Moral?" *Journal of Religious Ethics* (Fall 1989), 81ff.
6. John C. Bennett, *Christian Ethics and Social Policy* (New York: Charles Scribner's Sons, 1950).
7. Reinhold Niebuhr, "When Will Christians Stop Fooling Themselves?" *The Christian Century*, May 16, 1934, 659.
8. Ellen T. Charry, "The Moral Function of Doctrine," *Theology Today*, (April 1992), 43.
9. C. B. McPherson, *Possessive Individualism* (Oxford: Oxford University Press, 1961), 263. By permission of Oxford University Press.
10. Karl Barth, *Christ and Adam* (New York: Harper and Row, 1956), 91.
11. D. J. Hall, *Imaging God* (Grand Rapids: W. B. Eerdmans, 1986), 132. See also the stimulating study of the Trinity by Catherine M. LaCugna, *God For Us* (San Francisco: Harper, 1991).
12. J. P. Wogaman, *A Christian Method of Moral Judgment* (Philadelphia: Westminster Press, 1976), 140.
13. William Temple, *Christianity and Social Order* (Harmondsworth: Penguin Books, 1942), 44.
14. David Hollenbach, S.J., "The Common Good Revisited," *Theological Studies* 50, (1989), 87ff.
15. H. P. Santmire, *The Travail of Nature* (Philadelphia: Fortress Press, 1985).
16. B. C. Birch and L. L. Rasmussen, *Bible and Ethics in the Christian Life* (Minneapolis: Augsburg, 1989), 65.
17. The term is aptly used by Lloyd Gaston, professor of New Testament, Vancouver School of Theology, to describe Paul's view of sin and death.
18. This is developed more recently by Patrick Kerans, *Sinful Social Structures* (New York: Paulist Press, 1974), and Paul Riccour, *The Symbolism of Evil* (Boston: Beacon Press, 1967).
19. Reinhold Niebuhr, *Does Civilization Need Religion?* (New York: MacMillan Co., 1927), 133.
20. Walter Rauschenbusch, *A Theology for the Social Gospel* (Nashville: Abingdon, 1917), 72.
21. Gregory Baum, *Religion and Alienation* (New York: Paulist Press, 1975), 200-3.
22. Reinhold Niebuhr, *Nature and Destiny of Man* (New York: Charles Scribner's Sons, 1953),Vol. 1, 201.
23. Reinhold Niebuhr, *Moral Man and Immoral Society* (New York: Charles Scribner's Sons, 1932), 88.
24. See for example, J. P. Theisen, *Community and Disunity* (Collegeville, Minn.: St. John's University Press, 1985); Rosemary R. Ruether, *Sexism and God-Talk* (Boston: Beacon Press, 1983).
25. Reinhold Niebuhr, *Nature and Destiny of Man*, Vol. 2, 207.

IV. SITUATION AND CONTEXT

1. Daniel Maguire, *Death by Choice* (Garden City: Image Books, 1984), 65-96.
2. R. H. Preston, *Church and Society in the Late Twentieth Century: The Economic and Political Task* (London: SCM Press, 1983), 149.
3. Roger Hutchinson, "Study and Action in Politically Diverse Churches," in Cranford Pratt and Roger Hutchinson, eds., *Christian Faith and Economic Justice* (Burlington, Ont.: Trinity Press, 1988), 184.
4. W. W. Everett and T. J. Bachmeyer, *Disciplines in Transformation* (Washington: University Press of America, 1979).
5. *Ibid.*, 96.
6. See Cornel West, *Prophetic Fragments* (Grand Rapids, Michigan: W. B. Eerdmans, 1988).
7. Cornwall Collective, *Your Daughters Shall Prophesy* (New York: Pilgrim Press, 1980).
8. R. J. Schreiter, *Constructing Local Theologies* (Maryknoll, N.Y.: Orbis, 1985), 46.
9. Stephen Toulmin, *Cosmopolis: The Hidden Agenda Of Modernity* (New York: Free Press, 1990), and also Peter Berger, Brigitte Berger, Hansfried Kellner, *The Homeless Mind: Modernization and Consciousness* (New York: Random House, 1973).
10. See Gregory Baum, "Theories of Post-Modernity," *The Ecumenist*, Spring 1991. See also Peter Berger's analysis of the experience of being continually surrounded by strangers, no longer at home in the universe; C. B. MacPherson's critique of "possessive individualism," Philip Reiff's "therapeutic man," Christopher Lasch's "culture of narcissism," Alasdair MacIntyre's ethics of "emotivism," Robert Bellah's "culture of separation."
11. See Daniel Bell, *The Coming of Post-Industrial Society* (Harmondsworth: Penguin, 1976), and Allain Touraine, *The Self-Production of Society* (Chicago: University of Chicago, 1977).
12. See Lasch, Bellah, etc.
13. Charles Taylor, *The Malaise of Modernity* (Ontario: House of Anansi Press, 1991), 5.
14. A growing literature traces the rise and character of the modernist view. See, for example, Morris Berman, *The Reenchantment of the World* (Ithaca: Cornell University Press, 1981); William Leiss, *Domination of Nature* (New York: George Braziller, 1972); and Keith Thomas, *Man and the Natural World* (New York: Pantheon Books, 1983).
15. Jean-Francois Lyotard, *The Postmodern Condition* (Minneapolis: University of Minnesota Press, 1984).
16. Nathan A. Scott, Jr., "The House of Intellect in an Age of Carnival," *Journal of the American Academy of Religion*, LV/1, 7.
17. Charles Taylor, "Alternate Futures: Legitimacy, Identity and Alienation in Late Twentieth Century Canada" in Alan Cairns and Cynthia Williams, eds., *Constitutionalism, Citizenship and Society in Canada* (Toronto: University of Toronto Press, 1985), 185.
18. *Ibid.*
19. My approach is analogous to Augustine's method of appropriating philosophy. This contrasts with the other two approaches that are analogous to the methods of Aquinas and Barth, respectively.
20. Otto Maduro, *Religion and Social Conflicts* (Maryknoll, N.Y.: Orbis Books, 1982), 28, cited in Arthur F. McGovern, *Liberation Theology and Its Critics* (Maryknoll, N.Y.: Orbis Books, 1989), 144.
21. R. K. Thomas, *Getting to the Heart of the Matter* (Vancouver: Native Ministries Consortium, Vancouver School of Theology, 1990), 72.
22. McGovern, 146.
23. Jose Comblin, *The Church and the National Security State* (Maryknoll, N.Y.: Orbis, 1979), 142, as cited in McGovern, 146.

24. Z. K. Brzezinski, Foreword, in Vyacheslav Chornovil, *The Chornovil Papers* (New York: McGraw Hill, 1968).
25. See Joe Holland and Peter Henriot, S.J., *Social Analysis: Linking Faith and Justice* (Maryknoll, N.Y.: Orbis Books, 1983).

V. AUTHORITATIVE SOURCES

1. Bruce C. Birch and Larry L. Rasmussen, *Bible and Ethics in the Christian Life* (Minneapolis: Augsburg, 1989), 154.
2. *Westminster Dictionary of Christian Ethics* (Philadelphia: Westminster Press, 1986), 629.
3. Lisa Cahill, *Between the Sexes* (Philadelphia: Fortress Press, 1985), 6.
4. *Book of Discipline of the United Methodist Church 1976* (Nashville: United Methodist Publishing House, 1976), 79. The following two quotes are also from this book.
5. Max L. Stackhouse, *Public Theology and Political Economy* (Grand Rapids: W. B. Eerdmans, 1987), 10.
6. Cahill, 13.
7. Richard M. Gula, *Reason Informed by Faith* (New York: Paulist Press, 1989), 220-21. The following (including the quotes) is drawn mainly from his excellent overview. See 225ff.
8. For description and analysis of this see Owen C. Thomas, "Theology and Experience," *Harvard Theological Review*, 78:1-2 (1985), 179-206.
9. Paul Tillich, *Systematic Theology* (Chicago: University of Chicago Press, 1951), I, 40.
10. Thomas E. Clarke, "A New Way: Reflecting on Experience," James E. Hug, ed., *Tracing the Spirit* (New York: Paulist Press, 1983), 20.
11. *United Methodist Book of Discipline*, 80.
12. Thomas, 196.
13. Clarke, 20.
14. Cahill, 85, and following, 89.
15. Tillich, I, 44.
16. J. T. Burtchaell, *The Giving and Taking of Life* (Notre Dame, Indiana: University of Notre Dame Press, 1989), 6.
17. Tillich, I, 45, and the following, I, 46.
18. Cahill, chap. 1.
19. See David H. Kelsey, The *Uses of the Scripture in Recent Theology* (Philadelphia: Fortress Press, 1975).
20. Birch and Rasmussen, 173.
21. Lesslie Newbigin, *Foolishness to the Greeks* (Grand Rapids: W. B. Eerdmans, 1986), 62.
22. Richard B. Hays, "Scripture-Shaped Community" *Interpretation*, 55 (Jan. 1990), 51.
23. Newbigin, 60.
24. *Ibid.*, 62.
25. Hays, 51.
26. Newbigin, 60.
27. Hays, 49.
28. Lesslie Newbigin, *Truth to Tell* (Grand Rapids, Michigan: W. B. Eerdmans, 1991), 57.
29. Birch and Rasmussen, 131.

VI. THE ART OF DISCERNING THE WAY

1. For a useful description of this and some of the following methods named, see W. K. Frankena, *Ethics*, 2nd ed. (Englewood Cliffs, N.J.: Prentice Hall, 1973). For a briefer introduction, see T. L. Beauchamp and J. F. Childress, *Principles of Biomedical Ethics*, 2nd ed. (New York: Oxford University Press, 1983).
2. For a helpful description of proportionalism, see Richard Gula, *Reason Informed by Faith* (New York: Paulist Press, 1989), 272ff.
3. This is commonly identified with the work of H. Richard Niebuhr, James Gustafson, Bernard Haring, and Charles E. Curran.
4. Daniel C. Maguire, *Death by Choice* (Garden City, N.Y.: Image Books, 1984), 67.
5. See Jean Porter, *The Recovery of Virtue: the Relevance of Aquinas for Christian Ethics* (Louisville: Westminster/John Knox, 1990).
6. Gula, 305.
7. This draws on J. Philip Wogaman, *A Christian Method of Moral Judgment* (Philadelphia: Westminster Press, 1976), chap. 2.
8. For an exposition of this approach, see Albert R. Jonsen and Stephen Toulmin, *The Abuse of Casuistry: A History of Moral Reasoning* (Berkeley: University of California Press, 1988).
9. Gula, 304. Italics mine.
10. Daniel Bell, *The End of Ideology*, rev. ed. (New York: MacMillan, 1965), 333.
11. Roger L. Shinn, *Forced Options* (New York: Harper & Row, 1982), 231.
12. *Ibid.*
13. Reinhold Niebuhr in J. A. Hutchison, ed., *Christian Faith and Social Action* (New York: Charles Scribner's Sons, 1953), 236.
14. See Bell, 406; S. M. Lipset, *Political Man* (New York: Anchor Books, 1963), 453ff.; D. L. Munby, *The Idea of a Secular Society* (London: Oxford University Press, 1961), 30, 33; C. I. Itty, and Arend Th. van Leeuwen, in E. de Vries, *Man in Community* (New York: Association Press, 1966).
15. E. Heimann, *Reason and Faith in Modern Society* (Middletown, Conn.: Wesleyan University Press, 1961), 265.
16. Terence R. Anderson, "Christian Socialism Reconsidered," unpublished doctoral thesis, 1967, Union Theological Seminary, chap. 1.
17. Hutchison, 229, and following, 232.
18. Latin American liberation theology displays a similar spectrum of perceived connections between the Christian faith and socialist ideology. See A. F. McGovern, *Liberation Theology and Its Critics* (Maryknoll, N.Y.: Orbis Books, 1989), 180ff.
19. James Gustafson gets us started with the first three in *The Church as Moral Decision-Maker* (Philadelphia: Pilgrim Press, 1970), 83ff. I have added four more.
20. J. E. Hug, ed., *Tracing the Spirit* (New York: Paulist Press, 1983), 232.
21. J. C. Futrell, in Hug, 231.
22. Ellen T. Charry, "The Moral Function of Doctrine," *Theology Today*, (April 1992), 37.

GLOSSARY OF TERMS

agent. A person who acts; sometimes refers to a person who has power to act intentionally.

autonomy. Self-rule or self-governance. An autonomous person is one who acts according to his or her own freely chosen values and plan; that is, not controlled by others or prevented by personal limitations from acting freely. What constitutes a genuinely autonomous, self-directed choice is a matter of some dispute.

burden of proof. The prime responsibility for proving a controversial or contested point, e.g., overriding an important moral principle in favour of another. Determining which viewpoint in a dispute bears such prime responsibility is sometimes an important matter in ethics.

common good. A broad moral norm representing the shared values or goods of a political or economic association, such as a corporation, a union, a nation, or even the entire globe. It refers to the good of the whole — the conditions of social living essential for the true well-being of all within that whole.

common grace. God's freely offered, steadfast, and enduring love, which comes to us in the gift of life itself, in the gift of creation and the land, in the gift of family and one's people.

communitarian. Refers to a group of thinkers who assert that relationships are an essential characteristic of human beings in opposition to views (characteristic of liberal thought) that focus on human beings as separate, autonomous individuals.

consequentialism. An ethical theory claiming that actions are morally right or wrong primarily according to the results they produce. Utilitarianism is one common form in Western societies; situation ethics, popular in liberal Protestant circles in the 1960s, is another.

deontology. An ethical theory claiming that actions are morally right or wrong primarily according to their inherent features, such as truthfulness or fidelity, rather than according to the ends or consequences they produce.

dispositions. One aspect of moral character, a persistent tendency or stable readiness to speak and to act in a certain manner or way. Dispositions deemed good, such as hope and loving-kindness, are called virtues. Dispositions deemed undesirable, such as greed and impatience, are called vices.

Enlightenment. The term used to describe the dominant intellectual movement in western Europe from the mid-seventeenth through the eighteenth centuries. The major motifs of this thought shaped the prevailing worldview of Western societies. Some of the characteristic strands that make up this intellectual movement include the belief that human beings are primarily separate individuals and that the thought and conscience of each is important; a belief in a pre-established harmony between humans and the outer world of the cosmos; confidence in the capacity of human reason to understand this harmony and determine the good and achieve it; a belief in the progress and perfectibility of society.

ethics. The disciplined inquiry into how we ought to behave, questions of what is right, good, etc. More particularly, disciplined reflection on what does (descriptive ethics) and what should (normative ethics) go into answering such questions, including the meaning of such terms as the good and the right.

exegesis. Critical analysis of the meaning of words and passages in the Bible (or any other literary work).

goods. Moral standards used to assess the desirable consequences of an action or the ultimate ends that our actions should foster. In other words, objects or end-states thought to be worthy of human pursuit, such as friendship, health, happiness.

guidelines. A kind of moral norm or standard that recommends a definite action that is more specific than the general direction provided by principles. Indicating actions that are usually regarded as morally appropriate, guidelines are considered less morally binding than rules.

ideology. In its broadest sense, refers to any set of beliefs or ideas. Also used to refer more specifically to an idea system that relates beliefs and ethics to particular political goals and strategies, such as a liberal ideology, a conservative ideology, or a socialist ideology. A third use has to do with the social function of ideas and beliefs, especially their power to mask the true interests and operations of a group under the guise of lofty ideals.

liberalism. A loose term usually used to describe a particular, modern political doctrine or ideology. It comprises such convictions as belief in the supreme value of the individual, including certain freedoms and rights that belong to every person. This necessitates a limited and restricted government, subject to various mechanisms of accountability, to protect such individual rights and freedoms. This doctrine came into being through the Enlightenment movement of the seventeenth and eighteenth centuries in western Europe. There are a number of variations of liberalism, but the notion that human beings are primarily separate individuals, not defined by relationships and only secondarily members of groups, is central. The individual is to be guided solely by reason, detached from tradition, custom, religion, and prejudice.

metaphysical. Above or beyond the realm of what can be observed in nature, having to do with ultimate reality or the transcendent.

middle axioms. A type of norm that identifies social action goals that should be pursued, e.g., the abolishment of apartheid, thereby providing more specific guidance than the norm of the common good or principles of justice but less precise directives than particular strategies of action. The term first came into use through the ecumenical Oxford Conference of 1937, an important precursor of the World Council of Churches.

modernity. The culture, including worldview, that has accompanied technologically induced industrialization characteristic of the Western world since the seventeenth century. It includes a particular understanding of the cosmos marked by the assumptions of Newtonian science, combined with a particular view of the political order characterized by the nation state.

moral. That having to do with the good, the right, or the fitting way of being and behaving. What should I do? and What kind of person should I become? are moral questions.

morality. Behaviour and a way of being deemed to be right and good according to custom or code.

moral norms. Standards for guiding and assessing qualities of moral being (virtues and vices) and behaviour (actions that are right or wrong, obligatory or permitted).

natural law. That portion of the moral order that is built into the very nature of the universe and discernible by the exercise of human reason, especially the purpose of human beings and the way they are to live.

obligations. One type of moral norm, designating right actions deemed essential for the flourishing of human community, e.g., one should tell the truth, one should keep promises.

plausibility structure. The framework of belief shared by a community or society, largely taken for granted, that is the basis for assessing what is judged to be true or false, reasonable or unreasonable. The fundamental framework of a worldview.

pluralism. A social condition in which there are a variety of religious, ethnic, and cultural groups embraced within a single society.

postmodern. A loose term referring to a cluster of perceived changes in, not only the social and cultural conditions, but even the basic prevailing worldview of Western societies. Modernity, characteristic of advanced industrial societies of the West since the seventeenth century, appears to postmodern analysts to be breaking down because of fundamental flaws within its own foundations.

pragmatism. A philosophical theory maintaining that the meaning and truth of beliefs are to be assessed in terms of their effectiveness in making us more successful, or their benefit to the human condition. More generally, it refers to thinkers who emphasize what can be done in the world, rather than speculating on ideal possibilities.

prime face. On first appearance. In ethics, usually refers to basic moral principles representing prime obligations. They are *prime face* (on first appearance) binding and may only be overridden for very important reasons. What reasons should count is a matter of dispute in ethics.

principles. Moral norms or standards that provide broad or general direction for behaviour rather than indicating specific actions. Usually the term is used to refer to obligation-type norms; that is, those that designate actions as being intrinsically right or wrong in themselves. However, sometimes they also refer to actions deemed right or wrong in terms of the good or evil consequences they produce.

rights. Justified claims that individuals and groups can make upon others or upon society. They are characteristically claims of power, privilege, needed goods and services, those things of basic importance to human life. Rights are characteristically claims made for individuals, although they are also made on behalf of collectives and animals.

rules. Moral norms or standards that provide directives for behaviour by prescribing or prohibiting definite actions. They are distinguished from principles in that they are more precise in the directive given, and they are distinguished from guidelines in that they are more morally binding.

saving grace. God's freely offered, steadfast, and enduring love that is expressed supremely in Jesus Christ as God's mercy towards a disobedient and fallen humankind; the inauguration of a new creation including the forgiveness of sin and a fresh beginning for a new life of faith, hope, and love for every person; the promise to complete the new creation through the second coming of Christ, bringing a new heaven and a new earth — well-being, harmony, and justice in terms of right relations between human beings, humans and the rest of creation, all creatures and God.

theology. The study of God and matters relating to the relationship of God to humans and to the rest of nature; Christian theology is the systematic reflection on Christian believing, a conceptual depiction of the faith of the church.

values. A modern term for "goods" (see above). A type of moral standard used to indicate desirable consequences of an action, such as friendship, well-being, health, happiness, and the like.

worldview. The basic, operative understanding of reality shared by a society or body of people. Usually simply assumed, unarticulated, and held unconsciously. Includes deeply held, "of course" beliefs about the self, the world, and ultimate reality.

INDEX

930021